The Agony of Displacement

*Testimonies from the Survivors
of the Genocide in Gaza*

Nawal Halawa
Chief Editor

Ursula DeYoung
English Language Editor

ISBN: 979-8-9992568-0-5

Cover Art by Hanadi Bader

Sligo Creek Publishing
9039 Sligo Creek Parkway
Silver Spring, Maryland 20901
https://www.sligocreekpublishing.com/

DEDICATION

To the children who lived through war before they could live their childhoods.

To the little ones who grew up too soon, carrying heavy memories and broken dreams on their shoulders.

To Palestine, the land of martyrs.

To Palestinians, wherever they may be, across the ages and generations.

To the first family that was displaced, and to the last martyr who will fall before victory.

To all the martyrs, prisoners, and their families.

To the souls tormented by their bodies.

To the souls who loved their land and refused to ascend to heaven until their homeland smiled.

To the peoples whose hearts still beat with love for Palestine, Jerusalem, and Al-Aqsa.

To those walking with us in this valley—the valley of tears, hope, maturity, and pain.

This book tells your stories, not written in ink but etched in fire and smoke, in sorrow and hope. It is the voice of every child deprived of safety and childhood, and of everyone who resisted pain with a small smile despite everything.

With my warmest wishes that one day your laughter will fill the air again.

PREFACE

Penned in blood, rendered in tears…
~Vivian Yalda

Some may wonder how I became so deeply and emotionally attached to the children, women, and men of Gaza, and how the WhatsApp group for the Arab Heritage House in Canada changed into the Arab Heritage House–Palestine group. Its members immediately responded to the agony of the displaced and suffering people of Gaza. We quickly began initiating relief projects, hoping to alleviate their suffering as much as possible. We supported their commitment and resilience against the occupying entity, despite the bloody universal war waged against them by that entity and its allies, the leaders of Western countries, who built an air bridge supplying internationally prohibited lethal weapons to destroy the land and commit genocide. These armaments allowed the occupiers to penetrate brutally the Gaza Strip and practice ethnic cleansing against the defenseless people of Gaza, violating international norms and laws.

The idea for this book took shape after I began personally communicating with the families for whom we provided financial support on a monthly basis, at the expense of the members of the Arab Heritage House and with help of the proceeds from my latest novel in English (*A Girl's Paradise Lost*), which was published a week after the Al-Aqsa Flood—it is a story told by a child about the Nakba of Palestine in 1948.

As a researcher interested in Arab heritage and its documentation, and working in collaboration with donors, teachers, and educational supervisors, I started collecting the stories of displaced women, particularly the wives of martyrs, whose stories I received via email. The idea later evolved to include testimony from children and teachers from the Arab Heritage House Initiative for the Education of Displaced Children.

Many readers may not be familiar with the geography of the Gaza Strip before the 1948 Nakba, given that Gaza overlooks the Mediterranean Sea, with one of the most beautiful beaches in the world. Gaza City has a long history and many important landmarks, such as the Great Omari Mosque, the Church of Porphyrius (also known as the Cemetery Church), the Port of Anthedon, the Monastery of Saint Hilarion (Tal Umm Amer), and the Baptist Hospital, among others. It also contains the British army emetery, which holds the remains of four thousand soldiers killed by the people of Gaza while they were cooperating with the Turkish garrison against the British army, during the Mandate period.

The surrounding villages include many agricultural settlements that were a major source of food for the city, such as the Sheikh Ajlin neighborhood, famous for its sea grapes; Jabalia, well known for its almond orchards; Beit Lahia, known for its fragrant apples; and Beit Hanoun, known for growing Shamouti oranges. There are other cities in southern Gaza Strip, such as Deir al-Balah, known for its fine dates. Two cities, Khan Yunis and Rafah, were divided between Egypt and Palestine under the Sykes-Picot Agreement.

During the first Nakba, Zionist gangs displaced many people from the Gaza Strip with the aim of forcing them to settle in Egypt. However, the Egyptian authorities, under King Farouk, rejected the entire plan, which led to a backlog of refugees in the Gaza Strip. These refugees had no choice but to remain in camps, including the Jabalia camp in the north; the Shati camp on the seashore; the Nuseirat, Bureij, and Maghazi camps in the center, between Wadi Gaza and Deir al-Balah; the Deir al-Balah camp; the Khan Yunis camp; and the Rafah camp.

Due to its limited space, the Gaza Strip has one of the highest population densities in the world. That population has increased from a quarter of a million to more than two and a half million in seventy years. It consists of families living and moving continually, in an area no more than forty-one kilometers long and eight kilometers wide on average—distances easily covered on foot. The Zionists were well aware of the situation and repeatedly asked the camp residents to move from the north to the south, and from the center to the south. This was done to humiliate them, to kill the children and women, and to detain the young men in unknown locations, using immoral and unethical measures, in the hope of eliminating the Palestinians completely.

Given the significance of what these savage monsters did—actions that would later become known as one of history's massacres, recognized by the International Court of Justice—it has become imperative for us, the activists of the Arab Heritage House in Canada, to document their most recent acts of brutality and compile the devastating results in a book we have titled *The Agony of Displacement*. This book gathers tragic stories of the ongoing horrific events experienced by the people of Gaza, moment by moment, day by day, and month by month, from the Al-Aqsa Flood until the present.

On their behalf, we decided that this book should be a historical field document, stamping this racist, colonial movement with eternal shame, and expressing the resilience of the Palestinian people, who have set the highest example of bravery and resilience by upholding their land and legitimate national rights at the cost of tremendous sacrifice.

Nawal Halawa

Founder and President of the Arab Heritage House
Montreal, Canada
Arabculturalhouse@gmail.com

**Maison de la culture arabe
Arab Cultural House**

INTRODUCTION

We are the people who have never quenched our thirst for our homeland, yet nourish the entire earth with love for it. We stand here on the threshold of despair and pain. We are rebels for the sake of our homeland. We are bearers of rare blood and sacred soil. We are drowning in our blood until the earth cracks open.

O Phoenix bird, the tales wronged you when they called you a myth. And indeed, I see in my people the legend of life reborn.

On this land, there is much that makes life worth living. Do you, the occupiers, think you will triumph over our death, when we are the mighty giants? Never in history has a living body endured so much of what no human soul could bear, even in imagination. We will tell what the visual and written media have not said. We will recount to you our pain in our own words, and often with our own pens.

These are stories written to endure through the ages, stories that history will narrate about a premeditated genocide—crimes the likes of which humanity has never seen.

From the tongues of our children, I have captured their deep sorrow—some uttering their last breaths while insisting on telling their stories, others speaking of their grief while believing that their homeland is worth the struggle, and others still telling me about their future. As for me, I stand in awe before their strength. Believe me, these are children with unique smiles, and we have dedicated a special chapter to them.

The second chapter of the book holds the stories of mothers and young women, where you will find the tragedy's complexities vividly portrayed. You will witness such rampant evil that it may ignite your senses and make you question if these are truly the deeds of humans.

At the end of the book, we have included an appendix about the history of Gaza and its administrative divisions. The readers can refer to it to follow the routes taken by those displaced in the stories, as well as to familiarize themselves with the original places from which the survivors were displaced.

This book contains documented testimonies of real events, leaving no room for doubt. Palestine, despite the succession of catastrophes it has faced, continues to carry the banner of victory tirelessly. What pains us most is that our sorrow has sometimes distracted us from documenting our stories at the time. Yet, because we are a people who do not abandon our land, it has become necessary to document our pain and our suffering.

For those accustomed to reading stories, they will find that these narratives are rich in plot-lines and locations, yet unfold within a relatively short timeframe. You will also find that all of the stories converge on the same ending, a tragedy without resolution. For one of the pillars of our stories has collapsed, through no fault of our own; the oppressors persist in their tyranny, and the blood flows like a waterfall.

The crux of the matter lies here: Will you be one of those who speak up and push backagainst the injustice inflicted upon your fellow human beings? Will you rise up for humanity and good? Or will you remain a passive observer, composing the melody of despair?

This book contains numerous true and authentic stories. Dr. Nawal Halawa, President and Founder of the Arab Heritage House in Canada, was able to guide the supervisors of educational initiatives in the Gaza Strip to gather these stories from students, teachers, and parents, so that they can serve as a testament to the historical injustice endured by our Palestinian people—an injustice that still persists.

CONTENTS

PART ONE: GAZAN MOTHERS TELL THEIR CHILDREN'S STORIES

Heba Muheisen
Age: 9 years old

Today marks the start of a new week, and I want to be at my best. My father used to walk me to school every morning on his way to work. It was our special routine, one that filled me with warmth and security. But everything changed when terrifying sounds echoed through the streets—deafening roars that froze my blood. People were confused, some asking what had happened to our neighborhood, while others stood frozen in shock.

I screamed louder than ever before, begging my mother to protect us. She gathered my siblings and me into a corner of the house as the drums of war began to beat. Outside, people ran through crumbling alleyways as walls collapsed and flames rained down like ripe fruit falling from trees. Some fell as martyrs; others lay alive but too weak to rise. Eventually, we reached what they called a "shelter." At the time, I didn't know what that word truly meant. My mother reassured me that it would keep us safe, shielding us from harm.

But the truth was far different. There was no safety, no food, no blankets to warm us.Each day grew worse than the last. On November 8, a date we usually celebrated as my sister's birthday, fire and explosions arrived instead. We thought the earth itself had split open—a volcano erupting or an earthquake striking. Shrapnel scattered around us. Many fell as victims that day.

Among them was my cousin Mahmoud, just eleven years old, who had dreamed of becoming a footballer like Mohamed Salah. A piece of shrapnel struck him in the head, leaving him in a coma. But the most heartbreaking part of this tragedy unfolded later. My aunt, Mahmoud's mother, left behind her daughter Sila, who was trapped inside Al-Shifa Hospital for over two weeks. For fourteen days, she witnessed hell: fear, terror, and the unknown.

We were eventually ordered to head south, supposedly to a safer area. We fled, gathering whatever remnants of our belongings remained under the rubble. At the checkpoint, we waited for hours, feeling as though Judgment Day had come early. People were arrested in front of us, some collapsing from exhaustion, while bullets flew from tanks stationed on both sides of the road. Soldiers shouted insults, their faces twisted with hatred.

Despite all this, we finally arrived—but the reality in the south proved even harsher than we had imagined. My father disappeared for hours each day, searching for food. I remember sitting for days without even a piece of bread, our bodies growing weaker by the moment.

Then I contracted hepatitis. I wasn't alone—thousands of children like me suffered, unable to find nourishment or medicine. We stood in long lines alongside hundreds of others, hoping to collect contaminated water. The world watched and spoke out but failed to provide clean water—a basic human right.

We fought desperately to survive, scavenging for scraps of food wherever we could find them. I carried a bowl to bring back food from charity kitchens, meals unfit for human consumption, when I should have been at school playing sports with my friends. My heart ached for my grandparents, whom I hadn't seen in months. Every day I miss my grandfather, a martyr not only to war but also to inadequate healthcare.

Now, I stand at the edge of the road that once took me home in half an hour, and I think, *Coming back now is nothing but a dream.*

All I know is this: schools exist to educate, not to crumble on our heads. Walls are built to shield us from winter's cold and summer's heat, not to collapse upon us. Food and clean water are rights, not privileges. My home belongs to me, and no force on Earth has the right to evict me. Living free from disease and suffering isn't a luxury—it's my right.

I call upon courts of justice and international organizations: I demand my rights and the rights of every Palestinian child. Be the eyes of justice. Witness, O world, and do not stay silent. The Nakba of 1948 may have faded into history, but our stories must never be forgotten. Share them. Speak them. Spread them. Let them echo across the world.

Written on August 1, 2024

Naia Bahaa Zaqout
Age: 10 years old,
Told by Her Mother

Naia Bahaa Zaqout, ten years old, is just one of many children in Gaza who have witnessed the tragic transformation of beauty in the face of war. It's a story shared by every woman, every young girl, and every child in Gaza. Women around the world boast about their beauty and physical appearance, and the women of Gaza are no less beautiful; they too know how to appreciate and enhance their beauty.

Gazan women are, without exaggeration, among the most beautiful in the world. Yet, as life has become unbearable, has that beauty remained untouched? War has stripped us of everything that once completed our beauty—makeup, even the simplest cosmetics that gave us a sense of allure. The beautiful women of Gaza stand waiting for clean water, prepare food over burning paper, and endure long hours under the scorching sun. Can all of this leave them unchanged? Can beauty survive in these conditions?

The harshness of life has melted away everything that was once beautiful, everything these women once held dear. The cycle of deprivation continues, compounded by the relentless Israeli blockades that prevent cleaning materials from entering—as if cleanliness were a weapon of mass destruction they are determined to prevent us from using.

The suffering deepens, and as it grows the beauty of every woman and child in Gaza slowly fades. We live without soap, without shampoo. Even sanitary pads are a rare commodity.

The purest women on earth, in the purest land, are giving up their crowns, cutting their hair because they cannot protect it nor care for it properly. As a result, they are falling victim to contagious diseases, including hair loss and severe skin infections. We have become queens without crowns.

My daughter, Naia Zaqout, only ten years old, always had extraordinary hair, drawing the attention of everyone who saw it. Since she was little, she dreamed of having hair as long as the fairytale character Rapunzel. But now we had no choice but to let go of her beautiful and distinctive crown. How would I clean it?

I took the scissors in my trembling hands, filled with sorrow. She looked at me with painful eyes, full of sadness and loss. I moved forward, unable to retreat from the sorrowful gaze that spoke volumes. As I cut I partook in a story of thousands, a story shared by so many.

The beautiful women of Gaza today are dimmed, waiting for life and hope to be renewed. Is there any savior left for the crowns of these beautiful women?

Written on August 20, 2024

Majd Ahmed
Age: 28 years old

Today marks two hundred days of war.

I write this as someone who has been displaced ten times since the war on Gaza began, on October 7, 2023.

Our lives have been upended, our schools abandoned, with bullets whizzing over our heads and death lurking in every corner. We had no choice but to flee south, toward the central region, and then to Rafah, where we now live in tents, sleeping on bare ground with nothing but the most basic essentials. But all of this hardship pales in comparison to the loss of our home, our land, and the sense of belonging that once anchored us.

They burned my house to the ground. Nothing remains—no trace, no memory. Yet, despite the pain etched into every moment, our hope of returning to our homes and our land refuses to die. It burns quietly within us, a small flame defying the storm.

I am the mother of a five-year-old daughter. My widowed mother and siblings are my companions in this struggle. We have no income, no shelter, no semblance of stability or life. My daughter often dreams of the Israeli soldier she saw at the checkpoint when we fled Gaza for Rafah. She asks me, her voice trembling, "Does he want to kill us? What did we ever do to them?" Her innocent questions pierce my heart. How do I explain to her that the world seems indifferent to our suffering?

Our children's futures are being obliterated before our eyes, their dreams reduced to ashes along with their schools and homes. The trauma runs deep, leaving wounds that may never heal. My mother, diabetic and frail, struggles to obtain her medication. Each day brings new challenges: an empty stomach, an unhealthy diet, and the gnawing fear of what tomorrow might bring.

Not long ago, I fell seriously ill. The pain in my gallbladder became unbearable, and I was forced to seek help at a hospital. They told me I needed surgery, but in these impossible conditions—with hospitals overwhelmed and resources depleted—it was out of the question. So I endure the pain, both physical and emotional, silently praying for relief.

This war has worn us down to the bone. Every breath feels heavier than the last. Please, stop this madness. Let us return to our homes, to a life where laughter replaces tears and hope outweighs despair.

Written on April 7, 2024

Nawal Raaft Easa Fasfos

Age: 14 years old

On Saturday, October 7, 2023, we woke up to prepare for school, but the deafening sound of missiles shattered our morning. My father urged us, "Get out of the house and go to your aunt's house." At my aunt's house, we were told, "Evacuate this area." So we moved again, this time to my other aunt's home. The house next to hers was bombed, and we were terrified. We witnessed horrifying scenes of martyrs and body parts being pulled from under the rubble. The sight was unbearable, yet it was our reality.

Afterward, we sought refuge in a school, hoping to find safety there. But even in the classroom, fear followed us. They unleashed phosphorus bombs, smoke, and shells upon us. A shell struck the classroom next to ours, intensifying our terror. Panic overtook us, and we fled the school, stepping past the bodies of martyrs as we escaped.

We then headed south, desperate for safety. Now we are displaced in another school, praying that this will be the last time we are forced to flee. Insha'Allah, we will return to our family, to our home.

Written on August 12, 2024

Shahd Zaher Alhamadeen
Age: 15 years old

Praise be to Allah for everything. On October 7, 2023, the Israeli army and occupying forces sent evacuation orders for Beit Hanoun, a city bordering the fence that separates us from the so-called State of Israel. Under bombardment, destruction, and displacement, we were forced to flee.

Ambulances transported us out of our city to the Jabalia area, which was supposedly a "safe zone." Days and weeks passed, and sleep eluded us. The sounds of tanks, bombings, and gunfire, and the rising toll of martyrs and injuries, all filled the air. During this time, the army issued new evacuation orders, directing people to southern Gaza, specifically to an area known as "post-wadi," which they also claimed was safe.

Once again, we were forced to flee—this time to the Al-Nuseirat camp. We had no relatives there to take us in. When we arrived at the shelter in Al-Nuseirat, it was anything but safe, contrary to what the occupation forces had promised. The scene was tragically familiar: bombing, destruction, and devastation surrounded us.

Days turned into months, and the bombings continued everywhere. On December 27, 2023, evacuation messages were sent to the very shelter we were staying in. Once again, under bombardment, we fled, moving from one area to another until we reached Deir Al-Balah. Words cannot describe the hardships and challenges we faced during this displacement: the fear, the destruction, the sight of martyrs' bodies, the wounded, and the hunger that consumed Gaza due to the blockade of humanitarian aid by the so-called occupation.

A new year began—January 1, 2024—but the nightmare persisted. On July 26, an area near our shelter was bombed and threatened. For the fourth time, we were forced to flee. After the Israeli army finished bombing the area, we returned to our shelter, only to find more remnants of destruction and despair.

And so the days pass, the months change, and the killing, destruction, and bombings continue, targeting shelters for displaced people throughout Gaza. Yet, despite everything, we continue to live in hope—hope that this terrifying nightmare will end, that we will return to our homes, and that this unjust and barbaric war will finally come to an end.

Written on August 20, 2024

Zaheera Yaseen Alayoubi
The mother of two martyrs, Mai and Malak Badawi

They passed away without bidding me farewell. Perhaps Allah will bring them to me together. This prayer was etched deep within my heart, even before my tongue could utter it. But it is the will of Allah.

A short message came through: "Pray for me, Mama. I have an Arabic exam." Then, just hours later, everything changed. My children told me they had been called to evacuate their house immediately. They left everything behind, running in fear, their faces filled with panic, until they found temporary shelter with relatives.

Through my small screen, I watched the destruction and bombing unfold, but I didn't know if they were safe. I waited anxiously for the phone network to return, hoping to hear their voices—even a short message—to calm my racing heart.

The perpetrators of this destruction have wreaked havoc on everything. They have erased the landmarks of our roads and demolished buildings, the walls collapsing on the heads of their inhabitants. Cries echo in the air, but no one answers except Allah.

Finally, my phone rang again. It was my mother: "We left Aunt's house, and now we are in a tent made of the remnants of our home. Seventeen members of our family are cramped into a small tent at Al-Nasr Hospital for Children. There is no water, no electricity, and the bread lines stretch endlessly. The food is minimal, almost nonexistent. You can hardly imagine what it's like to sleep on a tattered mattress on the hospital sidewalk."

Despite their dire situation, they kept saying, "Praise be to Allah," their words of patience offering a fragile sense of security amid the calamities that had shattered their hearts.

My daughter told me that she would go back to the house, hoping to gather something useful. Accompanied by her aunt and her little cousin, Luma, they ventured out. When they reached the house—or what remained of it—they didn't recognize it. The earth itself seemed transformed. And as they began collecting whatever they could, death lay in wait. A bomb claimed the innocent Luma, only eight years old, tearing her body apart, leaving behind half of what she had once been.

The others fled, finding refuge in a corner of the tent. Their cries filled the air, mourning as though trying to delay fate itself. But there was no time to grieve. They didn't have the luxury of crying for their lost loved one. The sounds of bombs outside made them wonder: "Is it my turn now?"

When will this nightmare end? Their days began with everyone dividing the exhausting chores: some went for laundry, one stood in the bread line, another fetched water, while the women prepared a dish of lentils or pasta if some was available.

One night, as the noise outside deafened the ears, Malak sat reading the Quran. She smiled at her sister and said, "I'll finish it today, and then I'll be done."

Mai sat beside them, gazing at the sky, pointing her little hand at the moon. "It's complete today, Mama. Look at it every night. I'll share my messages for you with it, maybe it will reach you."

Malak adjusted their sleeping positions; she was afraid of sleeping near the tent's door. Everyone closed their eyes after a long, grueling day, utterly exhausted. In the early hours of that night, a treacherous missile pierced their tent. It claimed the innocent Mai, followed by Malak, who succumbed to shrapnel from the missile. They both became martyrs on November 6, 2023.

There are no words to describe the grief, except to say that it is a merciless enemy.

The survivors gathered their strength, which had almost faltered, and began their journey south. It's hard to embrace grief every day, but in this land you have no time to bid farewell to loved ones—one after another. Their path was littered with bodies being devoured by stray dogs and street cats. You have no right to scream, nor to look up. You walk straight ahead, hands raised, as if surrendering to whatever has befallen you.

After a long and painful journey, they arrived at their relatives' home in the southern governorate, and then their displacement continued to Khan Younis. Less than a month later, they had to leave their home again, this time heading toward Rafah. Under the burning sun, a nylon tent became their shelter, where the heat seared their bodies inside. They had nothing left but submission to Allah's will.

After months of torment—suffering illness, poverty, and lack of food—Allah granted them salvation. They left Gaza, beginning a journey of treatment and care for their many war-inflicted wounds, under Allah's protection and in my heart.

May Allah have mercy on the faces that once dreamed of being held. My condolences, for they are in the care of the Most Merciful.

My daughter Mai: I will look at the moon every night, hoping to receive the messages of love and longing from you, my beloved Mai.

Malak, my dear, my quiet and beautiful daughter: A mother will never forget her heart, and you are mine.

My children: Despite your wounds, you are writing in the books of steadfastness, creating masterpieces that even the greatest artists cannot achieve.

Written on March 21, 2024

Lama, Martyr
Age: 10 years old

I died in pieces, targeted directly. My scattered parts will bear witness against the oppressor on the Day of the Great Announcement.

They used to call me the girl with the enchanting smile. That's how many described me—beautiful, extraordinarily so, cheerful, innocent, and calm. My dream was to become like my beloved teacher, Walaa Zaqout. She had a way of making everything feel joyful, for she was always kind, graceful, and close to all her students.

I remember our school trips vividly, as some of my happiest memories. She made those days feel like paradise on earth. She made me fall in love with the Arabic language, and I would eagerly wish for time to pass quickly so I could grow up and become just like her.

I was my mother's closest companion—her confidante, the keeper of her secrets. Though young, I carried wisdom beyond my years, with a sharp mind that made our bond even deeper. Each night, my mother and I would share long conversations filled with laughter and quiet moments of connection.

But the occupation didn't give me enough time.

❀ ❀ ❀

As the October war raged on, we sought refuge in a hospital in Gaza. After a few days, we decided to return home to gather some belongings. We spent the night there, hoping for a brief moment of normalcy. The next morning, after we prepared breakfast, I stood on the rooftop, gazing at our house, at the neighbors, at life itself, longing for a sense of peace. And then—within moments—the earth shook violently beneath us.

I screamed in horror. "Lama... Lama..."

We found her—in pieces. Half a head, half an arm, half a foot and leg—half a body. It was the greatest catastrophe. How could my mind possibly endure such a sight? Should I weep for the pain of separation or for the tender little body that had never carried hatred or malice toward anyone?

You left me, my daughter, and your eyes still held the longing of unfinished stories and dreams we never got to complete. The cruelty of what I saw brought tears even to my tears. This was the harshest farewell I could ever endure.

We parted, but your spirit remains with me. The nights mourn you, remembering our long conversations and whispered dreams. I pray for your mercy and forgiveness, my beloved. Though my heart is burned with grief over your loss, Allah has granted me patience, steadfastness, and pride—for I am the mother of a martyr. My martyr, who was targeted by the occupation as if she were a fierce warrior, on October 23, 2023.

O fools… She was nothing but an innocent child, who never posed a threat to anyone. But your cowardice knows no limits; every Palestinian life is a target to you.

Despite my heartbreak, I stand as a witness to the truth. Record it. Write it down. Spread it. Our stories must be preserved and told—forever.

Written on December 2, 2024

Maram Abu Hasira, Martyr

Age: 10 years old

Before the days of the October 7 war, I used to speak passionately about children's rights—rights I deeply believed in. In our school lessons and during morning broadcasts, we often discussed them. How could I not care? They were my rights, meant to be provided to me.

But in the days after the war began, these rights started crumbling one by one. I lost my right to education, my right to safety. As time passed, I couldn't find food to satisfy my hunger: I lost my right to eat. Days later, my house was destroyed; I became homeless and lost my right to shelter. At the same moment, my family was martyred: I lost my right to live with them. When I suffered a severe injury, there was no one to tend to my wounds, which eventually led to my losing the last of my childhood rights: my right to life.

These rights are reserved for others. They begrudge us enjoying them, so they snatch them away without blinking an eye. Now I am in heaven, in a place more merciful and just. I've left behind the land of oppression and tyranny. I am now with Allah, the god of all beings, as a bird flying freely, high above. With Allah, all rights are preserved. Here I will speak, live safely, eat delicious food, enjoy good health, and gain useful knowledge. I am innocent in face and soul, betrayed by those who reduced me to a number.

Written on November 26, 2023

Sarah Ashraf Abu Jarad
Age: 10 years old

To the compassionate hearts of our oppressed people, we write to you, our own hearts bleeding with anguish over the daily reality we endure. Here is a glimpse of this harsh truth:

We live in a tent no longer than three meters and no wider than three meters—me, my twelve family members, and all our belongings. Among us is an elderly man, seventy-seven years old, his wife, age sixty-six, and children ranging in age from four to forty-one, along with their parents. We reside in a tent on the street, without even a curtain for privacy, while passers-by come and go around us. By Allah, we do not even have a mat to sit on, nor blankets to cover ourselves. How will we cope when the biting cold intensifies?

We have repeatedly tried to request mattresses or a better tent, but there is no way out, and no one responds. The sun scorches our bodies during the day, and by night we endure the chill. Only Allah knows our suffering.

The children are sick, and medical treatment is scarce, insufficient to meet our needs. Our bodies are riddled with skin diseases, ravaged by epidemics, and weakened by dehydration. Hunger has stolen our health. We cannot eat anything except the charity meals distributed at the camps.

Help us. Is there no savior?

Written on July 31, 2024

Abdul Qader Mohammed Al-Khatib
Age: 9 years old

I am from Gaza City. I once dreamed of living a peaceful, content, and secure life. I lived in a beautiful, clean home and studied at a UNRWA school in the An-Nasr neighborhood. I was an excellent student, dreaming of becoming a great doctor who would treat patients in hospitals. But war and occupation erased my dreams, leaving me homeless, living in a tent on the streets, displaced from place to place. Life has become unbearably difficult, filled with fear.

The first time we were displaced, we fled our home, my family and I—escaping death and hunger. We walked to Rafah on foot. Along the way, we saw the tanks of the occupation and soldiers in front of us, while planes bombed houses from above. After the arduous displacement from Rafah, we left for Deir Al-Balah, then went to Al-Bureij, and finally to Al-Nuseirat.

There is no safe place in Gaza, no place where my family and I can settle. Living in a tent is unbearable—full of diseases and germs. My body now suffers from sores caused by the intense heat and fever, and I battle constant illness and blood infections.

I don't want to live in a tent anymore. I dream of returning to my home and my beautiful city, Gaza. Where is my right to live in safety? Where is my right to education, healthcare, and nutritious food? Unfortunately, healthy food no longer exists. The war has destroyed our homes, schools, hospitals, and universities. Gaza has become uninhabitable.

As a Palestinian child, I wish for this war to end so that I can live like other children around the world. Peace be upon you, and may Allah grant mercy and blessings.

Written on August 7, 2024

Noha Khaled Ghanem
Age: 5 years old

My displacement story began in northern Gaza, in Beit Lahiya. On October 7, 2023, we fled from our home to my grandfather's house, where we stayed for five days. Then we moved to my uncle's house for four days, and after that we went to the shelters in Jabalia for another four days.

As the situation grew more dangerous, we relocated to southern Gaza, to my aunt's place in the new camp in Al-Nuseirat. We stayed there for eighty-six days—until the day the occupation forces dropped evacuation notices over the camp. Once again we were forced to flee, this time to Mawasi Khan Yunis, in the industrial area, where we stayed for a month.

One day the occupation forces suddenly entered. They surrounded the area for four days. By a miracle, we managed to escape and left the place. Afterward we returned to Al-Nuseirat, to the new market camp, hoping that it would be our final displacement.

With prayers to Allah, we hope this nightmare will end soon.

Written on July 30, 2024

Waseem Abu Haneen

Age: 6 years old

On the morning of October 7, 2023, at exactly 6:30 AM, we were preparing to head to school when the deafening roar of rockets shattered our routine. They came from every direction, shaking the ground beneath us and filling the air with terror. That day marked the beginning of unimaginable loss. Everything familiar in our lives began slipping away.

In the earliest hours, evacuation orders reached us. We were told to leave the area around the Abu Yusuf Al-Qouqa roundabout. With heavy hearts and trembling hands, we packed what little we could carry and left for our old house in the Beach Camp—a place now stripped bare of warmth or comfort. For nearly a week, it became our refuge. But even that fragile sense of safety was short-lived. Soon after this, residents of the Beach Camp received instructions to evacuate southward.

And so our journey of displacement began. We traveled to the Al-Nuseirat camp, where we stayed with relatives for four days. Desperate to reclaim some semblance of normalcy, we returned briefly to the Beach Camp, clinging to the hope that this nightmare would pass and life might return to what it had once been.

But instead of relief, we found chaos. The bombs grew louder, the skies darker, and death lurked closer than ever before. There was no choice but to flee again, this time heading south toward Rafah. On November 6, under relentless bombardment, we joined hundreds of others seeking shelter near the Return Roundabout at one of Rafah's schools.

For months we remained there—seven long months of uncertainty, fear, and survival against all odds. By May 2024, however, the occupation forces announced plans to invade Rafah. Once more we were forced to move. This time we returned to the Al-Nuseirat camp, carrying nothing but the weight of exhaustion and despair.

Here we are now, still waiting—unsure of how much longer this will last or what lies ahead. Each sunrise brings both hope and dread, as we pray for an end to this endless cycle of suffering.

Written on August 1, 2024

Omar Khaleel Salem
Age: 4 years old

Poverty and war—two relentless enemies of humanity. Together, they crushed our lives. The bombings grew louder, the streets emptier. Evacuation orders came in waves until we were finally told to leave the north, though we were promised that it would only be temporary.

My grandfather urged us to go. "Come on, Grandpa, hold my hand," I begged, tears streaming down my face.

"No," he said firmly. "I won't leave, even if they cut me into pieces."

"Grandpa, don't make us go alone!" I cried, clinging to him.

"Go," he insisted, pressing some money into our hands. "Use this to get by."

And so began our long, grueling journey—to Khan Yunis first, where we didn't stay long before being ordered to evacuate again. My father didn't have enough money to transport our belongings to Rafah, so we fled to Al-Hilal Hospital, clinging to the hope that hospitals might offer protection under international law. But instead of safety, we found a siege, beatings, and humiliation.

Finally we were forced to leave for Rafah. For months, my father searched tirelessly for work, and eventually found a way to secure some. One day, my grandmother warned him not to go to work; her heart felt uneasy. That same day, something terrible happened—he narrowly escaped death. His leg was severely injured, and part of it had to be amputated, leaving him unable to walk for a long time.

Now another evacuation order looms over Rafah. We didn't have the money to reach Al-Nuseirat—the cost for going just a few kilometers was over $800—but Allah sent someone to help us. And here we are, surviving against all odds.

I've started studying inside one of the educational tents, trying to hold onto a sliver of normalcy. I also help with household chores—carrying water, fetching food, doing whatever it takes to keep us going.

To you, and to the whole world, I say this: I'm only a child. How can I bear the weight of such hardships? I want to go back to my grandfather. Why do they stop me from returning to Gaza City? Stop this war, because if I die. If my grandfather dies before I see him again, I will never forgive you.

Written on August 1, 2024

Zain Ismail Totah

Age: 6 years old

I am Zain, the sole survivor of my family.

Before October 7, 2023, my life was peaceful and filled with love. My mother, my father, and I lived happily with our extended family in a modest but warm home. We never imagined that such happiness could be shattered so abruptly—until that cursed day arrived, October 7.

In a panic, we fled from our home to seek refuge at the Baptist Hospital, hoping it would shield us from the relentless shelling. For a brief moment, as we sat together—my parents, siblings, uncles, cousins, grandmother, and grandfather—we felt safe. But that feeling didn't last long. Suddenly rockets rained down on us like a storm, and everything turned chaotic. I don't even remember what happened next.

When I woke up, I was in a hospital bed, disoriented and lost in a fog of pain and confusion. It wasn't until later that I learned the devastating truth: every single member of my family had been martyred. My beloved mother, who was carrying a baby in her womb, left this world without saying good-bye to me or giving me one last comforting hug. My dear father, sisters, uncles, grandmother—all gone on that same tragic day.

The weight of their absence crushed me. There were moments when I wished for death, just so I could see them again, hold them again, and live among them once more. How can a child bear such loss?

Now I live with my grandfather in the Al-Nuseirat camp in the south. But what kind of life is this? The place is destroyed in every way imaginable—no shelter, no family, no warmth. Everything familiar has vanished. No mother to embrace me, no father to guide me, no siblings to laugh with. Nothing remains but emptiness.

Each day feels heavier than the last. Yet, through it all, I cling to hope. Allah is my only helper now. I pray for the strength to endure, and dream of a day when peace will return and I can find solace in memories instead of feeling only despair.

Written on July 21, 2024

Muath Jameel Siyam

Age: 6 years old

I am a displaced child from the north, a place called Zimmo. Our journey began when we fled our home, seeking refuge at my aunt's house in the camp. For three days we stayed there, hoping for some relief. But soon we had to move again, this time to my other aunt's house, where we remained for seven days.

As the war intensified, staying in that place became impossible. We left the camp and headed south to another aunt's home, in Rafah, where our story of suffering truly began. There was no shelter, no food, no water—and no money to buy even the most basic necessities. Prices soared beyond belief: a bag of flour reached 300 shekels, and sugar cost 70 shekels. Hunger gnawed at us daily as we survived on scraps—a small piece of bread sprinkled with thyme and crumbs. Illnesses spread among us, adding to our despair.

Then came the evacuation orders, delivered by leaflets dropped over Rafah. We were forced to flee once more, this time to Al-Nuseirat. With no money to transport our belongings, we walked—exhausted, broken, carrying only what we could hold in our trembling hands.

I wished for death many times during those days, but it never came. Instead we endured a life stripped of joy, dignity, and hope. Our childhood vanished under the weight of survival. Each day blurred into the next, consumed by standing in endless lines: waiting for food at charity kitchens, gathering firewood to cook our meager meals, and hauling water, all just to survive.

Now we live in a small tent in the Al-Nuseirat camp. My family and I huddle together, trying to shield ourselves from the harsh realities of displacement. The tent offers little protection from the scorching sun and biting cold, yet it is all we have.

Every night, I pray to Allah that this nightmare will end—that peace will return and we can go back to our home. Until then we endure, clinging to fragments of hope amid the ruins of our lives.

Written on August 2, 2024

Fares Mohammed Abu Eyada

Age: 10 years old

My displacement journey began on the sixth day of the war, when the area I called home became a target of relentless shelling. There was no sanctuary left—our house, our neighbors' homes, all were under threat.

We fled to Al-Nuseirat, hoping for safety. My father rented an apartment, but peace eluded us. On only the second day there, the market nearby was struck by a devastating bombardment. My brother and cousin were injured, the apartment was severely damaged, and I was thrown several meters by the force of the explosion. The scene that unfolded before me haunts me still: dismembered bodies, most of them without heads. It left a deep scar on my heart, filling me with terror and fear.

With nowhere else to turn, my father decided we should seek refuge in a school. A place that had once symbolized learning now became our shelter. For three painful months, we lived there, battling illness and despair. Then came another blow: a massive Zionist attack forced us to leave for Deir Al-Balah. We stayed there briefly, clinging to hope, but soon realized we had to keep moving.

Our next stop was Rafah, where our suffering took on new dimensions. Hunger, fear, and sickness became our constant companions. After two months, the toll on our bodies was evident—illness had changed us, leaving us unrecognizable even to ourselves. Unable to remain there any longer, we moved again, this time to my grandfather's house. But even there, safety was an illusion. Three months later, we relocated yet again, settling into a camp that would become another chapter in our story of survival.

Every step of this journey has been marked by pain and loss. We've wandered from one place to another, searching for a sliver of peace, a moment of calm. Yet the war follows us everywhere, relentless and unforgiving.

Now here we are, living in uncertainty, carrying the weight of memories too heavy for children to bear. All we can do is pray—to Allah, to fate, to anyone who might listen—that this war will end. O Allah, bring us relief.

Written on July 25, 2024

Habib Abdullah Habib

Age: 12 years old

I am in the sixth grade. In fifth grade, I worked on memorizing the Quran and hoped to solidify my memorization of it—but life had other plans. On October 7, 2023, I was on my way to school when the deafening roar of rockets filled the air. Fear gripped me, and we hurried back home. The school announced a suspension of classes due to the war on Gaza. That very day, we fled from Shujayea, leaving behind our books, notebooks, clothes, toys, and the beautiful home we had once cherished.

We sought refuge at my grandfather's house in the Zaytoun neighborhood. But soon we were forced to move again—this time to southern Wadi Gaza, then to Al-Nuseirat, and later to Rafah. Along the way, the news grew heavier with each passing day. My aunt and her children were martyred, as were some of my father's cousins. Every day brought news of another loved one lost. Then came the Baptist massacre, where over five hundred members of the Habib family were martyred. It was a tragedy too great to bear.

When the evacuation order came for Rafah, we left once more, returning to Al-Nuseirat. Now I study in a tent at the "Seeds of Goodness" school in Al-Nuseirat. Each day is a struggle, but we hold onto hope, praying for Allah to bring relief and an end to this war. We long to return to our schools, our homes, and the beautiful world of childhood that has been taken from us. Until then we endure, clinging to the belief that peace will one day return to Gaza.

Written on August 5, 2024

Loay Abdullah Habib

Age: 9 years old

I am in the third grade. I had memorized thirteen parts of the Quran and was working on Surah Al-Hajj, hoping to complete it soon. But then that cursed war began, on October 7, 2023, shattering my dreams and routines.

That morning I was on my way to school when the deafening roar of rockets and the terrifying bombardment forced us to turn back home. Fear gripped our hearts as we fled from Shujayea to the Zaytoun neighborhood, then to southern Wadi Gaza, and finally to Al-Nuseirat. Instead of our beautiful home, we found ourselves sheltering in schools—cold, crowded, and far from the comfort we once knew. Later we moved to Rafah, searching for safety that always seemed just out of reach.

One day my father received a call that struck us like lightning. My aunt and her children had been martyred. In that massacre, over five hundred members of the Habib family lost their lives. Allah was our only refuge in those dark moments.

The Gaza we left behind is unrecognizable now. Everything is destroyed—the schools, the homes, the mosques, even the trees that once shaded our streets.

Then came the evacuation orders, dropped by occupation forces over Rafah. We fled again, this time to Al-Nuseirat.

Now we live in the tents—flimsy shelters made of wood and fabric—that replaced our homes. They offer no protection from the scorching sun or the biting winter cold. Our greatest hope is to return to our normal lives, to our schools, to the sense of security we once took for granted. But nothing remains untouched in Gaza—every school, every home, bears the scars of bombardment.

We cry out to the world: hear our voices. Let this tragic war, which has stolen everything from us, come to an end. Let us rebuild what was broken and reclaim the peace we so desperately long for.

Written on August 3, 2024

Dana Hitham Freed Totah
Age: 9 years old

I'll share my story of suffering during the war.

I was preparing to go to school when, suddenly, the deafening sound of rockets filled the air from every direction. That's when my suffering began. The sounds terrified me. We were forced to flee from one place to another, overwhelmed by fear and dread. On top of that, we struggled daily to find food and water. I took on responsibilities far beyond my years: filling water containers, carrying them to the tents, waiting in long lines for food at charity kitchens, and gathering firewood or scraps of paper to light fires.

This unending war has aged me before my time. We've lost even basic rights, like proper clothing. The clothes we wear are torn, worn out, falling apart. The meals from charity kitchens are often just lentils or undercooked beans; they barely sustain us. Shoes are nowhere to be found in the markets, leaving us barefoot on harsh terrain. With no income, because my father cannot work, we scrape by with what little we have.

Now all I think about is gathering fuel and carrying water. Allah alone is our refuge and helper.

Written on August 3, 2024

Rimas Ramzi Aliwa

Age: 12 years old

The story begins on the morning of Saturday, October 7, 2023. I was getting ready to go to school when, suddenly, the sound of rockets roared in from every direction. My younger sisters and I were overcome with fear. Soon afterward the shelling grew heavier, and war-planes began targeting homes, bombing them with their residents still inside.

After a month of relentless Israeli bombardment, we made the difficult decision to head south, leaving behind everything we knew. When we reached the so-called "safe passage," the scene was horrifying—remains of children, women, and men lay scattered everywhere. On Thursday, November 9, we arrived in Rafah and stayed there for seven long months.

But in May 2024, the occupation forces began ordering evacuations in Rafah. We learned that a military operation was imminent, forcing us to flee once again. On May 12, we left for Al-Nuseirat. There, we settled in the Al-Balata camp and joined a school. Despite all we had endured, we found joy in returning to learning, clinging to the hope that education could still shape our future.

We dream of returning to Gaza one day, to rebuild what was lost and reclaim the lives we once cherished.

Written on August 7, 2024

Yazen Haitham Totah

Age: 10 years old

Despite my young age, I carry great responsibility. Since the war began, I have been suffering from deprivation and loss. I was forced to leave my home, displaced from one area to another, and on top of that I endure the daily struggle of carrying water and the challenge of securing food and drink. Every day I go to the market to sell bread. My mother prepares the bread for me each morning, despite being exhausted—she gave birth just a week ago—so that we can bring in some food.

I have lost everything in this war, including my rights as a child. This is my suffering in the war. Many children like me have endured countless displacements, witnessed the deaths of orphans and martyrs, and been deprived of even the simplest rights. Our lives have become exhausting, filled with fear and anxiety.

We still wait for relief from Allah, hoping for a ceasefire so that we can return to our home in northern Gaza and go back to our school and the life we had before October 7, 2023. That has become all we dream of in life—to return to how things were before that day.

O Allah, bring us back soon to northern Gaza.

Written on August 1, 2024

Lammar Mohammed Farid Totah
Age: 11 years old

I will share my story of suffering during the war. We, the children, have been forced to carry responsibilities far heavier than our young shoulders can bear. Our childhood has been stolen from us, along with our right to live as children.

Now all we think about is gathering fuel and water—tasks that leave our small bodies exhausted. We've lost every dream we once had. All we hope for now is to return to our homes and reclaim the childhood that was taken from us. We yearn for everything, yet are denied even the simplest things: food, clothing, anything familiar.

I dream of going back to school, playing with my toys, and wearing my own clothes again. But life in the tents has worn me down. The scorching summer heat tires my small body, causing rashes to spread across my skin. Diseases and epidemics are everywhere. And the constant buzzing of drones above my head robs me of sleep. It's unbearable.

We—the children of Gaza—have not enjoyed much of our childhood. Fear of death follows us everywhere. Honestly, death seems better than the life we endure now.

O Allah, bring us relief soon. You are our only help.

Written on August 4, 2024

Lana Eyad Abu Karsh
Age: 12 years old

I lived in Al-Zuhra, in the north—a beautiful, clean city where I had a modest but happy life. One day, a day like any other, I woke up, put on my school uniform, and went to wait for my school bus in front of my house—a house I will never forget. Suddenly, loud and terrifying explosions shattered the calm. Fear gripped me, and I ran back home. From that moment—on October 7, 2023—until today, I haven't known a single happy day.

For the first week we stayed in our house, hoping for the news that we could return to school and normal life. But then came the evacuation order. We were told to leave the city immediately. We ran as fast as we could, homes crumbling before our eyes, rockets raining down over our heads.

We walked a long distance on foot, through the pitch-black night. Exhausted, we rested briefly in a dark place. After an hour and fifteen minutes, we pressed on until we reached Al-Hasanayn School, in the central region. The school was overcrowded and rife with diseases, yet it was the only shelter we could find.

Not long after this, the Israeli army dropped leaflets ordering us to evacuate the area and head south to Rafah. There we lived in a tent, enduring freezing cold and severe shortages caused by the closed border crossings. We had no money to buy even the most basic necessities.

Later, yet more leaflets arrived, ordering us to evacuate Rafah and return to the central region. We left under dire conditions—no money, no medicine, no food. Back in the central region, we set up another tent, where life remained unbearably hard.

I wish I could have stayed in my home, close to my friends. But I left behind everything—my memories, my dreams, my ambitions, my childhood, and my home. I dream of waking up to safety, going to school, and living a normal life again. My beautiful home…I will never forget it, no matter how long this displacement lasts.

Written on July 31, 2024

Hala Majdi Mohammad Siyam

Age: 10 years old

I am from Sheikh Ajlin. We were sitting at home when suddenly, at 7:00 AM on October 7, 2023, the sound of rockets roared as if they were falling directly on us. Most of the shelling targeted our area because it was in a resistance zone. By Allah's mercy, we narrowly escaped death. Always we remind ourselves: "Praise be to Allah, always and forever."

After we had left for my grandfather's house and then departed from there as well, heavy shelling forced us to flee yet further. We went to Al-Shifa Medical Complex, where we stayed for two months. When the army reached us, we fled south to Al-Bureij, seeking refuge in a shelter school. The shelling was intense—I saw dismembered bodies and martyrs.

We finally left the school and went to the park, where we stayed for three months and eight days. Afterward we moved to Al-Nuseirat. In the camp we stayed for a week, but tragedy struck: my mother and younger sister were injured. I cried endlessly, until my sister was discharged from the hospital. Then we decided to move to Al-Zawayda.

We stayed there for two weeks, but the ants crawling on our faces while we slept made life unbearable. Finally we returned to the camp in Al-Nuseirat. I joined the "Seeds of Goodness" school, where we learn lessons that feel more valuable than ever—lessons of survival, resilience, and hope.

O Allah, may this be the last displacement for Gaza.

Written on July 22, 2024

Shahd Abdullah Habib

Age: 6 years old

I am Shahd Habib, a kindergarten student. I used to go to my beautiful kindergarten on a cheerful bus with my friends, laughing and singing along the way. But suddenly the hour of danger struck—an hour we never saw coming. The war began on Gaza, and we ran back home, hearts pounding with fear. That marked the beginning of our displacement story.

We fled to Al-Nuseirat, seeking refuge in a school, and then moved to Rafah. It was there that heartbreaking news reached us: my aunt and her children had been martyred. Then a call came saying that my uncle had been injured—his hand and leg badly wounded—and my cousin also had been hurt in his leg. Despite everything, they remained steadfast in Gaza, holding on to what little they had, while others, like us, were displaced to the south.

My father was heartbroken, longing for my uncles and aunts. But this cruel war has driven a wedge between relatives, siblings, and loved ones, scattering us far apart.

Then came the evacuation order from Rafah. The Israelis dropped leaflets ordering us to leave. In fear we fled again—my father, my mother, my siblings, and I—moving from one place to another, searching for safety. Finally we settled in Al-Nuseirat, where we now live in a small tent.

I dream of the day when this war will end. I want to return to my kindergarten to learn, play, eat, and live like other children around the world—not under the constant roar of shelling, planes, and tanks, but in peace and joy.

Written on July 31, 2024

Osama Mahmoud Mohammed Abu Han

Age: 10 years old
Told by His Mother

My joy was never complete, nor did my eyes find peace, after finally owning an apartment following fifteen years of relentless struggle. Barely three months I lived there before everything changed. The night of October 7, 2023, was calm and serene, with no sign of trouble.

At 5:30 AM we woke up for *Fajr* prayer, and afterward I woke my children to prepare for school. By 6:30 AM, everyone was ready to leave. Suddenly a deafening sound shook us to our core. My daughter innocently asked, "What is this, Mama?" I replied in a voice tinged with worry, "Don't be afraid. It's just thunder."

But soon rockets filled the sky, launching from every direction. In those early moments, we had no idea what was happening or who was responsible. Within hours, the situation became painfully clear. We were ordered to evacuate the area near Al-Quds Open University; our building would be bombed.

We left in disbelief, gripped by panic and fear, taking nothing with us. That day marked the beginning of our losing everything—every trace of life, in every sense of the word.

We fled to my uncle's house in the Beach Camp, where our journey of suffering truly began. After a week, more evacuation orders forced us southward. We went to my husband's relatives in the Al-Nuseirat camp, staying for four days before returning to the Beach Camp, still clinging to hope that life might return to normal.

But danger escalated daily. Fire zones, airstrikes, naval bombardments, and clashes surrounded us. The night of November 6 was our last in the Beach Camp. Death loomed everywhere, and we didn't think we'd survive.

The next morning, like many families, we fled south. Walking through Salah al-Din Street—the "Street of Death"—was harrowing. Corpses, charred bodies, destroyed vehicles, and collapsed buildings lined the road. Forced to abandon what little we carried, we walked on, defeated, heads bowed, heading straight to Rafah.

Arriving at sunset, we sought refuge in one of the schools but found no safety, no water, no food, nothing. We stayed in Rafah for seven grueling months. Our sole focus became survival—securing bread and water for drinking and washing. Prices soared beyond imagination, even for the simplest items. Humiliation weighed heavily on us, making death seem preferable. Day by day we waited, praying that Allah would intervene—but His will decreed that this trial was not yet over.

In May 2024, treacherous eyes turned toward Rafah, forcing us to flee again. This time we returned to the Al-Nuseirat camp. Here we have been since then, drinking the bitter cup of suffering repeatedly. We still breathe, though the war rages on, and we don't know how long it will last.

We ask Almighty Allah to treat us according to His mercy, not our deeds, granting us one of two blessings: martyrdom or victory over the enemies of humanity.

Written on August 7, 2024

Bilsan Shadi Sadi Abdul Qader
Age: 11 years old

I am Bilsan.

At the start of the war, our house was bombed several times. On the very first day we lost my uncle, a man we were deeply proud of for his work and character. At first we clung to hope, believing he had survived. But five months later, the devastating news shattered us: he had been martyred on that first day.

We endured hunger, thirst, relentless fear, and bombardment, facing death more times than I can count. Yet through it all we survived—praise be to Allah.

After five grueling months in Gaza's Shuja'iyya, we were ordered to evacuate to the south. Against our will, we left everything behind and headed south. There we faced unbearable hunger, thirst, and disease. In desperation, we resorted to eating animal feed. My brother fell ill from it, and the doctor urged my mother, "Go further south for your son's sake."

He was her only son; she couldn't bear to lose him, so, with heavy hearts, we decided to head south again. But the greatest shock awaited us at the so-called "safe passage." The Israelis intercepted us, took my father, beat him, stripped him of his belongings, and confiscated his phone and ID. To this day, since February 27, 2024, we have had no news of him. This is just one of the countless hardships we endured.

We have faced endless problems—not only with strangers but also with relatives. My mother bore the brunt of these struggles. She became our rock, our everything. We pray for this war to end so that we can return to our homes. I miss my father, my uncles, and my grandfather dearly. Their absence weighs heavily on my heart.

To our beloved Gaza—we miss you so much. We miss "Gaza of pride," a place we once called home.

Written on August 5, 2024

Balsam Shadi Sadi Abdul Qader
Age: 9 years old

I am Balsam.

At the start of the war, our house was bombed several times. On the very first day, we lost my uncle, a man we were deeply proud of for his work and character. At first we clung to hope, believing he had survived. But five months later, the devastating news shattered us: he had been martyred on that first day.

We endured hunger, thirst, relentless fear, and bombardment. Death loomed over us multiple times, yet by Allah's mercy we survived.

After five grueling months in Gaza's Shuja'iyya, we were ordered to evacuate to the south. Reluctantly we left, against our will. In the south we faced unbearable hunger, thirst, and disease. In desperation, we resorted to eating animal feed. My brother fell ill from it, and the doctor told my mother, "Take him south—he's sick."

My brother is her only son; she couldn't bear to lose him, so, with heavy hearts, we decided to head south. The greatest shock awaited us at the so-called "safe passage." The Israelis intercepted us, took my father, beat him, stripped him of his belongings, and shouted at us and my mother. They confiscated his phone and ID, leaving us standing in the scorching sun for hours. The Israeli soldier spoke to us in a terrifying voice. It was a moment I'll never forget.

My father has been held captive for five months. To this day, since February 27, 2024, we have had no news of him. This is just one of the countless hardships we've endured.

We have faced endless problems—not only with strangers but also with relatives. My mother bore the brunt of these struggles. She became our rock, our everything.

Now I am sick, suffering from intestinal issues and colon enlargement. Yet, because I have no official medical documentation, no one helps me. The weight of my illness exhausts me daily. My mother suffers from migraines and also desperately needs a specialist, but she lacks the money to see a doctor.

We pray for this war to end so that we can return to our homes. I miss my father, my uncles, and my grandfather dearly. My father is a prisoner; my uncle is a martyr; our house has been bombed. Their absence aches in my heart.

To our beloved Gaza—we miss you so much. We miss "Gaza of pride," a place we once called home.

Written on August 5, 2024

Mohammed Haitham Abdul Qader

Age: 11 years old

My name is Mohammed. My first displacement was to the UNRWA Al-Daraj School. From the very first day of the war, hunger and displacement became my constant companions. I've never known the sweetness of safety. I lost my shelter, my home, and every place I once called mine, moving instead from one location to another. My education slipped away, and here I am, enduring until the last moment, still in a school. Even after being shot in the back during a stormy, rain-soaked night, I survived. I fled to Al-Shifa Medical Center, only to face repeated Israeli attacks. With each displacement, life grew harder than before. The third time I fled to Rafah, only to face yet another attack there. Then I moved to Al-Nuseirat, settling near the New Balata Market. Here I remain, praying that Allah will bring an end to this war soon.

Here is my mother, Asmaa Jumaa Abdul Qader, sharing her story:

"I am a Palestinian woman from Gaza's Shuja'iyya. I fled with my son, Mohammed, through countless hardships, moving from one place to another as the occupation bombed, attacked, and tortured us without mercy. The suffering of displacement has grown unbearable. Hunger, oppression, and death have become the norm for so many. I pray for this war to end as soon as possible. My son was shot in the back, and I fled with him and my other children to the southern areas, reaching Rafah. But even Rafah wasn't safe; it too was attacked by the Israelis.

"Now I live with my children in Al-Nuseirat, near the New Balata Market. My heart yearns for peace, and I hope that the war will stop so we can return to Gaza Al-Hashem."

Date Written: August 1, 2024

Abdul Rahman Ramzi Aliwa

Age: 9 years old

The story begins on the morning of October 7, 2023. I was getting ready to go to school when a terrifying sound echoed from every direction. My younger siblings and I were overwhelmed with fear, but my father and mother reassured us, telling us not to be afraid or anxious. Soon after, the shelling and rockets intensified. Planes began bombing homes, striking directly over the heads of their residents. For an entire month we endured bombings, destruction, and relentless fear.

Finally we decided to head south with my family. On November 9, we reached Rafah, where we stayed for seven long months. But by early May 2024, Israeli forces threatened to invade Rafah. On May 11 we fled once again, this time heading to Al-Nuseirat and settled in the New Balata Market by May 12.

And here I am now, eagerly waiting for the day when I can return to Gaza, praying for peace and a chance to rebuild what was lost.

Written on August 2, 2024

Aisha Hussein Al-Hawajri
Age: 11 years old

On October 7, 2023, I put on my shoes and my uniform, ready to go to school. But when the sound of shelling reached us, I ran into my mother's arms, trembling with fear. The occupation forces warned us to leave our area. They burned part of our house and bombed the rest, leaving us homeless. And so began our journey of displacement.

We sought refuge at a relative's house, but we didn't stay long before moving on to a school sheltering displaced families. There we suffered from skin diseases and stomach ailments caused by polluted water and unsanitary, overcrowded conditions.

Later another evacuation order came, though we stayed that night. Eventually, as shells rained down on us, we were forced to flee again—to Khan Yunis, where we lived in a tent for two freezing months.

Fetching water became a daily struggle, and food and flour were scarce. Exhaustion weighed heavily on us. We lost weight and felt as though we had aged ten years. My childhood slipped away; I no longer played like I used to. Instead I stood in long lines for water, while my younger sister went to the charity kitchen for food. My mother washed our clothes and did everything she could to keep us afloat.

Suddenly Israeli forces dropped leaflets from planes, ordering us to evacuate once more. We fled to Rafah, enduring scorching heat during the day and freezing cold at night. Strange illnesses struck us, diseases we had never seen before.

This time, we didn't have to wait long before another evacuation order arrived. We headed to the central region, settling in yet another camp. My mother, drained and heartbroken, decided she couldn't flee again. She simply couldn't bear it.

I miss my home, my family, and my loved ones deeply. Will we ever return?

Written on July 31, 2024

Alya Shadi Nijib Hasan Al-Yazji

Age: 9 years old

On October 7, 2023, the Israeli Defense Forces sent messages ordering us to evacuate my beloved city of Beit Hanoun, at exactly 1:37 PM. By 2:00 PM, we were on the move, heading to Beit Hanoun Hospital under relentless bombardment. We stayed there until 6:00 AM the next morning, then walked from Beit Hanoun to my uncle's house in Jabalia Camp.

We remained at my uncle's house until 5:00 PM, but as the situation grew more dangerous and the shelling intensified, we decided to seek safer shelter. We moved to Hamad School in Sheikh Zayed City, near the Indonesian Hospital, where we found a classroom to stay in. For thirty-five days, we endured constant shelling and severe hunger.

The occupation showed no mercy—it bombed our school multiple times. With no other choice, we decided to head south in search of safety. Transportation was unavailable, so we walked from Sheikh Zayed City to Al-Mughazi Camp, then continued toward Rafah, which the Israeli Defense Forces claimed was the safest area. We stayed in Rafah for four months, in the Al-Jinina neighborhood, until planes dropped leaflets ordering us to evacuate once again.

We moved to Deir Al-Balah, hoping to find refuge, but safety remained elusive. Finally we ended up in Al-Nuseirat Camp.

Here we are now, struggling to survive day by day. Allah is our only refuge. I miss the smell of my homeland, the familiar streets, the warmth of home, and long for the day when the ceasefire decision will come, bringing peace back to our lives.

Written on July 25, 2024

Haya Ziad Al-Shanbari
Age: 7 years old

Will my father survive?

My father is my greatest role model, a mountain I lean on during every breakdown. Don't be surprised by my words, though I am young; this story will show you how the children of Gaza were made to endure unimaginable pain, teaching us resilience beyond compare.

Displacement after displacement... The pain of instability became my first breakdown. My father, a pillar of strength, works in civil defense. We rarely see him, for he risks his life on countless missions. Despite Israeli warnings, he has refused to leave the north, choosing instead to stay with my older brother, Bakri.

Before we left, hunger gnawed at our bodies night after night. To silence the growling of empty stomachs, we drank water mixed with salt, hoping it would keep us alive. As Ramadan approached, my father called my mother and said, "There's nothing left to feed the children. Go south, and I'll stay here in the north with Bakri."

We fled to Rafah, the farthest point in the south. But soon a devastating call shattered us: Israeli forces had arrested my father and my sixteen-year-old brother. Imagine a mother alone with her children in a thermal tent so hot that it burned our skin raw, receiving such cruel news. We prayed fervently to Allah.

The phone rang.

"Hello, who's speaking?"

"It's me, your brother."

"Did you get out of prison?"

"Yes, thank Allah."

"How was it?"

"We saw death pass by every moment. Our hands were bound with sharp plastic ties the entire time. Talking was forbidden. Eating or drinking was allowed only by their command. Showering was a luxury we didn't deserve. Rabid dogs attacked us hour after hour. We screamed while the soldiers laughed at us. Humiliation and degradation. Many prisoners had their limbs forcibly amputated, with brutal cruelty."

As my brother spoke, I thought, *How will my beloved hero endure all this pain?*

To this day, my father remains unaccounted for. Is he alive? What harm has he endured? These thoughts haunt me day and night. Imagining the torture he faces is unbearable.

Stop the war. Stop the killing. Stop all these crimes.

Written on July 31, 2024

Enas Haitham Totah

Age: 12 years old

My story of suffering in the war began on October 7, 2023. We woke up that morning to prepare for school when, suddenly, deafening sounds erupted from every direction. Fear gripped us instantly. That same situation continues to this day: we are surrounded by the relentless sounds of shelling and rockets, a constant reminder of the destruction around us.

The occupation has destroyed everything beautiful in my life. The laughter, safety, and dreams now feel like a distant memory. We've become burdened with responsibilities far beyond our years, no longer innocent children. This harsh reality has stripped us of the essence of childhood. We now search for worn-out clothes, rely on food from charity kitchens, drink polluted water, and bathe in the contaminated sea. Every beautiful dream I once held has died. The simplest joys of life have been replaced by survival and despair.

I've faced embarrassing situations while fetching water, moments that made me hate myself and curse the day I was born. The weight of humiliation and loss is too heavy for a child to bear. All I wish for now is to return to our destroyed home and sit amid the rubble, just to feel safe again.

Written on August 1, 2024

Maisaa Shadi Al-Yazji

\Age: 11 years old

On October 7, 2023, at exactly 1:37 PM, the Israeli Defense Forces ordered us to evacuate my beloved city of Beit Hanoun. By 2:00 PM, under heavy bombardment, we fled to Beit Hanoun Hospital. We stayed there until 6:00 AM the next morning, then walked on foot to my uncle's house in Jabalia Camp.

We remained at my uncle's house until 5:00 PM, but as the shelling worsened, we sought safer shelter in schools. We found refuge in a classroom at Hamad School in Sheikh Zayed City, near the Indonesian Hospital. For thirty-five days, we endured relentless shelling and crippling hunger.

The occupation showed no mercy—it bombed our school multiple times. Desperate for safety, we decided to head south. With no transportation available, we walked from Sheikh Zayed City to Al-Mughazi Camp, then continued toward Rafah, which the Israeli Defense Forces claimed was the safest area.

We stayed in Rafah for four months, in the Al-Jinina neighborhood. But when planes dropped evacuation posters, we were forced to leave again. We moved to Deir Al-Balah, searching for safety, but found none. Finally we ended up in Al-Nuseirat Camp.

Here we are now, struggling to survive day by day. Allah is our only refuge. I miss the smell of my homeland and long for the day the ceasefire comes, bringing peace back to our lives.

Written on August 5, 2024

Samia Al-Sharif
Age 15 years old

At the Beach Camp in Gaza, we were at home, surrounded by neighbors, when the war began. War-planes dropped evacuation posters, urging people to leave for safer areas. Many fled, but we stayed in our neighborhood. Every day the naval artillery bombarded us. My father and grandmother were injured. Finally we went to Al-Shifa Medical Center. At night we slept in a school, but soon fire zones struck the area. Everyone was injured except us; Allah saved me and my siblings. Afterward we fled to a UNDP facility.

On October 25, 2023, tanks advanced toward Al-Shifa, bombing the third floor of our building. Water supplies ran out, and we contacted the Red Cross to bring us water. Our greatest dream then was simply to drink water.

Under siege, the Red Cross coordinated with the Israelis, and we surrendered, raising the white flag. It was the first time I saw the Israelis. They told us, "Go either south or to Sheikh Radwan." We headed to Sheikh Radwan.

Later, on November 4, tanks advanced again, striking the area with fire zones. There was no flour or food for children—a bag of flour cost 600 shekels ($200). We couldn't afford it.

When we reached Nitsareem, the Israelis ordered us, "Stand still for five minutes." Then they let us leave. We went to a school, but the tanks kept advancing, spreading fire zones as we fled toward Al-Nuseirat. Then we fled to Deir Al-Balah, staying with relatives. When the tanks returned, we went back to Al-Nuseirat, settling near the market with other displaced families.

Then Al-Nuseirat was bombed. Special forces arrived to extract Israeli captives. Helicopters fired on people, and they took the captives. It felt like Judgment Day. Everyone scattered, fleeing death.

We continue to suffer to this day, dreaming of returning to our homes.

Written on July 31, 2024

Maryam Hazem Jouda

Age: 8 years old
Told by Her Mother

We have survived the war until this moment. Once we lived in a small, warm house, until it was bombed above our heads on October 10, 2023, shortly after the war began. By a miracle we escaped from under the rubble—my husband, myself, and our four daughters, all injured to varying degrees. Thus began our displacement journey, moving from one place to another in search of safety and shelter, after losing our home and without any source of income to meet our basic needs.

The situation worsened when we were forced to flee to Rafah, after our area in Al-Nuseirat was classified as a dangerous combat zone. There, in Rafah, we faced our hardest struggle yet, searching for shelter, food, and water. The endless queues were tormenting, but the most painful suffering was seeing my eldest daughter, Raghaf, who is thirteen years old and suffers from cerebral palsy, struggling to adapt and meet her special needs.

We stayed in Rafah for four months, living in a house with several other families. Then we returned to Al-Nuseirat, settling in a tent near our bombed house. But the war didn't spare us even then. The pain deepened when my husband, Hazem Jouda, was critically injured in an attack, leaving him hospitalized to this day.

Now I bear the responsibility of caring for our four daughters and managing the hardships of life, alone. The war hasn't ended, nor has our suffering, which renews itself every day as I look at my daughters and the painful conditions we endure inside the tent.

We pray to Allah to end this cursed war.

Written on August 3, 2024

Tameem Mohammed Abu Eyada

Age: 6 years old

My displacement journey began on the sixth day of the war, when the area I lived in was hit by unprecedented bombing. No place felt safe anymore, not our home or the neighboring houses.

We fled to Al-Nuseirat, where my father rented an apartment. On just our second day there, the market area was heavily bombed. My brother and cousin were injured, and the apartment we had rented was severely damaged. The force of the explosion threw me several meters away. I witnessed severed body parts and decapitated martyrs, a sight that deeply scarred us all, filling our hearts with terror and fear.

My father decided we should go to a school, as there was no other safe place left. We stayed there for three months, enduring illnesses brought on by harsh conditions. Then, after a major Israeli attack, we moved to Deir Al-Balah and stayed there briefly before heading to Rafah, where our pain and suffering reached new heights.

We remained in Rafah for over two months, but illness changed our appearance drastically. Unable to endure any longer, we moved to my grandfather's house, staying for three months. Then even that house became unsafe, so we relocated to this camp.

Every step of the way has been marked by suffering and pain. We ask Allah to end this war... O Allah!

Written on July 25, 2024

Jana Osama Al-Hawiti

Age: 13 years old

On October 20, 2023, we fled from Gaza to Al-Mughazi, where we stayed for a month. Then we moved to Khan Yunis and remained there for two months, followed by another two months in Al-Mawasi / Khan Yunis. From there, we fled to Rafah near the Egyptian border and stayed for a month before returning to Al-Mawasi / Khan Yunis for yet another month. Finally we settled in Al-Nuseirat, where we've now been for three months. Hopefully, this will be our last displacement, and the war will end with improvements for us.

We are utterly exhausted and fed up with our current situation. We pray for the war to end soon, because our financial situation is dire. My father is sick, my brother is sick, and we have no source of income. We lack money to buy clothes, cleaning supplies, or even a loaf of bread. There's no help or aid—our situation is below zero. No welfare checks or shopping vouchers are coming our way.

O Allah, may this war end, and may we find relief from the suffering, destruction, and war that has fallen upon Gaza.

Written on July 28, 2024

Lana Mohammed Abu Ajami
Age: 10 years old

On the morning of Saturday, October 7, 2023, at 6:30 AM, we woke up to the deafening sound of rockets being launched toward the settlements. Filled with fear and panic, we fled our home under heavy bombardment, seeking refuge in a safer area—my aunt's house in Al-Bureij. But when the shelling intensified, worsening our situation, we were forced to flee again, this time from Al-Bureij Camp to Al-Nuseirat Camp.

My aunt sheltered us for twenty days, until heavy bombardment targeted her house, leaving us no choice but to move to a new camp in Al-Nuseirat. There we stayed in my uncle's house for two months, sleeping and waking up to the sounds of bombs and missiles. Fear controlled every moment of our lives.

Then the Israeli occupation dropped evacuation posters on us. We fled to Rafah under fire, amid the sounds of rockets and the sight of martyrs' remains. We sought refuge in a shelter school, where we endured five agonizing months filled with terror and violence.

When the occupation ordered us to evacuate Rafah, we fled once more, to Al-Nuseirat Camp. Here we live in tents, enduring the worst days of our lives, constantly going back and forth to fetch water.

May Allah grant us relief in a blessed hour, end this war, and heal the bleeding wound... O Allah!

Written on July 20, 2024

Rahma Khaleel Al-Zayan

Age: 12 years old

I am a sixth-grade student. Before this aggression on Gaza, I was happy at home, waking up every morning to go to school with great joy. But everything changed on October 7, 2023. When the attack began, I fled from my beautiful home to southern Wadi Gaza.

Now, instead of studying or playing, I stand in long lines at the charity kitchen, hoping to bring food for my family. Sometimes I leave empty-handed. I also spend hours at the water truck, filling containers to meet our daily needs.

But the aggression hasn't ended. My father stayed behind in the north, and I'm not used to being without him. Thankfully, he's still alive. Yet there's no safety or security—bombings happen everywhere, and fear is constant.

I've been displaced four times. One day, during a displacement, planes bombed the house across from ours. Our home was damaged, and I was injured—my back and body still bear the scars. All my belongings and cherished memories were lost in the bombing.

After that we fled to Deir Al-Balah, settling in a zinc-roofed house. It was unbearably hot, offering no protection from the scorching sun. This tiny space belonged to my aunt, and forty-three of us lived crammed together. Water was scarce, so we resorted to fetching salty seawater and trying to make do with it. We ate only one meal a day—flatbread—and hunger became our constant companion.

Later we moved to Al-Nuseirat, where lighting fires for cooking became another struggle. Wood was expensive and unavailable, adding to our hardships. I sold canned goods and sweets to help my family, and my mother, who was pregnant, suffered alongside us. Due to pollution, we contracted many diseases, but treatment was out of reach.

We pray to Allah to end this war... O Allah!

Written on August 7, 2024

Dima Al-Sakani

Age: 10 years old

On the morning of October 7, 2023, my mother woke up me and my sisters so that we could go to school, but rockets began ascending into the sky. Fear gripped us instantly.

We stayed in our house for an entire month, until our home and our neighbors' homes were bombed. My grandmother was martyred; some of my cousins were martyred; others were injured; the tension rose beyond what we could bear. We packed our bags, taking only clothes, and fled to my grandmother's house in Al-Mughraga, where we stayed for two weeks. But soon the shelling intensified there, and her house was bombed too. Thank Allah, everyone survived. After that we went to Al-Maghazi School, where we stayed for four months—until it too was bombed. We witnessed the remains of martyrs scattered everywhere, a sight that left us terrified.

The shelling began again one night, and I couldn't believe the night would ever end or daylight come. Early the next morning, we decided to flee once more—but to our shock, the cost of a truck to transport us was $270. My mother handed over the money to the driver so we could escape the dangerous area for a safer place.

We fled to a development center run by social services on the street in Rafah, where we set up a tent amid freezing winter weather. We didn't have winter clothes, and the suffering was immense. Later we moved to Al-Nuseirat, settling in the Balata Market.

All praise is due to Allah. Now we wait for the war to end so we can return to our home, O Allah.

Date Written: July 21, 2024

Nada Ziad Al-Shanbari

Age: 12 years old

We lived in a small house filled with love, warmth, and affection—a place where peace reigned. On October 7, 2023, I woke up early to go to school. I put on my clothes and ate breakfast, and my father took me and my brother to drop us off at school.

Suddenly a loud noise shattered the calm. My father hugged us tightly and said, "Don't be afraid." We quickly realized what was happening: the occupation was attacking Gaza from every direction. Filled with fear, we rushed back home to take shelter with our parents.

My mother was waiting for us at the door, terrified and asking, "What are these sounds?"

My father replied gravely, "I don't know, but I think the occupation has begun to wage war against beautiful Gaza."

Our hearts sank under the weight of fear.

Soon after this, the occupation began dropping posters ordering us to leave our homes. My father, fearing for our safety, moved us to a shelter, where we started living among countless displaced families.

Later more posters arrived, ordering us to move south. My father resisted. He works in civil defense, risking his life daily to rescue and defend the innocent. He barely came home once in a month, and he stayed behind when we left.

Over time, life in northern Gaza had become unbearable—no food, no water, no safety. Suddenly my mother received a call from my father: "Ramadan has arrived, and there's nothing to fill our children's stomachs. Go south; perhaps we'll find something to feed them. It's better they die as martyrs than starve—it's more honorable for us. I will stay here because I cannot abandon my work. I will sacrifice my life for the homeland."

With heavy hearts, my siblings, my mother, and I left for Rafah, while my father and older brother stayed behind in the north. In Rafah, conditions were dire. On the first day we stayed in a small tent that burned with heat. After a short while, devastating news reached us: my father and my sixteen-year-old brother had been arrested.

We were heartbroken and prayed fervently to Allah. Thanks to His mercy, my brother was eventually released, though his condition was dire. I asked him, "How did the occupation treat you?"

He replied, with tears in his eyes, "They treated me as if I were worse than a dog. They beat us day and night. They didn't give us food or water. Our hands and legs were tied for about a month. They sicced dogs on us while we screamed. They didn't allow us to bathe, and they amputated the limbs of Palestinian prisoners from Gaza right before my eyes. But thanks to Allah, He relieved my distress. May He also relieve the distress of my father and all prisoners."

Two days later, the occupation dropped leaflets ordering us to leave Rafah again. We wondered where to go. No one seemed to care about us. Eventually we decided to head to Al-Nuseirat with people we had met in Rafah.

After a long and exhausting journey, we arrived and settled in the Balata Market Camp. There, my little sister fell ill again. We desperately need aid from the Red Cross, but no one has helped us. Our family remains divided—some in the south, others in the north.

When will this pain end? When will my father return safely, so we can reunite in peace?

Written on August 5, 2024

Mona Nidal Al-Sharif

Age: 11 years old

I am Mona, in fifth grade. I was ready to go to school on October 7, 2023, when the sound of rockets stopped me from continuing my education. The war on Gaza began with the Israeli occupation. I felt fear and anxiety, but my mother reassured me. We left our home in the Beach Camp as fire zones struck the area. I saw body parts and wounded people.

We spent the night in Al-Shifa Hospital, and in the morning we went to Al-Nuseirat. We stayed with my aunt, then moved to Rafah, and finally returned to a sandy area near the UN clinic in the market. Our lives turned upside down.

One night we woke up to the sound of rockets and the smell of smoke. We spent the night at my aunt's house and returned the next day. While I was playing, at noon, a missile struck us and my friend was martyred, during the operation in Al-Nuseirat. We were terrified—I saw tanks from afar, and the wounded, and an elderly man near me, who was injured and later martyred before the ambulance arrived. These were scenes I had never seen before.

My life became filled with exhaustion, humiliation, oppression, and a lack of all safety, protection, education, food, and hygiene. How long will this last? How long will our lives remain like this? We, the children of Gaza, stand in endless lines for bread and food from charity kitchens, fill jugs with salty and sweet water, and collect cardboard and nylon for our mothers to burn so that they can cook for us.

Despite the war, I study to make up for lost education, and keep myself busy instead of dwelling on the war and its pains. I pray to Allah to end the war and restore our normal lives before I lose anyone else from my family.

Written on August 5, 2024

Rimas Bilal Al-Hawiti

Age: 10 years old

My siblings—Anas, Jawad, Zain, and Rima—and my parents lived peacefully in our home in Al-Mughraga. On the morning of October 7, 2023, we set out for school, but on the way the sound of rockets and planes bombing unarmed civilians filled the air. Fear gripped us, and we ran back home in terror.

Artillery and planes bombed the houses next to ours. Shrapnel rained over our heads, and we fled in fear of the shelling. Seeking safety, we took refuge in Al-Maghazi School to protect our family. But soon the planes bombed the school, and tanks invaded Al-Maghazi Camp. Once again we were forced to flee—this time to Rafah. There we set up a nylon tent near the Ministry of Social Affairs.

After several months, Israeli forces launched a military operation in Rafah, destroying the city entirely. We fled yet again, this time to a government school in Khan Yunis. It was invaded by planes, tanks, and heavy weapons, demolishing homes and killing children, women, and men. Evacuation leaflets were dropped, leaving us hopeless, anxious, and scared.

We sought shelter with relatives in Deir Al-Balah for two months, but felt overwhelmed and decided to move to Al-Nuseirat. There, in the Balata Market, we set up a tent made of blankets and tarps. The heat was unbearable, and aid was nonexistent.

We have no income, no cleaning supplies. The prices are too high, and goods are unavailable in the markets. Malnutrition plagues us; healthy food is a distant dream. Vegetables, fruits, and meat are beyond our reach. Our social conditions are dire, and we desperately need someone to stand by us. Our clothes remain buried under the rubble of our destroyed home.

I hope Allah ends this war soon, so that we can return to life anew and try to forget the torment and horrors of this endless conflict.

Written on August 5, 2024

Mohammed Nidal Sharif Al-Sharif
Age: 5 years old
Told by His Mother

The innocence of a child at the tender age of five… Mohammed, the handsome boy, trembled in my arms when he heard the sounds of explosions on the ominous day of October 7, 2023. I kissed and embraced him, trying to shield him from the horrors unfolding around them. Repeated displacement within Gaza City became our reality. Hunger gnawed at us mercilessly, and Mohammed craved even a piece of bread, but our children couldn't find a single crumb. Every time Mohammed heard shelling, he ran and cried, his small heart overwhelmed by fear.

What is happening to us surpasses human endurance. What about the young ones? Hearts tremble. Mohammed spoke with anguish about the martyrdom of his friend Wadi', tears streaming down his face, gasps and breaks in his trembling voice. A small child carrying all this pain…

Days passed, and he alternated between hunger and complaints of the heavy burden of carrying water jugs and firewood. One day a cart pulled by a donkey passed us, loaded with the remains of children he knew. He cried and sobbed, and his tears nearly choked him. His heart was enraged and rebellious, wanting to escape the horror of what he had seen. He complained to Allah about the pain he was enduring, and I heard him breaking into sobs…

Pain accompanied my tears.

"What happened, Mother?"

"I miscarried… I miscarried due to grief, hunger, and displacement. How will I forgive all this misery?"

"I was going to name him Wadi', after my martyred friend."

"I can't bear the pain anymore. It's too much for me."

To those reading this story: Mohammed's kindergarten, home, city, friends, and brother—they're all gone. Why?

"Will Eid and Ramadan pass without my even noticing? Is this fair to you?"

"Can the world hold all my sorrow and pain, though I'm just a child of flowers?"

In the words of Mohammed, "I beg you, stop the war. Protect the few remaining friends and family I have. Let me live my life and grow up. I may be useful to you and to the nation."

Written on August 7, 2024

Hoor Khalil Al-Zayan

Age: 6 years old

At first I was the beautiful child Hoor. I lived in a lovely house with my father, mother, and siblings in the Safatawi area, enjoying peace and safety. I used to go to my beloved kindergarten, "Gaza Heroes."

But when the brutal and merciless war began and bombs rained down on Gaza—targeting the towers—we fled to my grandfather's house in Jabalia Camp. When the shelling intensified, we were struck by heavy bombing. I was injured in my left hand, and it was one of the hardest days for us. I endured immense pain, undergoing two surgeries with platinum screws.

Afterward we fled south. Our situation became extremely difficult, tragic, and dangerous, as it has been for so many Palestinian families. We then moved to Deir Al-Balah, where about forty of our family members stayed together. For over four months we lived without adequate water, food, or money.

One day the house across from us was bombed, but we narrowly escaped. Afterward we fled to Al-Nuseirat Camp because my mother was about to give birth. There were no suitable conditions for childbirth—the hospital wasn't equipped to handle such cases. The Al-Nuseirat area then faced multiple incidents of bombing and invasion, forcing us to flee again and again, until we finally settled in a makeshift shelter under a damaged roof.

The situation for me and my family remains incredibly difficult. Allah is our only support.

Written on August 7, 2024

Sharif Nidal Mohammed Sharif
Age: 7 years old

I am a child from Gaza, in the Beach Camp. The war on Gaza began on October 7, 2023, when I was in the first grade. My mother prepared my bag and belongings for school. Then we heard the sounds of explosions, chants of "Allahu Akbar," and shelling everywhere. I didn't understand what was happening around me. My mother hugged me tightly. My father, who was out at sea—he's a fisherman—soon returned with fresh fish, trying to comfort us. We sat down to eat, but since that day I haven't tasted the flavor of fish again.

The shelling intensified and got closer to us, so we fled to my uncle's house for a day. We returned briefly, only to flee again to Al-Nuseirat, staying at my mother's aunt's house for four days. The shelling worsened, so we went back to our destroyed home in the Beach Camp. For several days we lived amid ruins. Then came severe fire zones. After witnessing martyrs, body parts, and terrifying smoke, we fled. The place became deserted.

One night what remained of our house was bombed. I couldn't gather my toys or clothes. Our home, along with the surrounding houses, was destroyed. My friend Imad was martyred, as were my neighbor, grandmother, and uncle. I clung tightly to my father so I wouldn't get lost among the crowds in the streets. We slept near the Al-Shifa Medical Complex, and in the morning we went to my aunt's house in Al-Nuseirat. Then we fled from her house to Rafah, but soon returned to her house.

Conditions were bad, and the situation was ever more difficult. On some days I went to bed hungry because there was no bread. We were deprived of everything—we had no resources, no stability. At that time we had to carry water for bathing, due to the large number of people living together. We collected cardboard for my mother to use as fuel to cook food, when we couldn't get food from the charity kitchen. The situation was dire. My father couldn't provide for our needs, since he had no job opportunities.

Just before Ramadan, my friend Wadi' was martyred. I saw everyone around me crying. We left Wadi' in Allah's care. On Eid Al-Fitr, I visited his grave and distributed dates in honor of his pure soul. I miss playing with him.

I hope that the war ends and that the killing of children, women, men, and elders stops. The incident in Al-Nuseirat in June 2024 felt like Judgment Day. Everyone was running, fleeing death, unable to find a safe place. Those difficult hours finally ended, and we returned to the tents, continuing our hard lives.

The occupation has taken away all my rights as a Palestinian, and the world stands idly by. Shame on them—they watch us on TV screens, yet no one moves a finger.

A day will come when the war ends and I'll return to my home, retrieve my toys, and go back to school.

Written on July 30, 2024

Lama Nidal Al-Sharif

Age: 12 years old

I am Lama, an innocent child from Gaza, from the Beach Camp. I used to be happy, but October 7, 2023, stole my joy and laughter. That day I was getting ready to go to school when the sound of rockets shattered my world. Fear gripped me, and I ran to hug my mother tightly. Since that moment, I haven't been able to sleep unless I'm right next to her.

We fled the Beach Camp multiple times. The last time, fire zones destroyed our house and the homes around us, leaving behind many martyrs and wounded. I saw unforgettable, heart-wrenching scenes with my own eyes. We went to my aunt's house, seeking safety, but suddenly rockets struck a house next to hers. Filled with terror, we fled again, this time to the UN clinic in Al-Nuseirat. A friend of my brother was martyred.

Later we returned to the Balata Market, settling in a sandy area. Time passed, and Ramadan arrived. Despite the scarcity of food, I fasted with gratitude to Allah. But there was no joy or celebration during Eid al-Fitr or Eid al-Adha, just emptiness and sorrow.

During the war, I have suffered from skin diseases, ear infections, and eye inflammation, yet no treatment is available. Food shortages added to our suffering, and when food became available again, it was at prices we could no longer afford. I have been deprived of education, healthcare, safety, and a clean, healthy home. Life in southern Gaza has become unbearable.

I hope this war ends soon so that I can return to my school and my home. I miss you so much, Gaza.

Written on July 30, 2024

Nasser Mu'taz Abu Hashish
Age: 11 years old

We woke up to a breakfast lovingly prepared by my grandmother. We ate together, laughed, and got dressed to go to school. But soon they told us, "There's no school today, for security reasons." We returned home just as the sounds of rockets and shelling filled the air. Relatives sought refuge with us, crowding into our small space.

When the shelling intensified, rockets and shells struck the house across from ours. Tanks appeared in the distance, their presence ominous. Many shells flew through the air, and our windows shattered over us. Amid the chaos, we fled the house, clutching a white flag.

Trembling with fear, we stepped out in front of the tanks. When we reached a safe road, soldiers ordered us to leave via that route. As we walked, I saw a charred body on the ground, its legs and arms blackened. We pressed on, passing destroyed and burned houses until we reached a checkpoint. Tanks lined the streets, their barrels aimed at us, while shells fired around us. Through binoculars, soldiers selected young men, ordering them, "Take off your clothes."

Fear propelled us forward, step by step. My brother fainted, his lips turning blue, and my grandfather's blood sugar plummeted. Allah protected them. Along the way, we found a horse-drawn cart and rode in it toward Rafah, where we stayed with relatives for months.

When the shelling intensified again and we were told, "Evacuate Rafah," we fled to Deir Al-Balah, on June 15, 2024. Now, we anxiously await the end of the war and the opening of the border, so that I can reunite with my father.

Written on July 7, 2024

Oday Moemen Mohammed Helles
Age: 10 years old

In the Shuja'iyya neighborhood, where I lived with my family, the war began suddenly and destructively. We were asleep in our house when the sound of rockets boomed, shattering the night's silence. Shrapnel filled the house, while flames surrounded us from every side. Screams echoed everywhere, and I felt a fear I'd never known before. People around me said my mother had died. Shocked, I screamed and cried bitterly. Pain and terror consumed my heart.

We left the house in a panic. While standing outside, I discovered that my mother was still alive. I can't describe the joy I felt at that moment. I started jumping, screaming, and hugging her tightly, as if I had regained my soul.

Soon we began walking away from the area, but danger followed us. Suddenly planes dropped phosphorus bombs, choking us with thick smoke. We fled to my aunt's house, where we stayed for just one night. The next day we received a warning from the occupation, ordering us to evacuate to the south. We had no choice but to leave.

The shelling intensified, and with every step we took, fear grew. I saw martyrs lying on the ground, their faces covered in blood. The sight was horrifying—I couldn't hold back my tears. We walked over their bodies, each step filling me with sorrow and terror.

Finally we reached Suq Faris, but even there the shelling didn't stop. It was so intense that we couldn't bear it and had to flee again. This time we went to the south, to Al-Nuseirat. We stayed there for a month, but we weren't safe there either—the bombing resumed, targeting houses and towers.

We fled to the streets again, and the scene was heartbreaking. People fled in large numbers, the injured lay unattended, and children cried out of fear.

In January, we decided to flee to Deir Al-Balah, hoping to find some safety at last. But my heart remains attached to Gaza, longing to return. I pray for this brutal war to end. It has stolen our peace and comfort. All I want is to live peacefully with my family and return to my normal life, far from this constant fear.

Written on July 7, 2024

Rimas Tayseer Mohammed Abd Al-Rahman
Age: 11 years old

On the morning of October 7, 2023, the sky over Gaza seemed to collapse under the weight of rockets and explosions. My family and I scrambled to gather what little we could carry, stuffing clothes and essentials into bags with trembling hands. We left behind not just our home but also the laughter-filled evenings, the warmth of familiar walls, and the sense of security that had always shielded us.

Seeking refuge, we rushed to my aunt's house, clinging to the fragile hope that it would be safer there. But that hope was fleeting. Days later, tanks rolled into view, their ominous presence looming over us. The earth shook with relentless shelling, and fear gripped us tightly, like an unrelenting fist. With no other choice, we spilled into the streets, our feet pounding against cracked pavement as we fled blindly.

The world outside was unrecognizable. Buildings lay in ruins, their skeletal remains casting long shadows over the chaos. The air was thick with smoke, and the ground was littered with debris—pieces of shattered lives. Children wailed, their cries piercing through the cacophony of destruction. Adults ran frantically, clutching whatever they could save, their faces etched with panic and despair. It was a scene straight out of nightmares, yet it was our reality.

Eventually we reached Al-Nuseirat, hoping for respite. Instead, we found hardship. Clean water was scarce; food even scarcer. Hunger gnawed at our stomachs, and illness crept silently among us, preying on the weak.

Then came another wave of bombings, more violent than the last. People scattered like leaves in a storm, desperate for shelter. Above us helicopters circled menacingly, their blades slicing through the sky. When the dust settled, we made the painful decision to leave again. This time we journeyed to Deir al-Balah, each step heavy with exhaustion and uncertainty.

Now, as I sit here writing these words, my heart aches for what we've lost. I dream of returning to our home, to a life where laughter replaces tears and peace replaces fear. Until then, I hold onto hope—a fragile thread keeping me tethered to the belief that better days lie ahead.

O Allah, bring an end to this suffering and guide us back to the embrace of safety and normalcy.

Written on July 7, 2024

Hala Basel Jaber Abu Salem
Age: 12 years old

On the edge of a restless night, as the first hints of dawn tried to pierce through the darkness, our home in the Biet Lahia Project was jolted awake by the thunderous roar of explosions. The silence that had once cradled our small neighborhood was shattered, replaced by the deafening chaos of rockets raining down. Despite the fear gripping my heart, I dressed in my school uniform, clinging to the hope that this day would unfold like any other. But deep down, I sensed that life as I knew it was about to change forever.

When I reached school, we were quickly sent back home, for the shelling showed no signs of stopping. My chest tightened with worry as I returned to find my uncles at our door, their faces pale with panic, having fled the destruction that had swallowed their neighborhood.

Despite the turmoil around us, my sister, my cousin's daughter, and I decided to step out briefly, seeking a fleeting sense of normalcy by buying falafel from a nearby shop. We walked down the street, exchanging nervous words, trying to distract ourselves from the horrors surrounding us. For a brief moment, it almost seemed that we could escape the nightmare.

Then, without warning, the earth shook violently as rockets struck a house nearby. Shrapnel flew in every direction, and thick clouds of dust swallowed the world around us. In the midst of the chaos, a searing pain shot through my face—a shard had pierced my skin. Blood poured freely, relentless, like a fountain I couldn't stop.

Worse still, my hair caught fire from the blast, leaving it beyond repair. When doctors shaved off my remaining hair, I felt as if I were losing a piece of myself—a blow too heavy for my young heart to bear.

Tears streamed down my cheeks as I stared at my reflection in the mirror, unable to recognize the person staring back. Nightmares crept into my sleep, and even my waking hours felt shadowed by despair. Each glance at myself reminded me not only of my physical scars but also of the innocence I'd lost.

My mother bore her own silent agony. Her eyes carried the weight of my suffering, and I saw how it broke her, little by little. She tried to comfort me, but some wounds are too deep for words to heal.

Now, ten months after the war that changed my life, all I pray for is for my hair to grow back as it once was and for the peace of mind I lost to return. Every sunrise brings a prayer to my lips: may this land heal, may this pain end, and may we find the safety and joy that once belonged to us.

Written on July 7, 2024

Abdullah Saadat
Age: 12 years old

In the quiet dawn of what seemed like just another day in Beit Hanoun, we gathered around the breakfast table, clinging to the fragile rhythm of normalcy despite the looming uncertainty. None of us imagined that this day would carve itself into our memories—a scar too deep to fade.

At 2:00 AM, the piercing ring of a phone shattered the silence. My father answered, his face pale as he listened to instructions from the Israeli occupation forces: evacuate immediately. Their command felt like a thunderclap, propelling us into a frantic scramble to pack whatever we could carry. With heavy hearts, we left behind the home we loved and fled toward Jabalia.

Our journey was far from safe. Planes roared overhead, raining destruction on houses near us. Shrapnel flew like daggers, yet somehow Allah shielded us. We pressed on, arriving at a school in Jabalia, hoping it would be a sanctuary.

But peace remained elusive. The relentless shelling crept closer, forcing us to flee yet again—this time to an apartment in the Sheikh Ajlin area. For a week we clung to hope, only to find ourselves under siege once more. When neighboring buildings were bombed, we received orders to evacuate the structure sheltering us. Hours later, it was reduced to rubble.

Each return to Jabalia weighed more heavily on our souls, every step shadowed by mounting fear. One fateful afternoon, I ventured out with my cousins to buy supplies. On our way back, chaos erupted when a nearby house was struck. Miraculously, we escaped the deadly shrapnel, but fate wasn't done with us. As we ran for our lives, another strike followed. In front of my eyes, my cousins fell—some martyred, others grievously wounded, their limbs severed, their faces scorched.

I froze amid the wreckage, my body paralyzed by shock. Panic surged through me as I screamed for help, but my cries were swallowed by the void. We buried the martyrs, their loss a wound that refuses to heal. Among them was my best friend and my beloved cousin, whose laughter I long to hear again. Each memory of that day brings waves of despair.

Later, while walking through the streets, still haunted by the echoes of rockets and drones, disaster struck again. A drone appeared and targeted the house next to the school where we had sought refuge. The explosion was so powerful that it robbed us of breath. Bodies lay torn apart. The scene defied comprehension. Once more we resolved to flee, this time to Deir al-Balah.

Now, as I stand among the remnants of everything I've lost, I pray fervently for this war to end. I yearn for my cousins, longing to relive the days when laughter filled our lives instead of sorrow. O Allah, bring relief to our suffering and restore the peace we've been denied!

Written on July 7, 2024

Judy Saffi
Age: 11 years old

On the morning of Saturday, October 7, 2023, I woke up expecting just another ordinary day in our small, cozy home, a place brimming with laughter and warmth. I ate breakfast with my sister and my mom, the air calm and familiar. For a brief moment, life felt normal.

Then, without warning, the sky erupted. Rockets began raining down on Gaza, their thunderous roars shaking the ground beneath us. Fear and unease gripped my heart as the sense of safety we'd always known slipped away. The catastrophe that unfolded forced us to flee, leaving behind our home, our school, and the beautiful streets where we had once played.

The nights that followed were unbearable. Darkness swallowed our world; there was no electricity, no relief. The relentless shelling echoed endlessly, leaving no corner untouched by fear. What was once a peaceful sky now felt like an unending shadow looming over us. For seven agonizing days we stayed inside our home, trembling with fear, unsure if we'd survive the next hour.

Then came the day we had to leave. Our journey of displacement began. With nothing but the clothes on our backs, we abandoned the home we cherished, fleeing first to Al-Nuseirat, then to Al-Maghazi, followed by Az-Zawayda, Khan Younis, and finally Deir al-Balah. Each place brought new hardships; each step was heavier than the last. Exhaustion became our constant companion, and hope grew fainter with every passing day.

These simple words cannot capture the depth of my pain, the bitter loss of everything I held dear. My friends, my school, my cherished memories, my neighborhood, my grandmother, my toys, my room, even my bed—all are gone.

As a Palestinian child, don't I deserve to live in peace? Don't I deserve a life free from the horrors of war? All I want is to return to my home—to wrap my arms around its walls and reclaim the life that was stolen from me.

I'm so tired. So very tired. All I ask is for this injustice to end. I want to live like other children—free, happy, and safe. I dream of peace for my homeland and long to return to my neighborhood, which feels farther away with each passing day. I dream of a tomorrow where laughter replaces tears, where schools instead of shelters welcome children, and where no child has to endure the weight of war again.

Written on July 7, 2024

Rose Dhaheer

Age: 12 years old

On the morning of October 7, 2023, my brother and I were getting ready to go to school, our backpacks slung over our shoulders as usual. But before we could step out, the world around us erupted into chaos. The deafening roar of rockets and explosions filled the air, and confusion clouded our minds. Our home was in Tel Al-Zatar, a quiet area in northern Gaza. What started as an ordinary day quickly turned into a nightmare.

As the situation worsened, we were forced to leave everything behind and flee south to Rafah, seeking refuge in a neighborhood known as Harat Hajjazi. For nine long months, we tried to build a semblance of normalcy amid uncertainty. But peace was fleeting. When the threat drew nearer and Rafah came under attack, my family and I had no choice but to flee once more. My father stayed behind in Rafah, while the rest of us sought safety in Deir al-Balah.

We found temporary shelter with my cousin's son. A week later, my father joined us after a harrowing escape. He and the others were supposed to leave at dawn, but the occupation forces struck in the dead of night, forcing them to flee their home. Two of our family's cars were seized, but still they refused to surrender. Under the cover of darkness, they rented a cargo truck and embarked on a perilous journey to Khan Younis. Exhaustion weighed heavily on them, and fear shadowed every step until they finally reached safety.

Now we are scattered—some in Khan Younis, some in Deir al-Balah, and others still in the north. Our hearts ache for the ones we've lost and the life we've left behind. All we ask is for this war to end. We dream of returning to our home in the north, where laughter once filled the air, and reuniting with those who remain.

O Allah, bring us back together, whole and unbroken.

Written on July 25, 2024

Hala Ihab Abu Shannab

Age: 12 years old

On the morning of October 7, 2023, my sister and I were walking down the stairs, ready to head to school, when unfamiliar and terrifying sounds filled the air—rockets raining down, voices shouting, and school buses retreating hastily.

Terrified by the chaos unfolding around us, we hurried back home. As we watched the news, the reality of what was happening began to sink in. That day marked the beginning of a painful journey of displacement for everyone in Gaza, fleeing toward the southern part of the Strip in search of safety.

Our first stop was Deir al-Balah, then Al-Mughraqa. We spent one harrowing night there before deciding to return to our home in Gaza—a night etched into my memory with fear and uncertainty. The next day, we sought refuge at my grandfather's house. It was there that we received devastating news: my aunt's home had been bombed. She had survived but had lost her daughter and husband instantly. Her injuries were catastrophic—she'd lost all four limbs, and, overwhelmed by her pain, she passed away the next morning, joining them in martyrdom. Other family members were also wounded in the attack.

A week later, the bombing reached the Taghreed Tower, where my other aunt lived with her children and grandchildren. They were all martyred, and their bodies are still buried beneath the rubble to this day.

Soon after, the area where we were staying was declared unsafe, as bombardments intensified across every corner. With heavy hearts and tearful eyes, we begged my father to let us leave. Reluctantly he agreed, and we fled to Khan Younis.

But safety remained elusive. The house where we stayed in Khan Younis was bombed, forcing us to move again, this time to the industrial area. Even there, no peace could be found. After brutal attacks and massacres carried out by the occupation forces, the area was evacuated once more.

Finally we made our way to Deir al-Balah, where we have remained ever since. Now we hold onto hope—the hope that this war will end and we can return to our home and loved ones in Gaza. Until then we wait, burdened by longing and loss.

Written on July 7, 2024

Nuzha Al-Bawwab

Age: 12 years old

On October 7, 2023, my world turned upside down. The deafening roar of rockets and explosions jolted us awake, leaving us bewildered and terrified. What followed were some of the hardest days of my life.

The occupation forces demanded the full evacuation of Gaza. We sought refuge at Al-Shifa Hospital, a place that should have been safe but instead became a battleground. Night after night, fear consumed us as soldiers invaded neighborhoods, spreading chaos and destruction. The cries of the injured and the sight of martyrs haunted us, while the stench of death filled the air.

When Al-Shifa Hospital itself was evacuated, we fled south to Rafah. The journey was grueling, every step laden with fear and uncertainty. We arrived in Tel As-Sultan, only to be told yet again to leave. Our next stop was Deir al-Balah.

And this isn't the end of my story, because the war rages on. Will there ever be peace? For now, I hold onto hope—that one day we'll return home and this nightmare will fade into memory.

Written on August 1, 2024

Noor Shaldan

Age: 10 years old

On October 7, 2023, the echoes of war shattered the tranquility of Gaza. It wasn't long before the streets filled with panic-stricken families fleeing their homes. Among them was Noor, whose name symbolizes light but whose life was plunged into darkness.

On October 13, a day now known as the "Great Exodus," thousands poured out of their neighborhoods, desperate for safety. Noor's family, the Ridwan Shaldans, joined the throngs of displaced individuals. After hours of searching, they boarded a crowded truck, their fragile vessel of hope on Salah al-Din Road.

Tragedy struck near Kuwait Roundabout, when the vehicle was targeted. Lives were lost and many were injured, including Noor's beloved mother, Hiba Shaldan, and other close relatives. Noor herself survived but emerged bearing both emotional and physical scars. Now she dreams of returning to her warm home and reuniting with her mother, whose absence haunts her every thought.

Despite her hardships, Noor remains resilient, embodying the spirit of Handala—silent yet defiant. She holds onto hope, believing that dawn will break through these dark times.

Written on August 5, 2024

Yasmeen Hendawi
Age: 10 years old

Our home in Gaza was reduced to rubble, forcing us to flee. First we took refuge in schools scattered across the north, then moved to Al-Shifa Hospital. Even there safety eluded us. Threats loomed large, and we were forced to leave once more.

As we walked barefoot along Salah al-Din Road, fear gripped our hearts. Tanks surrounded us, and the bodies of martyrs lay abandoned on the roadside. Tears streamed down my face—not only from fear but from witnessing horrors that no child should ever see. Finally we reached Shuhada Al-Aqsa Hospital, where a tent became our temporary shelter.

My struggles didn't end there. My weak heart, unable to bear the weight of displacement and fear, faltered. And despite urgently needing surgery, I remain unattended, caught in limbo.

Why must we endure this? What crime have we committed to deserve such suffering? Even during Ramadan and Eid the war raged on, stealing joy and leaving behind emptiness. We've lost everything—our homes, clothes, memories, and dreams. Will we ever reclaim what was taken from us?

Written on August 6, 2024

Lina Dhaher
Age: 12 years old

On October 7, 2023, the world as I knew it shattered. The war erupted suddenly, and rockets began raining down on us from every direction. The sound of explosions echoed through the streets, shaking the ground beneath our feet. For a week, we clung to the hope that things would calm down, but fear eventually drove us from our home. The enemy spared no one: young or old, none of us were safe.

Our first stop was Jabalia, in the Al-Fakhoura area, where we sought refuge. But safety was fleeting. From Jabalia we fled to Al-Shifa Hospital, a place that should have been a sanctuary, yet it too became unsafe. The relentless bombing forced us to move again, this time south to Deir al-Balah. There we found temporary shelter at Al-Shuhada Al-Aqsa Hospital.

But nothing could shield us from the harsh reality of what we had lost. Our home in the north was destroyed, reduced to rubble by the bombs. Now we live in a tiny tent, a fragile shelter that offers little protection from the elements. It lacks everything—clean water, electricity, all the basic comforts. Every day feels like a struggle, and every night is filled with fear. We go to bed knowing that nowhere is truly safe; every corner of Gaza has become a target.

Despite everything, I hold onto hope. I dream of the day when this war ends and we can return to our normal lives. I want to live like any other child—to laugh, to learn, and to feel safe. O Allah, please bring an end to this suffering and restore peace to our land!

Written on July 31, 2024

Basma Abu Zeid
Age: 11 years old

On the morning of October 7, 2023, as the first light of dawn crept into our home, we were preparing to head to school. At exactly six o'clock, everything changed. Without warning, the deafening roar of explosions shattered the calm. Confusion spread like wildfire—people ran out of their homes, children cried, and within minutes, the life we knew was flipped upside down.

I remember that day vividly; it's etched into my memory like a scar. It marked the moment we lost not just our homes but our childhoods too. Since then I haven't seen my house, my friends, or my school. They were all destroyed by massive military vehicles. Even my favorite doll, the one I loved more than anything, was taken from me forever.

The horrors I witnessed haunt me still. I'll never forget the sight of a small child lying motionless in his mother's arms, his face streaked with blood. Her cries echoed in my ears as my own mother and I hurried away from that scene. But no matter how far we ran, the image remained burned into my mind.

We moved from one school to another, each stop bringing new heartbreak as we watched homes collapse on their owners. Eventually we set off toward the south. The journey was terrifying—I struggle to put into words the fear that gripped us every step of the way until we reached An-Nuseirat.

It was there that we learned the heartbreaking news: my grandfather and uncles had been martyred in Gaza. Grief weighed heavily on us, yet we had no time to mourn.

Soon after, we were forced to move again, this time to Deir al-Balah, where we lived in tents. Even there, peace eluded us. When the area was threatened once more, we fled to Khan Younis, then to Rafah, and finally back to Deir al-Balah. Each move brought fresh suffering, each day filled with anguish and despair.

Now we endure unimaginable hardships, burdened by pain and frustration. All I wish for is an end to this war. I dream of returning to my home, my toys, my school, and the loved ones who remain. O Allah, bring us relief and restore the life we've lost!

Written on July 7, 2024

Reem Al-Salibi

Age: 12 years old

On October 7, 2023, the war erupted without warning. For a week we remained in our home in the Al-Shati refugee camp, clinging to the hope that things might calm down. But the situation grew increasingly dire. Shells exploded around us, shaking the very foundations of our lives. On the seventh day, my uncle arrived in a panic, urging us to leave immediately. "The area is too dangerous," he warned. Reluctantly we packed what little we could carry and left the only home I'd ever known.

We sought refuge at my aunt's house, staying there for two days. That brief respite ended abruptly when we heard the heartbreaking news: my beloved aunt had been martyred. I sobbed until my throat felt raw, overwhelmed by grief and disbelief.

Then came the gas canisters, fired indiscriminately by the occupation forces. As they filled the air with their suffocating fumes, we ran for our lives, dodging bombs and the deafening roar of explosions. Our next stop was a UNRWA school in the An-Nasr area. For three long weeks, we huddled together inside its walls, praying for safety. But the bombing continued relentlessly, reducing our home—and the homes of so many others—to rubble.

When the ground invasion began, targeting areas near Al-Shifa Hospital, everything changed. Israeli soldiers stormed into the school, smashing doors and instilling terror in everyone present. We hid in the administration office, hearts pounding, as chaos unfolded outside. When we finally emerged, tanks and bulldozers surrounded us. Raising white flags and holding our hands high, we surrendered—not out of choice, but out of sheer necessity.

We walked southward, battered and exhausted, until we reached Deir al-Balah. That first night we slept on the bare ground beneath a staircase in a school, shivering from the freezing temperatures. It was the hardest night of my life.

By morning, we were told the school wasn't safe anymore. So we moved again, this time to Al-Shuhada Al-Aqsa Hospital, nestled within the sprawling displacement camps.

Now we live in a tent, surviving day by day. Every moment reminds me of what we've lost—our home, our belongings, our sense of security. Through it all, I hold onto one wish: to return to Gaza and embrace my family once more.

Written on July 30, 2024

Mumen Saad
Age: 12 years old

I'm Mumen, a boy from Gaza's Al-Shuja'iya neighborhood. Let me share with you the story of my family's displacement—a journey filled with fear, loss, and longing for home.

It began on the evening of Friday, October 6, 2023. I went to bed excited about the next day; I was supposed to host my school's radio broadcast, something I'd been preparing to do for weeks. But instead of waking up to excitement, I woke up to chaos. After I had prayed *Fajr* and put on my school uniform, the sound of rockets pierced through the air. Their thunderous echoes shook me to my core.

My siblings and I trembled with fear, running straight into our mother's protective embrace. She worked hard to comfort us, turning to her phone to find out what was happening outside. That's when reality hit us— it wasn't just random explosions; it was war.

My father told us to gather our most important belongings and prepare for the worst. Meanwhile, my mother baked za'atar and cheese manakish for lunch, trying to keep some semblance of normalcy alive. Soon after this, my grandmother and uncle arrived, urging us to leave the house. They warned us that everyone else in the neighborhood had already fled.

Finding transportation was nearly impossible, but somehow we managed to secure a ride. We headed to my grandmother's house in Tel Al-Hawa, where she greeted us with tears in her eyes, overwhelmed by worry for our safety. For a week, we stayed there, hoping things would calm down. But on the afternoon of the following Friday, we were forced to move again.

This time, our destination was An-Nuseirat, to my aunt's house. The journey was harrowing. Planes roared overhead, and bombs fell relentlessly around us. Children screamed, adults wept, and people ran aimlessly. It felt like the world was ending.

At my aunt's house, we lived with fifty other family members, packed tightly together. The bombing grew fiercer each day. One horrifying moment stands out vividly—the enemy bombed the house next door. Rubble and shards of glass rained down on us, and amid the darkness and confusion, we discovered that my uncle had been fatally injured. He bled out before our eyes, becoming yet another martyr in this endless tragedy.

As conditions worsened in An-Nuseirat, staying there became unbearable. We were forced to flee once more, this time on foot, heading toward Deir al-Balah. Israeli drones hovered menacingly above, firing bullets at us, while rockets continued to fall from all directions. We spent nights sleeping in the open, drenched by rain and freezing from the biting cold. Fear and exhaustion consumed us completely.

Eventually we reached Deir al-Balah, moving between tents until finally settling in one at the Al-Shuhada Al-Aqsa Hospital displacement camp. Now here we are, living day by day, hoping against hope to return to our home and loved ones in Gaza.

Written on July 31, 2024

Kareem Totah
Age: 10 years old

I am Kareem, a boy from the Al-Zeitoun neighborhood in Gaza. My story begins on October 14, 2023, when my family and I were forced to leave our home in Gaza and head south to Khan Younis. For four days, we tried to find some semblance of safety there, but it wasn't long before we felt compelled to return to Gaza, for a brief week. Our fleeting sense of normalcy was shattered when the occupation forces began dropping leaflets that warned us to evacuate immediately. We had no choice but to abandon everything we held dear—our home, our dreams, our hopes, and even our future. All we could think about was staying alive.

Our next destination was Deir al-Balah, where we sought refuge near Al-Shuhada Al-Aqsa Hospital. There, amid the chaos, we pitched a small tent that became our temporary shelter. But life under that tent was far from livable. The biting cold of winter pierced through the thin fabric, while the scorching summer sun made the days unbearable. For four long months, we endured these harsh conditions, clinging to whatever hope we could muster.

The occupation forces didn't stop there. Once again they dropped leaflets, ordering us to leave. This time we packed up our meager belongings and fled to Rafah. For four more months, we tried to rebuild our lives in this new location, only to face yet another wave of bombing. Bombs rained down around us, forcing us to flee yet again. And so we returned to Deir al-Balah, back to the displacement camp at Al-Shuhada Al-Aqsa Hospital. Here we are now, living in uncertainty, wondering if we'll ever have a place to truly call home again.

Written on July 27, 2024

Name: Dima Khaled Abu Jabara
Age: 10 years old

I am Dima, a ten-year-old girl from the Bureij refugee camp. My story begins on October 13, 2023—a day that changed everything. Our home was bombed, and in an instant I lost nearly everyone I loved. My father, my six siblings, my uncle, his wife, and their children were all martyred. Somehow my mother and I survived, and crawled out from under the heavy rubble that had buried us alive.

I remember feeling paralyzed by fear, my heart pounding as if it might burst. I was in complete shock, unable to comprehend the enormity of what had just happened. The world around me felt surreal, like a nightmare I couldn't wake up from.

From there we embarked on a journey of displacement. First we went to a new camp, then to Al-Razi School in An-Nuseirat. Safety remained elusive. We moved again to Al-Shuhada Al-Aqsa Hospital, then fled south to Rafah, and eventually settled in Deir al-Balah.

Now my mother and I live in a small tent. Life here is unbearably difficult. Every day is a struggle—physically, emotionally, and mentally. The grief of losing my father and siblings weighs heavily on my heart. Their absence is a constant ache, a void that can never be filled.

But amid the pain, I hold onto hope. I dream of the day when this war ends, when I can visit my father's and siblings' graves and pay my respects. I want to honor their memory by living a meaningful life. My dream is to become a journalist—to tell the stories of my people, to speak the truth, and to serve my homeland. Though the road ahead feels uncertain, I cling to the belief that better days are possible. Until then I endure, carrying the weight of my losses while nurturing the hope of a brighter future.

Written on August 7, 2024

Hanaa Mahran Antiz
Age: 12 years old

On Friday night I slept peacefully, unaware of the storm that awaited us. On Saturday morning, the deafening roar of rockets jolted me awake. I rose from my bed, trembling with fear. Suddenly the occupation forces began bombing, and terror gripped our hearts. Our home, a small tin structure, offered no protection from shrapnel.

Fearing for our lives, we fled to my grandfather's apartment on the first floor. But the explosions grew louder and closer. Each blast shook the ground beneath us, and we realized that staying wasn't an option. We packed quickly and set off for the schools, remembering how crowded they had become during previous wars. This time, we decided to go to them on the very first day.

We drove to the nearest school in our car and spent the first week there. Then came the evacuation leaflets, urging us to move south toward Wadi Gaza. At first we ignored them, hoping the situation would improve. But by the second week the fire zones and explosions had intensified, forcing us to flee to my maternal grandfather's house in the Al-Zeitoun area. There we stayed for two weeks, clinging to each other for comfort.

Soon the evacuation orders came again—this time through text messages on our phones. Fear overwhelmed us as we realized we had nowhere safe to go. My father made the decision to take us to my aunt's house. Her home was small, crammed with displaced families, but we stayed there for a month.

When the occupation forces threatened evacuation again, we returned to the Al-Zeitoun area, staying for two more weeks. But as tanks and shells drew nearer, we knew we had to leave once more. On our way to my aunt's house, we passed through streets littered with the bodies of martyrs and wounded civilians. Homes lay in ruins, and the sight sent waves of terror through us. Yet we pressed on, walking fearfully until we reached her house. We stayed for a week before deciding to seek refuge at the Hope Orphanage Institute on Unity Street.

For about a month and a half we lived there, finding temporary solace. But when they evacuated Al-Shifa Hospital nearby, the area was surrounded, and we were forced to wander again. Walking on foot, we eventually reached a school in the Al-Tuffah neighborhood. We stayed there for ten days, but then the occupation forces struck again, bombing the school. We woke to the cries of women and children, and soon people began fleeing. We decided to head to the UNRWA school, where we spent a week at the Al-Shuja'iya Boys' School.

One fateful night, the occupiers bombed a section of the school. The sound of the shells echoed through the halls, and we spent the night praying and seeking Allah's mercy. The next day we were told to evacuate to western Gaza—but everyone had already left. With no other options, we returned to the Hope Orphanage, the only place we knew. We stayed there for two more weeks until new evacuation orders came, this time demanding the complete evacuation of the hospital and western Gaza. As people fled east, we decided to return to our home on Al-Shaaf Street.

When we arrived, tears streamed down our faces. It had been so long since we'd seen our home. Though partially destroyed, it still felt like a sanctuary. We moved into my grandfather's apartment on the first floor, breathing a sigh of relief. "We won't leave again," we promised ourselves.

But life grew increasingly difficult. Food prices soared, and basic necessities like flour disappeared. Hunger gnawed at us, and we resorted to eating animal feed and soybeans. My daily ration was a single small piece of bread, barely enough to sustain me. My siblings cried from hunger, and we struggled to survive on one meal a day. When we heard that food and flour were available in the south, and knowing that Ramadan was approaching, we made the heart-wrenching decision to leave.

Crossing the sea and navigating checkpoints filled with tanks and soldiers, we journeyed in fear and exhaustion until we reached Deir al-Balah.

And so our story continues—a tale of survival, resilience, and hope. It will not end until the war does.

Written on July 28, 2024

Sundus Abdullah
Age: 13 years old

On the morning of October 7, 2023, the sky seemed heavy with foreboding. War was looming, but none of us could have imagined its devastating reach. By the next day, we were trapped under relentless bombardment, unable to move as night fell. In those moments, it felt like the end of everything. Yet what awaited us was far crueler than we could have envisioned.

Thus began our journey of unimaginable suffering. We fled on foot, carrying nothing but the clothes on our backs, seeking refuge at Al-Shifa Hospital. Days blurred into one another, each marked by fear, uncertainty, and an overwhelming sense of loss. Our hearts were shattered by the absence of family members who had departed—without a final hug, without a last word. Which was harder to bear, their departure, or their leaving without saying good-bye?

Each day brought the same anguish, the same struggle. After some time, we became trapped inside the hospital itself. When we finally stepped outside, we carried nothing with us—not even hope. We walked along roads labeled "safe," only to find them lined with tanks and soldiers. Destruction and death surrounded us at every turn.

Our family scattered during the chaos, and we sought temporary shelter wherever we could. But safety remained elusive. Finally even the most fragile haven was taken from us, leaving us homeless yet again. Grief and distrust settled deep within us, blending together like shadows merging with light.

Do you think the story ends here? It doesn't. I've lost count of how many times we've been forced to flee, moving from one place to another. The worst part of it all has been sitting on the curb, waiting for scraps of mercy from strangers—people who might have once been like us. We sat there, hoping someone would offer us a corner to rest in.

And still, to this day, we continue to search for shelter amid the turbulence of life and the endless stream of heartbreaking news about loved ones lost in the north. Thankfully, we've found a place to stay—for now. But based on everything we've endured, I know it won't last long. Just like every other time, we'll probably lose it soon enough.

Still, through it all, we cling to whatever hope remains, praying for an end to this nightmare.

Written on July 22, 2024

Sama Al-Shakhriti
Age: 11 years old

I am Sama, an eleven-year-old girl from Gaza. At the start of the school year, I was excited to begin fifth grade. One morning I was studying hard for an upcoming exam and helping my siblings get ready for school. Everything seemed normal until, suddenly, the earth-shattering sounds of explosions ripped through the air. Fear gripped us tightly as we ran in every direction, desperate to escape the relentless bombing. Living near the border made each blast feel as if it were piercing straight into our souls.

My parents quickly decided that we needed to leave. They led us to my uncle's house, the first time we had to flee our home. For a while, we thought we might be safe there—but safety is a fragile illusion in times like these. By nightfall, the Israeli army had sent evacuation orders to Beit Hanoun. With heavy hearts, we packed what little we could carry and fled again, this time to Beit Lahiya. There we found ourselves in an abandoned house, a shell of a building unfit for human habitation.

Four agonizing days passed under the shadow of war. Then came a phone-call that shattered what remained of our peace: my cousin had been martyred. My father, grandfather, and uncles rushed to pay their final respects. Just as they left, news arrived that our current location was now under threat. Panic surged through us as we prepared to flee for the third time.

This journey was the most harrowing yet. We crammed into a truck with other family members, the road ahead fraught with danger. Occupation forces targeted vehicles indiscriminately, turning every mile into a gamble with death.

Back home, my father refused to abandon the north. He stayed behind, clinging to what little he could protect. Meanwhile, my siblings and I traveled south with my uncles, seeking refuge at a relief center. Eventually we ended up in a UNRWA school already overflowing with displaced families. Conditions were unbearable—no clean water, no functioning toilets, and certainly none of the comforts of home. Each night we lay on the bare ground, shivering from both the cold and the weight of uncertainty.

For two long months, we endured this existence. Then we were forced to move again, this time to Deir al-Balah. There we pitched a tent, a flimsy shelter offering little protection from the elements. The heat inside was suffocating, making it feel less like a home and more like a tomb.

One fateful day, my father received a call that struck us like lightning: our home had been bombed. Every cherished memory, every piece of clothing, every toy—it was all gone. The emotional toll was overwhelming.

Despite everything, I still dream of returning to the north, to the ruins of my home. Every night I pray for the war to end, hoping that someday I'll be able to walk among the rubble of my past and rebuild my future.

Written on August 22, 2024

Misk Abu Aita
Age: 12 years old

I am Misk, a twelve-year-old girl from Gaza. October 7, 2023, was a dark day in our lives. I was getting ready to go to school when, suddenly, a fierce war began.

We stayed in the north for forty-five days of the war, during which I experienced the hardest moments of my life. Fear controlled us completely, and we refused to leave the house. But fate had other plans. After the occupation forces bombed part of our home and committed numerous massacres at the nearby Al-Fakhoura School, my father decided to save us. He made the decision for us to flee to the south—our first displacement.

We fled to Al-Qarara School, where we spent one night. Then we moved to Al-Aqsa University, which was also filled with displaced families. We stayed there for another night before moving to Khan Younis, specifically the industrial area. We lived there for about two months, until the cursed occupation forces surrounded the area and bombed the buildings. Many martyrs fell that day, but once again we survived, by a miracle.

We evacuated the area, waiting for a car to take us to Rafah. Unfortunately, occupation tanks surrounded us, and we couldn't take our belongings. We fled on foot until we reached Rafah. We stayed there for three and a half months, living in agricultural sheds unfit for human life. The heat was unbearable during the day, and the cold was biting at night.

Later the occupation forces decided to invade Rafah, forcing us to flee again, this time to Deir al-Balah. Now we are in Deir al-Balah, living in a tent under the scorching sun. Life is incredibly difficult, and every day I dream of returning to the north.

Written on July 7, 2024

Ahmad Hussein
Age: 10 years old

On the morning of October 7, 2023, I woke up at exactly six o'clock. I put on my school uniform, had breakfast, and then walked to school. Suddenly I heard the sounds of explosions and rockets. School was canceled for the day, and we returned home, terrified. The entire day passed while we were gripped by fear.

People were told to evacuate Beit Hanoun—it was considered a dangerous area—but we refused to leave our home. We stayed through the night, which was unbearably hot. Text messages and calls from the Israeli occupation forces were sent to our phones. We stayed until the next morning, then fled to Jabalia Camp, where we remained for four consecutive days.

On the fifth day, one of my uncles was martyred, and the house we were staying in was threatened. We fled to the Al-Mashrou' area, spending one night there before moving further south, to Deir al-Balah. We became displaced wanderers, moving from one place to another, eventually settling in an abandoned house.

On our first day there, another of my uncles was martyred. We stayed in the house for only a short while before moving to the Deir al-Balah Relief Center. While we were there, the nearby Deir al-Balah Camp, located next to the school, was targeted. My sister's leg was injured, and we were forced to flee again, this time to a tent in the Akila Relief Camp, where we remain to this day.

Later we received news that my aunt and cousin had been martyred. May Allah have mercy on them. We are still in the same place, suffering from a lack of water, extreme heat, food shortages, and constant fear. Allah be our support, and may He grant us patience in the face of these trials. All praise is due to Allah, no matter the circumstances.

Written on August 3, 2024

Reem Ayad
Age: 11 years old

I am Reem, an eleven-year-old girl from Gaza. On the morning of Saturday, October 16, 2023, the treacherous occupation forces launched several missiles at a place right in front of our home. The window grills shattered, and half of the house collapsed on top of us. By a great miracle we managed to escape from the rubble, but we were all seriously injured.

My sister's arm was severed. Unfortunately, no one could reach us due to the intense shelling and piles of debris blocking the roads. My father carried my sister and rushed on foot until he reached an ambulance, which then took them to the hospital to save her life. As for the rest of us, despite our injuries and bleeding, we walked on foot until we reached Wadi Gaza. There we called for help from the ambulance services.

An ambulance eventually picked all of us up and took us to Al-Shuhada Al-Aqsa Hospital in Deir al-Balah. After leaving the hospital, we fled to the Nuseirat Camp, where we stayed for a few months.

Unfortunately, life in the Nuseirat Camp became unbearable. Then the occupation forces ordered us to evacuate the camp, so we left on foot once again, reaching Deir al-Balah just before sunset. We didn't have time to set up a tent, so we slept in the street that night. The next day we built a tent, but living in it has been extremely difficult.

All I want is to return to my home.

Written on July 7, 2024

Raghad Mohammad Jundiyah

Age: 12 years old

On Saturday, October 7, 2023, I was sitting with my mom, dad, and siblings in our living room. My father and brothers got ready to go to school, while I went to the palm tree in our field to gather some fresh dates to eat. When I returned home, I found Israeli shelling coming from every direction. We were all shocked—what was the reason for this?

Later we learned that the resistance had confronted the Israelis and captured soldiers. Since we live in the eastern border area, in the industrial zone, we fled our home and went to my grandmother's house in Al-Muntar. We stayed there for the first week of the war, taking only two schoolbags with us. Afterward we moved to Al-Bureij City, on October 14, and stayed there for two and a half months. The people there were kind, and aid was abundant.

After that we went to Rafah, where we lived in tents for three months. Prices were extremely high, and the weather was unbearably hot. I couldn't even fast during Ramadan. Then came the evacuation orders, and we fled to the Nuseirat Camp, paying 1,000 shekels for transportation. I later joined Buthour Al-Khayr School to continue my education.

I pray to Allah to relieve our suffering, bring us out of this war safely, and reward those of us who endure patiently.

Written on August 14, 2024

Asmaa Al-Hawajri

Age: 11 years old

Hello. I am from Gaza, and I am eleven years old. At such a young age, what can I do to fight against the occupation? And how can I express the tragedy, sorrow, and burdens that weigh so heavily on our hearts during these difficult times? Today, I have decided to tell my story.

I was heading to school when, suddenly, I heard the sounds of rockets being fired everywhere. I didn't know the reason. My father came to pick me up from school. Since our home was tall and located in northern Gaza, near the occupation's borders, my father took us to my grandfather's house, near Kamal Adwan Hospital. We stayed there for two weeks, then evacuated to the Nuseirat Camp, near my aunt's house, in the same neighborhood. We stayed with her for two months, then moved to my uncle's house. After three months, the occupation forces dropped leaflets ordering another evacuation, and we fled to Rafah, where we lived in tents in Tel al-Sultan. We stayed there for two months, then returned to my uncle's house.

What did I do during all this time, you ask? I was always standing in line for bread, struggling to get a single loaf, even though I often felt suffocated. I also stood in line for clean water and salty water, returning drenched but still going out again to try to bring food from the charity kitchen.

And what else do you think we endured, besides all this suffering? Our lives continued like this. To make matters worse, the occupation burned down our home. How long will we remain like this? Will we ever return? All of this is for the sake of beloved Palestine. I love it deeply, and I will continue to love it, though I don't know how to fully express that love. We will keep defending it and caring for it.

I hope that this dark cloud will pass and that we will return to Gaza.

Written on July 7, 2024

Lana Hamdi Al-Yazji
Age: 10 years old

I thought it would be just another ordinary day. But it wasn't. I woke up and prepared to go to the school I loved so much. I was ready to take my first monthly exam in fifth grade. Suddenly, out of nowhere, we heard loud noises. We thought it was thunder announcing the arrival of winter, but it turned out to be the beginning of a complete upheaval in our lives.

The first sign was the Ministry of Education's announcement suspending classes indefinitely. Since my father was abroad, my grandfather insisted that we come to his house for safety. That was the second big change in just one hour. We left our home and all our belongings behind, as we usually do for visits to my grandfather's house.

Two days later, in the middle of the night, the strikes and bombings intensified. We couldn't sleep, and most of these attacks targeted the area around the home we had abandoned. Five days later, a neighboring house was targeted. I woke up to find my mother carrying me, to protect me from flying glass shards (I have a mobility disability). We fled to a distant house. In the morning, we returned to my grandfather's house under the threat of planes. Leaflets ordered us to evacuate to "safe areas"—the biggest lie of all—in the south.

On October 13, 2023, we set off with my grandfather to Nuseirat. That date remains etched in my memory—it was the last day I spent in my beloved Gaza. I will never forget the hardship of our journey. It felt like the trip itself was warning us that the worst was yet to come.

In Nuseirat began the real suffering. We lived in a single apartment with nine families—crowded together, sleeping on the floor, using one bathroom, praying, eating, and sometimes playing. Our problems grew worse as food became scarce and water supplies dwindled.

Weeks and months passed. I rarely left the apartment, sometimes not even stepping out of my room except to use the bathroom. My mother brought coloring books and crayons to keep me occupied while others played. I couldn't keep up with them because of my mobility challenges.

Winter arrived, and we were still wearing summer clothes, freezing in the cold. We shared pieces of bread and wrapped ourselves in thin blankets, without proper bedding. Our limbs froze despite my mother's attempts to keep us warm. This led to intestinal issues, colds, and fevers.

Even though we had left our homes to seek safety, airstrikes and constant shelling followed us. The sounds were louder, more frequent, and higher-pitched. We never knew peace or sleep. One night, after evening prayers, we were preparing to sleep. Many children and their mothers from my extended family were in one large room when, suddenly, an explosion shook the building. The door slammed shut on us, and every window shattered, with stones flying inside and out. After some time they managed to open the door, but I was screaming in the heart of terror. I tried hard not to scare my mother, but the fear this time was too much for me to bear.

Due to the extensive damage to the building, which had housed many displaced families, everyone rushed downstairs, thinking the house itself was the target. I stayed behind with my mother, who was frantically searching for my siblings, unsure where they had gone or how to carry me and escape. My uncle soon returned to carry me, and we ran through the streets. Everyone was screaming, and I was overwhelmed with shock and panic. That night will never fade from my memory. Thankfully it finally ended, and we survived.

Days later, the occupation forces advanced into a nearby area and ordered everyone to evacuate. My grandfather and the other elders were confused: where could we go, being such a large group? They decided that we should flee to Deir al-Balah; this was our third displacement.

We lived there for a few months in a shared house, where I contracted chickenpox and several skin diseases. My mother decided that we should live in a tent so I could have some independence, without the need to climb stairs and have her carry me (she struggled with both). She couldn't bear seeing everyone else go out to play, while I couldn't even see them from the window. So the tent became our fourth home, and with it came new struggles.

Life in the tent was incredibly difficult. Necessities like lighting a fire, carrying water, cleaning, and cooking were all almost impossible in a place lacking the most basic resources. And my mother bore all of this alone, amid overcrowded conditions and widespread pollution. I contracted several illnesses, including hepatitis A, which caused me immense suffering. With limited transportation and the hospital far away, I didn't receive proper treatment. We all endured, especially my mother, until we eventually recovered. We tried to get a new wheelchair and treatment for my needs, but to no avail.

Now, after all this time, I try to pass the time by writing and memorizing the Quran. I go to a learning tent, where I study drawing and participate in recreational activities. But the overcrowding in the camp makes it hard for me to move, especially after the displacement from Rafah. Still, my mother insists I attend, and she works with the organizers to accommodate my condition.

At this point, I can't bear it anymore. I feel tired, frustrated, sad. How can they provide only the bare minimum for life? I miss my father, my home, my relatives in the north, my old life, my school, and the future my mother worked so hard to build for me—a future where I wouldn't feel different. No matter how much I write, I cannot fully describe the suffering imposed on us, nor find justice for it.

Every day we pray to Allah; He is our only refuge. I wish I could wake up from the nightmare of October 7 to find my school, my teachers, and my old life waiting for me. Right now, I feel like a stranger in my own homeland.

I hope the war ends soon so that I can continue my treatment and walk again. My final message is to my mother: O mountain of strength, O divine care and kindness sent to protect me, may Allah keep you with me and reward you for your patience and perseverance!

Written on May 1, 2024

Dareen Saleh Siyam
Age: 11 years old

On October 7, 2023, my brother and I were getting ready to go to school when something unexpected happened—the hateful war broke out. From the very first day, we witnessed the worst things imaginable. The Israeli occupation forces called us, ordering us to evacuate our home. So we left, heading to my grandfather's house in the Al-Shati Camp, though it wasn't truly safe: they were bombing relentlessly, day and night, in all areas.

Then they began dropping leaflets that urged us to head south, and they cut off our food and water supplies. Eventually we were forced to leave our home and head south. We went to Al-Mawasi, where we lived in a tent. We suffered from sandstorms, bitterly cold weather since it was winter, rain pouring into our tents, and a lack of water and hygiene supplies. Despite all this, we endured, holding onto the hope of returning home.

But then the unimaginable happened. The occupation forces threatened Khan Younis, forcing us to flee again—this time to Al-Mawasi in Rafah, as summer approached. We suffered from insects like mosquitoes, lizards, and the unbearable summer heat. Sometimes we even saw death with our own eyes.

Soon after this, the occupation forces threatened Rafah and we fled once more, to the central area, settling in Nuseirat Camp / Al-Balata Camp. We pitched the same tent that had traveled with us from place to place.

Here, too, we suffer greatly from the summer heat and insects. And that's not all—obtaining water has been another ordeal. We stand in long lines for hours upon hours, just to get what? A single jerrycan (twenty liters) of water. And let's not forget bread, which is as scarce as water. One of us goes to fetch water while the other waits in line for a loaf of bread. Sometimes, an entire day passes before we can secure a single loaf! What can we do? This is Allah's will.

Our dear principal, Dr. Maisa Halas, opened Buthour Al-Khayr School to continue our education, which had been interrupted by the Israeli occupation's aggression. We were overjoyed because it has kept us busy and distracted us from the summer heat. Sometimes, though, I wonder: Will we ever return home? Will this suffering end? Will the war ever stop?

Written on July 7, 2024

Aseel Abdullah Habib

Age: 8 years old

I am Aseel, an eight-year-old girl from Gaza. October 7, 2023, was no ordinary day for us. We took the bus to school as usual, but at six-thirty in the morning we heard the sounds of many missiles. We were terrified. My mother, especially, feared for our safety and didn't know what to do. The rockets roared like thunder. The bus turned back and took us home. My father sat listening to the news, and we realized that the hour of war had struck.

My mother gathered some clothes, and we fled to my grandfather's house in Al-Zaytoun, leaving behind our home, belongings, books, and everything else. We stayed at my grandfather's house, listening to the sounds of F-16 airstrikes and phosphorus bombs, which are internationally banned. What more could happen?

On Friday, October 13, the Israeli occupation dropped leaflets over Gaza, ordering everyone to evacuate and head south. With Allah's help, we carried our burdens and moved to Nuseirat, where we went to the schools to begin our journey of displacement outside Gaza.

Oh, how it hurts! Where is the house that once sheltered us? Where are its walls, my room, my books, my belongings? Oh, the pain in my heart!

We stayed in Nuseirat for thirty-five days, waiting for hope to return—but hope vanished. Even bread became scarce. The occupation refused to allow flour and gas into bakeries, and we were reduced to eating one meal a day.

Eventually my father decided that we should go to Rafah. We attended schools there, nearly forgetting our home—or rather, we did forget it! The only food we received was canned goods distributed by the school. Flour was rare, almost impossible to find. A loaf of bread cost two shekels, expensive in the south and nonexistent in the north.

We stayed in Rafah until December, when they announced a ceasefire. But what happened next? We don't know! The occupation invaded Khan Younis, destroying it completely. I remained in Rafah for six months, until the day came when leaflets were distributed over Rafah again, forcing us to flee once more, to Nuseirat. There we set up a tent that became our new home.

All we do now is either collect food from the charity kitchen or fetch water. The school year has ended, but we are still living through the war. Everything is destroyed—the schools, the houses, even the water and sewage networks. Nothing remains but destruction wherever you look. We wait for Saladin al-Ayyubi to come and liberate us from the unjust, brutal occupation that shows no mercy—to children, to women, to elders, or even to animals. How long must we endure this suffering? To whom can we complain but Allah?

Written on July 7, 2024

Sewar Mohammad Matar

Age: 5 years old

On the morning of October 7, 2023, I woke up to go to my beautiful school, Al-Basma School. Suddenly I heard the sounds of explosions launched by the occupying forces on Gaza City. These attacks were violent, resulting in massacres and widespread death and destruction.

Later the occupation ordered the people of Gaza to evacuate the area and head south, claiming it was safer there. We left, spending the first night sleeping in the street. After two days in the open, a school welcomed us, but we had to pitch tents between classrooms. We often waited in long lines for the bathrooms.

One day I went with my cousin Wadea' to get fresh water. After hours of waiting, we finally got some. On our way back, the occupation bombed the area, and Wadea' was martyred—only his foot remained! What a horrifying scene. I will never forget it for the rest of my life! He evaporated into pieces before my eyes, leaving only his foot behind, while I escaped death by a miracle.

We've grown up so fast. Death is everywhere, and blood stains the streets. My mother cuts my hair periodically because we have no shampoo. The war has robbed us of our basic rights. I dream of a glass of milk and a heartfelt laugh.

Bring back our home. Bring back Gaza. Bring back Wadea'. Bring back my happiness!

Written on August 13, 2024

Ala'a Siyam

Age: 5 years old

On the morning of October 7, 2023, I was heading to Al-Basma Modern Kindergarten. Suddenly, while we were on the bus, the driver turned back, due to intense shelling. It seemed that war was looming on the horizon, but we didn't yet grasp the full impact it would have on us. The next day, we found ourselves surrounded by intense bombing at night, unable to leave. At that moment we thought it was all over—death felt closer than the sunrise itself.

After some time, we fled to my grandfather Abu Ala'a's house, near Carrefour Mall. We spent dark days there due to relentless airstrikes. Every day blended into the next; fear and anxiety consumed us. I couldn't even grieve for the family members who had passed away without saying goodbye. Which is worse—their loss or losing them without a farewell?

Every day brought the same pain and suffering. And soon the occupation dropped leaflets, ordering us to evacuate again. This time we walked on foot to Rafah. Reality was harsher than any description. Our journey of suffering unfolded clearly before us. We left with nothing but our souls, walking along roads supposedly "safe," yet surrounded by tanks and soldiers. Even here, destruction and death awaited us.

Our family scattered, and we found temporary shelter. But Rafah wasn't safe for us—we were driven out again, left homeless once more. Sorrow and despair intertwined in our hearts like night and day.

Do you think the story ends here? Truthfully, I've lost count of how many times we've moved from one place to another—and so it continues. We found ourselves searching for new shelter amid life's turmoil and the constant news of deaths among our relatives in the north.

After fleeing Rafah, we settled in a tent in the Nuseirat Camp. Life inside the tent was unbearable—the scorching heat, waiting in long lines for sweet and salty water. Oh, how difficult those days were!

I wish we could return to our beloved Gaza home, filled with memories. How I miss kindergarten and childhood! O Allah, bring us back to our home as soon as possible, after we have lost so many precious days!

What I fear most now is that, just like every other time we've found shelter, we'll lose it again after a short while. Displacement and instability fill our hearts with sorrow.

Written on April 19, 2024

Sandra Mohammad Matar

Age: 8 years old

On the morning of October 7, 2023, I woke up to go to school like all the other students. Suddenly I heard the sounds of explosions launched by the occupying forces on Gaza City. These attacks were violent, leading to numerous massacres. Death and destruction began, and I returned home crying. My mother hugged me, and we cried together. The occupation bombed our neighbors' house late at night. When I went outside, I saw two friends torn apart—they were no longer whole! Kanzie and Miraal, my childhood friends, were gone, leaving only their hair behind. Their bodies had vanished! What a heartbreaking sight it was.

The occupation ordered the people of northern Gaza to evacuate and head south, claiming it was safer. I won't describe the hardships of life in tents and the war—you've already heard about them in the media. All I'll say is this: What we endure is far harder than anything you've read, seen, or heard in the news. Far harder!

I'm tired. Yes, I'm exhausted. Where do we go? Allah is our only hope.

Written on August 13, 2024

Diyala Mohammad Tafesh
Age: 12 years old

My name is Diyala Mohammad Tafesh, a Gazan girl from the heart of Gaza City. I am an ambitious and hard-working student who dreams of becoming a doctor. I know this is a dream shared by many. I have chosen it not because of my family's aspirations or the prestige associated with the profession, but because I genuinely want to practice medicine. I have been walking steadily toward this dream, knowing with certainty that this career aligns with my abilities. It will allow me to support my mother in her old age, make my father—the wise one—proud, and perhaps even surpass him in success. It will also help my sister when she feels weighed down by illness or the suffering of loved ones. I will not let sadness overcome them.

One day, however, my steady steps toward achieving my dream were halted and strained; the cancer of the enemy began to invade my dreams and my life. Yet it did not defeat me—far from it. The enemy launched missiles at our neighbors' house, causing part of our home to collapse and injuring my sister, whom I had promised never to let be burdened by sorrow. Thank Allah, she survived!

Days passed, and we moved from one displacement shelter to another. But I will not leave Gaza, no matter what. I cling to my land until death. I am that stubborn girl who refuses to let the cancer take over my homeland.

One morning, which we had thought would be peaceful due to deceptive negotiations, I woke up wanting to prepare breakfast for my family. All I found was dried thyme and a stale piece of bread. *No problem,* I thought. We had agreed that the cancer would not defeat us. We ate our breakfast and thanked Allah.

As usual, my father went to work. A man with a mission, he is fearless even in the darkest circumstances. Between my prayers, I asked Allah to protect him. The day went on, and the sound of artillery grew louder. Though distant, it was intense. I turned on the radio, and shocking news struck my ears: they were besieging Al-Shifa Hospital! *What?*

"Father...Father!" I screamed, and so did we all—prayers, tears, and wailing filled the room. Then I stopped. I had promised myself that the cancer, in any form, would never take over my homeland.

We learned that the Israeli army had taken my father prisoner while he was doing his job, tirelessly working to ease the pain of the wounded and bereaved alongside a team of other doctors, wise individuals, and nurses. That was the tragedy—how could we bear the thought of my father enduring all the forms of torture we had heard about inside the occupiers' prisons? Questions began swirling in my mind.

Is the profession of medicine, which I aspire to, a curse? Or is it an unforgivable sin, for which my father must suffer such torment? My father, whose heart is tender and holds no hatred, not even for the worst of humanity—and now he had become their target!

I stopped questioning. I am determined to remove the cancerous tumor sooner or later. It will never defeat me. But my beloved father, the man with the tender heart…

Father, you have been absent for five months now, still held captive. I know you are alive, and I reaffirm it: the Zionist cancer will never defeat us. Stay strong, and do not worry about us. My mother is a woman of immense strength. But—I won't hide it from you—we are hungry, very hungry. Sometimes my mother feels extremely weak and frail, and so do we. We haven't tasted fresh vegetables or meat in a long time. Our bodies have been deprived of the balanced diet they taught us about.

Still, no matter what, nothing will drive me away from the flower of my heart—my beloved Gaza. I repeat it often, even if it bores my readers: the malignant Zionist cancer will never defeat me. My homeland is like my body: pure and capable of expelling every evil.

Written on August 4, 2024

Maram, Miyar, and Umm Ibrahim

Told by Umm Ibrahim (Martyr)

I am described as the ideal mother by everyone who knows me. My children are Ibrahim and my twin daughters, Maram and Miyar. Few can tell them apart, except for my heart, which distinguishes between them even without seeing them. I won't hide it—I am deeply attached to my twin daughters. I pay close attention to every detail of their lives. Every day revolves around them: I braid their hair, help them with their lessons, and care for countless other small details.

Their teacher, Wala Zagout, was our favorite—a teacher and a friend. She knew how to distinguish between them, just as my heart could. She shared many moments with us and understood that my girls suffered from an extreme fear of missile sounds and other noises. She always supported them, acting as a second mother. When the war erupted, she tried to comfort us with prayers and activities to ease the heavy burden of those times.

On a long November night, we started drawing our dreams. Ibrahim drew himself as the owner of a company, while Maram and Miyar drew themselves as doctors. Their dream was to heal the sick. They were identical, even in their aspirations. The roar of planes grew closer, and the sounds of missiles never ceased. I tried to hide my fear so that my children wouldn't panic, especially since I was pregnant. But the sounds kept getting louder and closer.

We froze. My daughters clung to each other, burying themselves in my embrace, while Ibrahim ran to his father's arms. Moments later the roof collapsed on us, and everything turned to ashes. I heard Maram calling out to Miyar, "Why aren't you answering me?" Another brutal blow followed, and after that I no longer heard anyone's voice.

Miyar was martyred instantly, as were Ibrahim and their father. Maram was still fighting for her life. The doctors separated her from Miyar with great difficulty to treat her injuries. But there was no hope—her wounds were too severe.

She opened her eyes. I reached out to her, and Miyar extended her hand as well. Together, we took Maram away from a world that shatters childhood dreams and the dreams of families who lived in the warmth of pure hearts. Here, in this better world, there is no oppression or cruelty.

I am Umm Ibrahim, the martyr.

Written on November 26, 2023

Naya

Age: 11 years old

My name means "the beautiful Syrian gazelle." I am in the fifth grade, deeply loved by my parents. I have one sister who is incredibly beautiful, and I love her very much. Before October 7, 2023, my life was very beautiful. I had my own room, which resembled a Disney castle, and clothes carefully chosen by my mother with love. I adored my school. But all of that changed one morning, when we woke up to terrifying sounds. My mother, as usual, said they were just fireworks, but she didn't know that this round of conflict would last so long.

We went through extremely difficult times. I could see my mother trying to hide her fear from us, but I felt it deeply—especially since the sounds outside were very different from previous conflicts. They were truly horrifying. And every day they came closer. My parents tried to maintain a façade of strength, until the fateful day came—the day when we left our warm, beautiful home after the war machine approached our neighborhood.

We headed south, where I saw all the terrifying scenes my mother had tried to shield us from. The streets had completely changed. We passed by the sea road, and suddenly bullets rained down on us from every direction. O Allah! I will never forget that day. Even now, I can still hear the fearful cries of my sister, my mother's prayers as she collapsed, and my father's trembling moans. Unforgettable moments.

We arrived at a friend's house in Deir al-Balah. My mother was exhausted; out of sheer fear, she miscarried the baby she had long awaited, and cried for him a great deal. Soon afterward, my stomach started to hurt badly. My mother made me herbal tea, thinking I had caught a cold. But the shock came when it turned out to be my period! How could this happen when I was only nine years old? We consulted a doctor. It seems the war had also affected my body—I became a woman with the mind of a child!

I wish this nightmare would end. It has consumed my dreams and stolen my childhood; I am no longer the carefree child I once was. Why are you waiting to stop all of this?

Written on November 11, 2023

Nagham Mohammad Fareed Al-Shafi'e

Age: 10 years old

The war began on October 7, 2023. Since then, we have been living under harsh conditions. We have faced many difficulties and lost countless loved ones. On January 4, 2024, we fled to Rafah, when the occupation invaded the Nuseirat area. Later we returned to our home in Al-Zawayda, but life there became unbearable due to severe hardships and rising living costs.

On Friday, June 7, my father was martyred while heading to work early in the morning. His death was one of the most painful moments for us. Now we live without a father, enduring continuous suffering because of his absence. We miss him dearly at home.

We pray that Allah grants mercy to our martyrs and ends this cursed war on our besieged people. Allah has been our only support.

Written on July 27, 2024

Tala Loay Abu Al-Judean

Age: 12 years old

I was on my way to school with my friends when I heard the loud sounds of missiles. I felt terrified and ran back home, crying. My beloved mother hugged me, trying to calm my heart. The next day we heard women and children crying and screaming. They were trapped under the rubble. An ambulance rushed to the scene. There were four martyrs and two injured.

After a week of war, the occupation began random bombardments and dropped evacuation leaflets over Beit Lahiya. We fled to Kamal Adwan Hospital and stayed there for three days. But eventually we couldn't endure the situation any longer, due to the overwhelming number of martyrs and casualties. We were extremely afraid of the dangerous shells being fired.

At exactly 2 PM, we returned home. In the morning, we decided to flee to Al-Zawayda. We stayed there briefly before taking the coastal route to my aunt's house, where we spent eight months. Afterward, we returned to Al-Zawayda, and I enrolled in a beautiful school to continue pursuing my education.

Written on July 31, 2024

Naia and Lujain Yarib AlZaneen

Ages: 7 and 8 years old

We thought it would be just another school morning—breakfast, uniforms, the usual rush. The smell of warm milk drifted from the kitchen. My mother was already standing at the kitchen table, making sandwiches for her four kids. I was waiting for my sandwich. Nothing felt unusual, until a fast and unrelenting burst of rocket fire roared outside.

I was chewing my breakfast, and swallowed at the sound. My mother froze. Her eyes darted toward the window. "No one is going to school today," she decided, out of fear. That was the morning of October 7, 2023, and this is a tale of displacement from Beit Hanoon, the northern section of the Gaza Strip.

The next day the bombings got closer and louder. We woke up to massive explosions. The ground shook. The walls groaned. All I knew was that we couldn't stay any more. My mother grabbed a few clothes and a little food, and we headed out to nowhere. The city we had left behind dwindled to a black speck on the horizon. We went toward southern Nuseirat, where Ain Jalout towers are.

It was far away from the so-called "unsafe" area, yet our feelings during the three months we spent there were stronger than terror. A nearby bombing isn't only a loud sound that hits the ears; each one felt like someone shaking the tower violently until all the windows were shattered and everything swayed inside. We were on the seventh floor, and we were forced to dance by each bombing.

Then warning messages arrived by phones: we had to evacuate immediately. This was our second journey of displacement: we headed to Rafah. As we went on our way, we received the news that the tower we had just left had been bombed to the ground.

Then, for the first time, I saw Rafah. The tents were vast and inaccessible, ranging in front of me as far as the eye could see. The ground cracked like a desert, stretching far away, miserable, stale, and tired at the same time. That desert was breathing, burning my body in the daytime and freezing it at night.

In January, the beginning of every new year, heavy rains flooded out people wearing tattered clothes, their faces pale. Only then did I realize that a new year was a new misery in Rafah. A tent to live in was the last thing that remained to us.

Hungry for life, we were chasing hope in whatever fragile form it came. We struggled with the scarcity of water, the lack of food, and the endless swarms of biting insects. The streets overflowed with garbage.

Sewage water crept into every corner. While everyone was waiting in lines, kids stole moments of joy by playing on the sandy hills of displacement and hardship, laughing and flying from the top to the bottom. Their giggles turned to screams as they raced toward the hot-food kitchen when it opened its door to distribute scraps of food.

In Rafah we had run away from the war—but it followed us. The army launched an operation to invade Rafah. We had to flee once again, to search for somewhere, anywhere, that would be safer. We packed our few belongings and pitched a tent in Al-Zawaida, on a patch of farmland owned by some of my father's relatives. They welcomed us with warmth, and soon we made new friends. We enrolled in a local educational center called Jaffa AlEzza Camp, determined to continue learning despite everything.

Even there, in Al-Zawaida, we weren't spared. We had to flee from our tent again and again, running from flying shrapnel. The house next to ours was bombed. Still, we tried to live as normally as we could. My father built us a swing beside the tent. My siblings, my friends, and I took turns flying through the air, laughing, kicking a ball across the dust. Sometimes my mother would prepare us sweets, if a little supply of sugar was available in the market.

Our home in Beit Hanoun looks so amazing and beautiful in the photos in my phone. Now it is half-burned, shelled repeatedly, stripped of anything it once held.

Yet hope remains. Hope that one day we will return and rebuild. Hope that we will make new memories in the place where the old ones were left behind.

Written on July 7, 2024

Nisma Hani Naif Abu Aun
Age: 9 years old

I live in the displacement world, since October 7, 2023—an open-air prison, that is. We thought the war would last a week or two, the way it had before. But this time it turned out to be a genocide.

Within a week, we started fleeing from one house to another. Finally we settled at a relative's home, where we stayed nearly three months.

Then calls to evacuate again kept hunting us everywhere. Our shelter was among the targeted areas. Three days later, we fled to Rafah. We didn't know where we were going. We just walked, guided only by Allah. We stayed in Rafah for about seven months.

Then we were displaced again. This time we went to Al-Zawaida. And here we are, still away from home, more than three hundred days later. By God's grace, we are still holding on. We ask Him for one thing: to let us return home, soon.

Written on July 8, 2024

Lana Loai Abu Al-judian

Age: 11 years old

My feet took a step back. I didn't look back. I was on my way to school when the resistance rockets rumbled in the sky. The next night we went to the hospital, seeking safety. The explosions got worse. Israel was bombing us intensely and dropped phosphorus bombs that burn things, even bodies.

One after another, I lost many of my family. When the area around Kamal Adwan Hospital was hit, some of my family members were there. They didn't survive. Paramedics were trying to carry the bodies, and an Israeli plane fired another rocket at the ambulance. The medic died too. He just was trying to help.

My cousin was working at Yemen Al-Saeed Hospital in the north. While he was carrying a martyr's body, a helicopter shot him—once in the head, once in the stomach. He died on the spot.

We have been displaced to the middle area. Death is here too. Another cousin of mine was martyred while trying to bring water from the hospital.

Dear Allah, please let this war end soon! I want to go home. I want to sleep in my bed. I want my family back.

But I am still waiting to take the next step forward.

Written on July 7, 2024

Rital Hasan Aliwa
Age: 11 years old

Our home was obliterated by a bomb. My toys drowned in the rubble. My schoolbooks turned to ash. My clothes curled up in flames. My dreams, small and bright, were scattered like burnt paper in the wind. My friends faded away. My school, which had taught me to dream of being a math teacher, and our neighborhood, AlShujaya, both vanished. All the homes, mosques, hotels, and markets I knew were flattened.

And my beloved eldest uncle, the kindest man in my world, was killed at Abu Mazen Roundabout in Gaza, struck down by an Israeli bomb. He will not return; his laughs and playfulness will no longer be heard. We hear nothing but the roar of his loss. The place where he played with us is far away now, under the rubble. Only the dust remains.

So many children in Gaza, like me, sleep without fathers, and their mothers wear black eternally. So many dreams are lost in the space between death and the will not to die.

I pray: May this war stop. Our dreams wait in our sleep through the night. My home waits for me to return alive. And may Allah hold to account every coward who watched and did nothing.

Written on July 7, 2024

Mayar Alaa Darwish

Age: 10 years old

The inhabitants in Gaza have endured one of the most brutal wars in history. On October 7, 2023, our lives were turned upside down. Among us now are the martyred, the wounded, the orphaned, and the poor.

Our sorrowful people are living a paralyzed life. Schools, homes, and mosques have been bombed. We have lost the dearest things we owned, our homes, and now we live in tents, suffering through the scorching heat of summer and the bitter cold of winter. We struggle to find water, which we must fetch from faraway places because it is not available where we are. The same difficulty applies to food, made worse by the lack of money.

All of this unfolds before the silent eyes of the Arab world.

I pray to Almighty Allah that this war waged upon us will come to an end.

Written on July 7, 2024

Nisreen Mohammed AlYazji

Age: 10 years old

A bombing sound shut up our minds while we were getting ready for a new week at school. It was a beautiful day. I still remember our screams as we headed to school on what had seemed like a normal day. One rocket was followed by another. The bombing was getting worse.

On the second day they stole a home filled with safety. People were screaming at midnight. Neighbors warned us that the home next to us was about to be bombed. We swung displacement backpacks over our shoulders and ran out into the streets. People screamed out of fear, and strangers took us into their home for an hour.

Safety is absent in the presence of war. We thought that maybe our home, though its roof would fall upon our heads if it was bombed, would be safer than the street. Then my grandfather came to take us to his home, and we stayed there for two days.

As the bombing grew more intense, the occupation forces ordered us to evacuate Gaza on Friday, a day that had once been a warm family day. Now all of its features have faded away. Without hesitation, we went to the last property remaining to my grandfather, a stretch of land in the south.

Still, a second and third and fourth journey of displacement were waiting for us. We stayed in a building in Deir El for a month. We headed later to Rafah, where a friend of my father received us on his land for five months. The last time, we settled in a displacement camp in AlZawayida. There I met new friends in Yafa Camp, and we started learning together.

Written on July 7, 2024

Maria and Rima Abdallah Shafiq Al-Sarahi
Age: 8 and 6 years old

It was 6:30 AM on a day like any normal day for me and my sister, on our way to school. Suddenly loud explosions shook our ears. Terrified, we turned around and ran home as fast as we could. For several days we stayed indoors. We ran out of food and clean water to drink. The bombing in Al-Shujaiya grew worse, so we went to check on our grandfather. After that, we moved to Al-Nuseirat in the central area, but we didn't stay for long.

Problems started to arise as the tragedy started to reach our bodies—all our bodies. The happy, strongly bonded family we had once been was left behind in the old house. We left for Al- Zawyda, where we stayed at the house of my father's friends. The number of displaced people there grew to thirty-five, living in a single place. There was no space for us to sleep; we spent an entire night inside a car in the Al-Sawarih area. We had no access to water for a whole week.

Then destiny decided to help us. It came in the form of our kind new neighbor, Abu Amir, who generously gave us some water. Day by day we became closer neighbors, like family.

As a ground invasion began in Al-Bureij and bombing intensified, we went to Deir al-Balah and stayed on a piece of land owned by my father's friend. There I became close friends with a girl living in a neighboring tent. She became like a sister to me, and we used to go together to fetch water.

One day my uncle and I went to the sea. When we returned home at sunset, an explosion hit our neighbor's house. The sound was terrifying— I was really scared. We went back to Al- Zawyda, and my father insisted that it must be our last displacement journey. I started to live there. Later I found my way to Yaffa Camp. Now I go to school every day.

Rama Raed Musbeh
Age: 12 years old

I thought it would by a normal day. But that thought was cut off by the sudden roar of rockets. We endured more than what any body should carry, more than what the soul should bear. I remained in my home for nineteen days, despite the constant threats, despite the fire that rained down without pause, as if our flesh were food to keep the blaze alive. We finally fled barefoot at three in the morning, our hearts beating faster than our steps, thanking Allah that we were not being hurt.

Before heading south, we were displaced many times within Gaza. Displacement is no different whether it leads to Rafah, the far south, Deir El-balah, or Zawyda in the middle. All of these places are bloated with the displaced, becoming regions where life has no pulse. About forty people share the same bathroom and sleep in the same place overnight.

One night was very hard. They hit our neighbor's house with phosphorus bombs. I saw children rolling, their small bodies ablaze, their screams carving the sky open. The children couldn't breathe. The burns seared deep into their skin.

Isn't burning our children alive enough to stop the war? Is there any righteous soul who can bring this war to its knees? Stop the war.

Bian Abu Garkhoud

Age: 9 years old

The Zawaida area, October 7, 2023: We woke to the sounds of sharp, unrelenting, and terrifying explosions, as if the Day of Judgment had arrived. Someone told us that resistance fighters had breached the borders. They had entered the occupied lands, storming the enemy houses beyond our borders.

I watched, frozen. Later, in the heart of the afternoon, the enemy opened fire, and they have continued until this very day, the 310th. The flames have spared nothing, swallowing children, elderly people, women, students, doctors, and journalists. None have escaped. This is not over yet.

The whole world is watching with naked eyes a real story of resistance. This is not a movie. Shame on everyone who is watching.

Written on July 7, 2024

Ma'ather Qusai Ibrahim Al-Za'anin
Age: 11 years old

We didn't know the war had begun. We went out for a visit to Grandpa's home. The war broke our holiday, just as carrying the heavy displacement backpacks broke our backs, while we fled from one place to another.

The terrifying war began on Saturday, October 7, 2023. We were no longer visitors; we had become displaced. We stayed in Gaza for a month, then escaped to the south through scenes that looked like the Day of Judgment. We walked all the way to Al-Zawaida. I'll never forget that day, November 9. The bodies of martyrs lay scattered across the roads, pieces of flesh flung toward an unknown fate.

Later came another displacement order to leave the area where we had taken refuge. A big van stopped in front of the door, and what we still had was thrown into it. As a displaced person I reached Rafah, the city that embraced all the displaced from the north and south of Gaza. We spent there the holy month of Ramadan and Eid al-Fitr.

But even that didn't last. Soon the occupation threatened Rafah too, and the occupation forces began their assault. So we were forced to flee once more, back to Al-Zawaida on May 15, 2024.

Another displacement may await us, who knows? A life-loving people, we will never lose our hope, despite the agony: that we will return, that we will rebuild, that we will go back to our beautiful home in Beit Hanoun.

Written on July 7, 2024

Said Belal Saleem Al-shafee
Age: 12 years old

I didn't understand what was happening when intense rockets flew into the sky. Fear crept into the sky with them. That night I started to gather the threads of the story. I thought that I would have to be in school in the early morning, but the truth was that resistance fighters had snuck over the borders. Gaza Strip was under Israeli attack. Things started to look different. The news brought nothing.

I have never gone back to school since that day. I have never gone back to my home. We were heaped up in makeshift tents, withdrawn from our childhood, taken away from the land of our homes. Evacuation leaflets fell down on my city. Our feet carried us south, toward Al-Zawaida. We left our dreams, our childhoods, and our laughter behind in Gaza.

After that day life passed slowly, without safety, electricity, health, or shelter. We lived day by day, looking for water, food, and wood. Evacuation orders never stopped chasing us in the so-cold "safe area." The occupiers seized Gaza's crossings. They tightened the noose on trade. They starved us of food, of soap, of the most basic things. Prices soared. People fell.

We are deceived by a world that calls Muslim resistance fighters, who are sacrificing themselves for their land, "terrorists," while labeling the killing of innocent children and the destroying of homes and mosques "self-defense."

We say, as always: *Hasbiyallahu wa ni'mal wakeel.* God is enough for us, and He is the best disposer of affairs.

Written on July 7, 2024

Juwan Jamal Youssef Rayan
Age: 7 years old

I don't remember how many times I have survived death. I'm a little girl, but I've survived a lot. Shrapnel has pierced through our home's asbestos roof more than once. I don't know how many times the stones and sharp pieces flew into our safe little home.

I don't get scared when I hear the sound of bombing. Sometimes I even laugh out loud when I see Mama frightened. I try to comfort her. I'm a kid, but I understand deeply what *displacement* means. I know what life looks like when you live in a tent. I understand how it feels when the buzzing drones in the sky are separated from you by only a thin piece of fabric.

I understand what's happening around me. I know our life is very hard. I don't want to end up like Noonoo, my cousin. She is alone, for her mother was martyred.

I'm not afraid of the bombing, but I miss my old life. I miss my teacher. I miss my school and my friends. I only want to have fun. I miss what it felt like to feel safe in my homeland.

Written on July 7, 2024

Ibrahim Qusai Ibrahim Al-Za'anin
Age: 6 years old

The brutal war began. I was in kindergarten. My life wasn't the same.

The war swallowed the most precious things we had. It took our lives, our time, our loved ones. We left everything behind, a month after the war started, and headed south to Al-Zawyda at first, followed by a displacement journey to Rafah. Then we returned once again to Al-Zawyda, on May 15, 2024.

The war hasn't put down its weapons. It is a war that doesn't end. Nothing is clear. Everything is dark and confusing. Will this war ever stop? Will we ever go back to our home and rebuild it with our own hands?

I pray to Allah, always and forever.

Written on July 7, 2024

Hamza Ahmed Yusif Albrdini
Age: 9 years old

I'm a third-grade student. At first, after October 7, 2023, I thought I was enjoying a nice break from school. I was wrong. As the days passed slowly, I realized we had been roped off from school and withdrawn from our own childhoods. We became like grown-up men, waking up every day to carry water, not schoolbooks, from faraway places. Standing in long lines for flour and bread was exactly like standing in the morning lines in school. But we had been pulled away from the days of play and innocence.

Without electricity or clean water, we are displaced, living in a small house with just two rooms. We are heaped up with sixteen people and their belongings, in one room. All the time there is shouting, suffering, and no privacy.

My father left our home long before the war. I have become a wall for my mother, who was cunning enough to know the importance of giving her nine-year-old the responsibility of carrying heavy gallons of water. Every day I have to go to the water desalination station, next to Kuwait Hospital and near our displacement place. It's become a daily routine.

I know that it's too heavy for her to be father and mother for me at the same time. Fear would pierce my heart whenever she went out for a bit of dignity. To stand in endless lines for oil, sugar, and flour was very dangerous, and I waited for her return each time with a longing heart. I couldn't stop thinking that she might be like so many other parents in Gaza, who go out but do not come back.

I sat at the edge of the tent, chewing a dry piece of *saj* bread. It crumbled in my hands, like the displacement struggles breaking the soul. I miss the soft, warm bread from home, the kind that smelled like comfort and rose with love. The kind that tasted like real life.

Bombs! I remember when the house next door was bombed, and everyone rushed to help. I saw the little bodies of my friends torn to pieces in front of my eyes. We carried them in plastic bags as shrouds. For days after that, I couldn't sleep. Those images wouldn't leave me. My mother kept holding me, trying to comfort me. She prayed, "I hope, if we must die, that our bodies stay whole." That made her cry. But it's the truth. Here in Gaza, we die every day. In Gaza, we are the Living Dead. The agony of waiting for death fills every second of our lives.

The day they bombed the Ali Ibn Abi Talib Mosque was one of the worst we've lived through. The bombs fell without warning. I was in the kitchen with my mother. She was making food. The sound of bombing was terrifying, unprecedented. What was that? A second intense missile. I couldn't believe how terrifying it was. We thought they were targeting homes one by one. We said *Shahada* and sat silently, waiting for death.

When the sounds stopped, we stepped outside. The street looked nothing like it had before. A gray area. Everything had been swallowed by destruction. Desperately we ran back inside. Better to die at home than out there.

Eventually we left our home in Rafah, separated from my cousins and friends. Nothing can describe the pain of that farewell. We fled because Rafah was unsafe, but the place where we went was even more dangerous. We came to the middle area of Gaza, where the bombs rain down every day, louder, closer, deadlier. We always say to each other, "Stay close, so that if we must die, we die together."

Many people never will come back. Others homes were bombed, like my uncle's. His wife and four children too were martyred. So was my best friend. My mom had just left their house ten minutes before the missile fell. When I think about it, I realize how much danger we live in. I don't know who's next. I don't know who'll be burned by the next rocket, like my cousins were.

Some things can't be forgotten, no matter how hard you try. May Allah have mercy on their innocent souls. They were children—they did nothing wrong. And maybe I'll be next. Here in Gaza, there's no safety, no shelter, no protection. We are dead, just waiting for our execution.

To the free people of the world: Stop this cruel death. We are children.

Written on July 7, 2024

Rimas Rami Zuhair Abu Jabara
Age: 10 years old

Gazzah Aleizha, a land of pride, resilience, and defiance. But they trapped us. They stole our water. They stole our food and every lifeline in Gaza.

Once upon a time, our home was full of warmth, happiness, and peace. To Rafah our feet ran away, escaping hungry death and bombs falling on homes, hospitals, and schools.

The Zionist Occupation has trapped us here, cutting off water, food, and every lifeline. The cloth of our tent breaths cold at night and heat in the day. The days have begun to stretch on as we go daily to search for water and firewood.

Hope and resilience are all that remain. But Victory shall come.

Written on July 7, 2024

Kajeen Husny Naser Albouab
Age: 10 years old

We walked with no water, no food, and no clear direction. Forty kilometers of exhaustion, like walking through a long dream that wouldn't end. Our feet moved slowly, feeling that the ground didn't want to carry us. There were no cars, no shelters, just an empty road and people like us, walking, each wearing a scared or silent face. We knew we were leaving home, but we didn't know where to go. Five months of fleeing from place to place wasn't our choice. We ended up moving to a piece of land in Al-Zawayda. It was crowded, but we had no other choice.

Before, everything felt normal. On the morning of October 7, 2023, we woke up as if it were any other day, put on our school uniforms, and got ready to go. Suddenly we heard strange sounds: rockets flying from different directions. Everything changed, and fear filled the house. We turned on the TV and found out that the war had started.

We stayed home for two days, listening to the sounds of bombs. Then came an order to evacuate our area. We went to my grandma's house, but not long afterward another evacuation order came. That night we ran through the dark, not knowing where to go. We ended up in a neighbor's house. When the sun came up, we went back home. The warning had been false.

But after a full day without water or electricity, another evacuation order was announced for the whole north. We sat by the window watching people leave—some in cars, others walking. We got scared, and we left too. We walked south, over forty kilometers, until we reached a school crowded with displaced families. We stayed in one of the classrooms for about a month, not sure if we would ever go back.

One morning we were woken up by the school principal shouting through the microphone: "This area is dangerous!" We had been hearing loud, close bombing, and the school shook sometimes. We left again, this time to Khan Younis. The road was full of danger—explosions, flares, and fear.

After a few days, we had to flee once more, to Rafah. We stayed in the Qatari hospital, but there was no water, no electricity, no sanitation. The place was very crowded. At first there was no food. It was winter, and we had no warm clothes, no blankets. We tried to sleep on the cold floor.

Now we are still in Al-Zawayda, watching our fate, waiting for the war to end.

Written on July 7, 2024

Bisan and Erada Mousa Ebraheem Alzaneen, Twins
Ages: 9 years old

That morning, my mother laid out our new kindergarten clothes, neatly folded, smelling of soap and hope. The plan was simple: a warm bath, breakfast, and then off to our new classroom, where letters and colors waited to meet us. The world still felt so kind.

But instead of brushing our hair, she packed emergency bags. Instead of tying our shoelaces, she tightened the zippers on our only suitcase. By nightfall, the dreams of our first day at school had turned into a nightmare of smoke, sirens, and silence.

The roar of rockets coming from inside, toward the occupied land, was shocking—a sound unlike anything I had ever known, as if fear itself had a voice. My heart trembled. Then my mom grabbed her phone, her hands shaking as she dialed my father. He was outside at work, as usual. She asked if he was safe. He was, but he warned her not to take us to the kindergarten. A heavy silence filled the room. I didn't understand all the words, but I knew something was breaking, something bigger than just our plans for the day.

The next morning came with no promise. The sky, once blue, now seemed uncertain. The bombardment had started, and it wasn't stopping. Darkness started to fall, and the night was awful. Everyone was talking, and one word kept echoing—*evacuation*, for areas near the border. Instead of packing our lunchboxes and coloring books, my mother began to fill small bags with clothes, important papers, and necessary things we needed. She had done this before, many times. After the noon prayer, a nearby building was hit and completely destroyed. It was getting worse by this time. They started to bomb areas successively and intensely. It was a new kind of bombing.

My father came home that afternoon with a decision already written on his face: "We're leaving." We each carried a bag that my mom had prepared the day before. We walked on foot until we found a taxi. We had no destination, just away from the edges of danger. Fighter jets circled above us, loud and low, like shadows that could strike at any moment.

We stayed in a new spot for five days, and moved later to another in the Al-Zaytun neighborhood. We stayed for ten days where my cousin's family lived—her grandmother and brothers welcomed us kindly. But the situation quickly deteriorated. The sky darkened with war and the clouds of bombing.

Then came a rare chance: we were offered a place inside Al-Rantisi Hospital, where my uncle worked. Fourteen days passed there. Then the bombs came for the hospital too. The occupation forces targeted it without mercy. We fled again, to my aunt's home nearby. It wasn't far, but safety had become a mirage. We stayed there just two days before tanks rolled into al-Nasr. So we left, escaping death again.

November 9, 2023, is a date carved into my bones. We fled south, toward Wadi Gaza. We had no car and no protection, just feet. We walked, carrying what little we could. The road was long, endless, and strange. We were tired. I walked beside my mother, and I was so very tired from the weight of the bag on my back, from the heat, from the silence on the road. What I saw along the way I will never forget.

Eventually we reached al-Zawaida. We stayed there for fifty days, until the very end of the year. Then we moved again, to Rafah, the displacement city. The sun there was cruel during the day, dry and sharp, and at night a terrible cold took over, a cold that crept not only into our bones but into our hearts.

We remained in Rafah until May 15, 2024. Then we relocated to al-Zawaida. And here we are, still breathing, still alive. We don't know where life will take us next. But all of us carry the same hope, to return to where we belong. I miss my home. I miss my clothes, my room, my toys. I miss everything. And still we dream of going back.

Praise to Allah for everything.

Written on July 7, 2024

Joudy Udai Alzaneen
Age: 10 years old

A bale tent made of worn-out old clothes. As the scorching sun climbed higher, its rays poured down like fire, melting the brittle body of the tent. Inside, the suffocating heat wrapped itself around my skin, seeping into my bones, until I felt that I too was dissolving under its weight. Black and red ants crawled up my legs, biting without mercy. Hoping to find some compensation for the long months of suffering, I walked to a makeshift school.

It was the beginning of a new school day, or so I thought. But the roaring of rockets came from every direction, followed by screaming, shattering the morning stillness. I had thought the war was only rockets and the sounds of bombing. I didn't know what it really meant until a missile reached our neighbor's house without warning, in Beit Hanoon, and my family fled to my grandparents' home. Then the war became crueler, and it has never stopped chasing us. The evacuation leaflets caused us many displacement journeys, starting from our neighborhood far away in the north of the strip until the last spot we ended up in, Al-Zwayda.

At first we stayed for several weeks in Al-Zaytun neighborhood. Then we fled to Omar Al-Mukhtar Street, to the home of my mother's uncle. Just one day later, we returned to my grandparents' house, but the bombing was fierce and merciless, so we sought shelter in Al-Rantisi Hospital, where my uncle managed to find us a room so we could stay safe. Even there, we tried to carve out fleeting moments of joy laughter, play—a fragile sense of normalcy.

Boom! A war-plane struck the floor above us, the nephrology department at the hospital. That night we lay in silence, still and breathless, as if already dead. The next morning we fled again, this time to my aunt's house in Sheikh Radwan, where we stayed for two days. But soon a ground invasion swept through the area and forced us south. We witnessed things we had never seen before. We walked over six kilometers, with nothing to shield us but an empty road and the open sky. I saw things I had never seen before. There were bloody martyrs, scattered belongings, dead people.

126

Months passed, and even in Al-Zawayda evacuation orders chased us once more, forcing us to flee again to Rafah. There hunger came for us. When the flour ran out, famine began to spread. We used wheat and corn as substitutes to make flour for bread.

Thanks to Allah that it didn't last longer. I pray this war won't last anymore.

Written on July 7, 2024

Rinad Husnai Aliwa
Age: 13 years old

Days passed in my city. The agony of waiting. The war hasn't come to an end yet. Is it winter who brought the bitter cold, the heavy rains flooding the tents of displaced people, and the storms that take away belongings to another world? Why did Ramadan this year come without mosques where we can pray all together? Where are the joy and happiness that used to brighten the faces of children in my city during Eid Aldha and Eid Alfiter each year?

Where are the people I love? Why did they kill my uncle? He was a gentle man. I miss my school. I miss my friends. I miss my old home.

Written on July 7, 2024

Mohammed Husnai Naser Albouab

Age 12 years old

The night was quiet. We had just fallen asleep in my grandmother's house, trying to escape the fear and ongoing bombing in our area, the Southern Al-Rimal neighborhood. Suddenly loud voices broke the silence. "Evacuate the house!" neighbors shouted from the street. My heart raced. We got up, gathered what we could, and left quietly, like shadows slipping through the dark.

In the early morning we returned to our house, though our area still in danger. Things were still, as if nothing had happened. The quiet made me uneasy, like the calm before a storm, as I went back to my grandmother's. Not long afterward, the phone rang. The bombing was repeating over and over; all of my uncles and their families fled their homes and came back to ours. That night we were all together under one roof. There was no electricity, no water. But we felt safe, just because we were together.

The morning came heavily, like a gray wall. That day the Israeli occupation announced an evacuation order: "Go south." They claimed the south was safe. But bombing was chasing us everywhere. We sat in silence for a long time, just staring into the hollow air. There was nothing to pack, nothing to carry, except a fragile thread of hope. Maybe one day we would return north, maybe something of our life would still be waiting for us there.

We started walking. When we reached Wadi Gaza, we were exhausted. We collapsed by the gate of a hospital, right on the cold pavement. Everyone looked tired, dusty, and lost. Papa walked around, looking for a car to take us the rest of the way. The night was creeping in from the edge of the sky like a beast when at last we found one. We squeezed in and rode to the southern part of Wadi Gaza. There we found a school overflowing with displaced families. We stayed for almost a month—no water, no clothes, no food. Some tried to return to the north, but we couldn't. It wasn't safe.

One day the school director stood on the platform and shouted into a microphone, "This area is dangerous!" He didn't need to tell us. We had been hearing the bombs falling nearby every night. We packed again and moved to Khan Younis, running from one danger into another. Flares lit up the sky, and the sound of shelling followed us like a shadow.

Our fifth displacement was to Rafah. We stayed in the Qatari Hospital, crowded with people. No clean water, no electricity, no bathrooms. At first even food was hard to find. It was winter, and we had no warm clothes or blankets. We shivered at night, hungry and cold.

After five months, we moved to a piece of land in Al-Zawayda. It was packed with people, but we had no choice.

We are still waiting for some solution to materialize from around the corner and bring this war to end. I don't know if this is the end of our displacement journey, or if I'll ever go back to my home in Gaza.

Written on July 7, 2024

Rwida Mohammed Adel Almasri

Age: 9 years old

We woke up to the footsteps of an uninvited guest.

It was early morning, and war had arrived without warning, slipping through our street like a shadow. I had gone to bed excited: tomorrow was supposed to be the first day of the new school week. I had prepared my uniform, my bag, and my dreams. But none of that mattered anymore. The air had changed. The sounds outside weren't the usual morning noises. They were heavy, sharp, and final.

I was heartbroken. School was canceled. Life was canceled. The next day, fear grew so loud that it echoed between the walls. Our neighbors came running to our house, hoping the basement could shield them. The walls were thick, they said; maybe they could quiet the bombs a little, maybe they could slow death down.

We stayed for about a month. Then things grew even worse, so we all fled to my grandfather's house. Two days later, the bombing reached us there too. And so we left again, heading to Al-Zawaida, in the central region. The road was a nightmare. We walked past swollen bodies, unrecognizable, abandoned by the world. The stench of death clung to our clothes and followed us like a second skin. Tanks roared past us, crushing everything in their path—trees, cars, walls, and our memories. The road shook beneath us. I held my breath for hours.

Eventually we reached my uncle's house and huddled in the ground floor. But nothing lasted. A few months later, even Al-Zawaida became unsafe. We fled once more, this time to Rafah. There we built tents from old, worn-out fabric. The heat was unbearable. Poisonous insects crawled over our things at night. We barely slept. We barely spoke. It felt like the earth itself had rejected us.

After months of exhaustion, we returned to Al-Zawaida. Not to a house, but to tents again, fabric shelters trembling in the wind. Now we struggle even to find water. Everything is scarce, except our prayers. Still we are grateful. We are alive. And in a world like this, that alone feels like resistance.

Adel Mohammed Adel Al-Masri
Age: 6 years old

A big-minded boy with a bag of crayons—that's who I was. But then I couldn't go back to my beautiful preschool, Beit AlTofola in Gaza. I was so scared. The rockets were screaming in the sky, louder than anything I'd ever heard. I was often afraid. When the fear got big, Mama reminded me that I should pray so that the bad people would go away. One time she took a video of me praying for the war to come to an end. I was sitting on the couch in the living room.

Our neighbors came to shelter with us, hiding from the sounds of bombs. We had Warda, Sham, Salah, Tamim, Samira, my dad's cousins, Rawda, Marwa, Uncle Abdulrahman and his children, Aunties Najwa and Niveen, and Grandpa Abu Osama Farwana with his kids, Malek, Adam, Rahaf, and Nada. There were so many people in our home. We cooked together, baked bread, played games, read stories, told jokes, and acted out silly plays with my cousins Adel and Ameer. Mama brought crayons, drawing books, a little whiteboard, puzzles, dolls, and even a puppet theater. War doesn't, I think, love colors, but we tried to cheer each other up every night of the war.

When the ground invasion started and the tanks reached our neighborhood, my grandmother, uncles, and their children came to stay with us too. They had escaped death when Al-Rantisi Hospital, where they were sheltering, was bombed. I was so happy to see them. But things were getting worse. Our house and the basement became so crowded with people fleeing the fighting. Bullets slammed into the walls. My grandmother couldn't go down to the basement—she was too old to handle the stairs. Glass shattered over their heads. Calls kept coming, telling us that we had to evacuate to the south.

We left, somehow, by a miracle. The tanks were firing at my brothers as we ran. We walked through what they called the "safe route," Salah al-Din Street. I saw martyrs on the ground. I saw tanks. We walked for a long time. I didn't cry. The whole way Mama held my hand and whispered, "We're almost there. Just a little more. If you stop, they'll shoot us. Don't touch anything on the ground, not even if it's yours."

All the neighbors had already left. We finally reached my mom's uncle's house, exhausted from walking. We hadn't brought anything with us except small backpacks, just a change of clothes on each of our backs. I had brought my crayons and coloring books in my preschool bag.

On the way, we'd seen a man, my uncle, lying on the ground. I knew he was a martyr. But when we arrived, I told Mama that my uncle must have been really tired from all the walking. Why else was he resting instead of walking the way we did? He was sweating a lot. I knew he was gone, but I didn't want Mama to be afraid.

She hugged me tight and said, "God keep that fate away from you. Pray for him, and pray that God takes the bad people away."

We played a lot in the basement of my uncle's house. At night the four of us—me, Mama, Yara, and Roweida—slept on one mattress, covered with our jackets. We had no food. My brothers bought some supplies, and we lived off the flour until it ran out. Then we started cleaning wheat, mixing it with rice, grinding it, and baking our own bread. My dad was in Khan Younis with my uncle Osama, staying at a friend's place. The bombing there was heavy, less than in Gaza but still terrifying.

Then tanks trapped my dad in Khan Younis. He escaped, somehow, and reached Rafah, but he didn't manage to get to us in Al-Zawaida. Later we were told to evacuate again, to the far south, so we rode in a big truck to Rafah. My grandmother and uncles had bought a lot of kitchen supplies and other things.

In Rafah they built tents from old cloth, wood, and nails. I learned how to poke holes in empty cans of beans and peas, and we planted corn, wheat, lupine, even purslane. I learned to light fires, because Mama and Grandma cooked over open flames. I gathered firewood from everywhere. We drew on stones we collected from Al-Mawasi and Rafah. We ran wild on the sand, pouring all our energy into play. I stood in the line for drinking water. We'd go to the Japanese Garden to fetch salty water. Yara and I walked to the soup kitchen. The heat was unbearable, and the walk was long.

Mama told me that we are, in reality, much older than our age. I fasted during Ramadan, but we didn't hang lanterns or decorations the way we did every year at home. The bombing didn't stop, a reminder that the Israelis were lying. There was no such thing as a safe place. Still, we become careless about being afraid. God was with us. He was the one protecting us.

We stayed in Rafah for five months and in Al-Zawaida for fifty days. Seven months of exhaustion. I missed my home, my bed, my toys, our new TV, the trips, and the breeze kissing my face. I missed riding in the car, going somewhere nice. I missed Mama's delicious cooking. I don't like these unhealthy canned foods. But even that food, I've learned, it is a blessing. May God protect our blessings and keep them from slipping away.

The bombing in Rafah got worse. The agony of waiting for a ceasefire that never came was much worse. We refused to leave Rafah until a month after the invasion. When we saw how bad things were, we returned to Al-Zawaida. This time we lived in tents, on land owned by my uncle. Other people were already using the basement. But the bombing was intense.

We had to flee more than once because we were too close to Salah al-Din Street, and the Israelis are treacherous. A piece of shrapnel landed in my uncle's tent, next to ours, and bullets from a quadcopter hit the trees nearby.

We still cooked over fire. The fabric of our tent melted in the sun. My skin broke out from the heat. The sand was filthy. Finding water was still a struggle, and everything was expensive.

It's been ten months of war, and it still hasn't ended. I wish my teachers could see me now—how well I can trace letters and write in neat handwriting. But I'll be starting first grade without even going to kindergarten. I go with my sisters to the Yaffa Al-Azza Camp to study, so that I don't waste my life on useless things. I memorize the Quran with my sisters. I finished *Surat Al-Fajr*, and now I'm learning *Al-Ma'un*. I play with the blocks, crayons, and coloring books they gave me at the camp.

I pray for this war to end, so that we can go back to our homes and see you all in Gaza—in better days. We have to fight the Israelis with knowledge, resilience, and defiance.

My name is Adel. I was born in Gaza, the land of war and stubborn hope. I am just nine, but I've lived many lives already. Mama, Papa and my two sisters, Yara and Rwida, are my family. I love you so much.

Written on July 7, 2024

Dima Jihad Fathi Juma
Age: 11 years old

The moment I climbed into the car, I froze. A masked man sat beside me, clutching a round, black bag, the kind you'd see in negotiation scenes in movies. My sister Sara was already inside, her face pale, her hands trembling. She had told the driver to stop when she heard me calling her name over and over: "Saaaara! Saaaara!" Only then did I catch up and jump in.

School had closed its doors, and everyone was heading home. The masked man didn't speak. He simply glanced at us once, then looked away. A heavy silence filled the car as it drove through streets echoing with fear and confusion. I could feel Sara's fear pressing against mine. We didn't say a word.

We couldn't believe it when we made it back home. The building was quiet, but the air was heavy with dread. I harried to turn on the TV. Rockets were still flying. The sky rumbled without rest.

We had heard a strange, terrifying bombing sound on our way to school that morning. We had thought the day would be normal. That morning, October 7, 2023, Sara and I had left early. It was our turn for the morning duty of cleaning the classroom before the rest of the students arrived. The routine was familiar: we'd walk halfway, then catch a ride from near Abu Jabara's shop to get to school on time. We laughed together on the way, unaware that the world around us was about to change forever.

We reached the school and hurried to find a place at the front of the morning line. I waited the day to begin. But the headmistress stood in the middle of the schoolyard, shouting at the top of her lungs: "Go back to your homes! All of you! Why did you come?!"

Fear started to creep in as students screamed in the hallway, fleeing, crying, and shouting. She started to push them away to their homes, and I looked for my sister so we could leave. Resistance fighters from Al-Qassam Brigades had launched a large-scale operation in the settlements surrounding Gaza. They had killed soldiers, captured others, and taken hostages. The air was thick with uncertainty.

Then the retaliation came. The Israeli bombardment started with a madness we'd never seen before. Entire neighborhoods were wiped out: Al-Rimal, Al-Zaytoun, Tal Al-Hawa, Al-Karama, Al-Shuja'iyya, Jabalia Camp, Azza, and Al-Sumoud. Leaflets fell from the sky, ordering inhabitants to evacuate to the south. But we didn't leave, not right away. We stayed home for two days, trying to convince ourselves we were safe.

135

But the strikes kept getting closer and closer. One missile hit a house just a hundred meters away. The building we lived in shook violently; windows shattered all around us. Barely an hour later, another strike hit even closer. This time the shockwave rattled every nerve in our bodies. Women and girls screamed in terror. Families rushed to pack what they had and flee. One by one, the apartments emptied. Soon our building was completely deserted except for us.

We lasted ten days. Then we packed what we could and left for Khan Younis. The journey was terrifying. War-planes circled above us. Bombs fell to the east and west of Salah al-Din Street, the main road south. Eventually we made it to a small apartment that belonged to my grandmother's relatives, the Abu Al-Reesh family. We stayed there for two months. There was no water. There was no safety. Shrapnel tore through windows, even pierced the bathroom wall. Every second felt like a gamble, but by some miracle we survived.

Then tanks advanced into the eastern parts of Khan Younis, Abasan, Bani Suheila, and Khuza'a. We couldn't sleep at night. The sky was a battlefield of sound: explosions, gunfire, flares that turned night into red daylight. The flames crept closer. The Israeli soldiers were moving in. We heard the earth groan under their boots. They came with fire and intense bombing. We had no choice.

Again we packed our bags. Again we searched for a car. Again we fled, this time to Rafah. We arrived late at night. Our relatives greeted us with warm hugs and heavy hearts. We thought we might finally find rest. And for seven months, we did. We had water, blankets, food, things that were real luxuries at that time. But war doesn't sleep; it only waits. One day the order came: evacuate Rafah. We evacuated again, to Al-Zwayda.

I pray that Gaza is our final stop. I pray for our martyrs. May God have mercy on their souls. May He comfort their families and give strength to their hearts. May He heal our wounded. And may He plant our feet firmly on this land, no matter how many times they try to make us run.

Written on July 7, 2024

Yara Mohammed Adel Almasri

Age: 11 years old

We rushed to the concrete house next to our worn-out fabric tent, its fibers faded and frayed by ten relentless months of sunlight. We were seeking protection. I sat quietly in a corner, facing my mother, my grandmother, my uncles, and their wives. Memories started to unfold, bit by bit. Getting ready for school was the last thing I had done, exactly five minutes before a deafening noise filled the air. I thought it was thunder, maybe. But how could it be thunder in October? My mother had told us that the sky would be warm and clear in October. Only moments later, we realized it wasn't thunder. It was the sound of rockets. The sound that meant war had knocked on the doors of Gaza.

It all began on that historic day. We were very happy about what had happened that morning. We were supposed to head to school, but chaos started and has lasted ever since. The occupation forces, after seven hours, started to fire areas so intensely that the earth shook us as if there were an earthquake, or as if Judgment Day had started. Still, we thought it wouldn't last that long.

I remember wearing heavy winter clothes, even though the heat was suffocating, as if we were papers held over a flame. We packed our school bags with just one change of clothes and walked on Salah al-Din Road. We kept walking until it felt as if our backs were carrying burning mountains. My brother, Adel, looked at one of the killed people lying on the side of the road and said, "Mama, that man is tired like us from walking so much. That's why he stopped to rest. That's why he's sweating." But he wasn't sweating. He was a martyr. And the red pool around him wasn't sweat, it was blood.

Along the way we saw things that we, as children, should never see: lifeless bodies, pools of blood, charred corpses, decomposed remains, scattered limbs. Blood-stained clothes were strewn across the road. Tanks rolled past us, and others fired from behind earthen mounds. Soldiers warned us not to turn back or pick up anything that fell. They forced us to evacuate from the north to the south.

Walking seven kilometers to arrive at my mother's uncle's house in Al-Zawayda was exhausting, and we woke up the first day early, unable to pack our things. We sheltered in a ground-floor shop, and we had no bedding to sleep on. After a while we managed to buy some. The whole family shared one thin mattress and two blankets.

Slowly we began to adjust, trying to carry on with our days. But soon our food supplies started to run out. We had no flour, so we bought wheat and ground it ourselves. Each morning at dawn, we'd wake to knead dough for our family and my grandfather's household, about two hundred loaves a day. Each person could have two small loaves. We baked them over an open fire. Wood was expensive, painfully so. We used to go out together, scouring the land around us for fallen branches. All families were doing this. The area was packed with displaced families.

After fifty days, the people in the middle area of the strip were ordered to evacuate. Rafah was a strange city to us. How could someone who once owned a home, a plot of land, maybe even a villa, live now in a tent? In a place that felt like the desert, where the sand burned beneath your feet? And the news wasn't good. The bombing came closer. This was a place where we didn't own a single olive tree, even though it was still our homeland. After losing our house and belongings, I wondered what was left to protect?

We left Al-Zawayda for Tel al-Sultan in Rafah. The so-called Mawasi Rafah, meaning the "safe zone." We had to build our own tents. A large group of us shared the same toilet—a deep pit dug into the ground. Setting up the tent for my cousins was a kind of joy. It was like a camping trip, just like the cartoons, like those forest expeditions they'd shown on TV. None of us could realize the reality of that tent. It was our fate, in the shape of torment and a lack of water.

I, Ya'rob, Ibrahim, Iradah, Ma'athir, Rowaida, Shadia, Lujain, Naya, and my little brother, Adel, worked together at first to fill water containers. We were learning how to take responsibility. My father bought a water tank just for our small family, separate from the shared ones with my uncles, because the kids were playing with the water. I was the eldest son of my father, and I didn't mind. One day my mother told me, "We are the ones who raise real men. And Palestinian girls are the sisters of those men." I started going with my father to the Japanese garden to fetch salt water, and sometimes we'd go together to Yasin Station near the barracks and the Egyptian station for drinking water, if no charity water truck came to our area.

As for food, there wasn't much we could eat except canned foods filled with preservatives and salt. I tried to help my mom cook and bake over the fire. Sometimes I would walk long distances to go to the hot-food kitchen, hoping to find something decent that could save her from the exhausting routine of cooking. But in five months, I can remember only two or three times when they had enough cooked food. My mom said, "They cook ten pots just to feed as many displaced people as they can. They think everyone enjoys mushy, half-cooked food, the kind you see dumped at the roadside for stray animals." Then she added, "If they'd just cooked five pots of good food, they would have earned a real reward instead of creating so much waste."

On my displacement journey I have come to know many different areas, like Al-Nuss Street, the Saudi neighborhood, the Japanese garden, the Tiara, the Barracks, Swafi, an area with sandy dunes, and the Philadelphi Corridor. We even spoke to some Egyptian soldiers, but their words were few, restrained by fear of their commanders.

On the dunes, we children would steal fleeting moments of joy—climbing, running, laughing, trying to shake loose the heavy sadness inside our small chests. Somehow it made us feel human again. And after the torment of nights sleeping on the bare ground, surrounded by insects, we would gaze out from the highest points and see the beauty of our homeland. For a brief moment, we could pretend to forget what we were going through, clinging to the hope that one day we would return and that our land would be free again.

We awaited the month of Ramadan with great anticipation, praying that maybe there would be a ceasefire. But this year it carried none of the joy we had known before. The situation was dire: unbearable heat, and so little food and drink. No refrigerators, no juices, none of the delicious Ramadan dishes we once loved. Even vegetables and fruits were nowhere to be found. Still, we didn't complain. We accepted any meal we could find and ate enough to survive.

Then Eid arrived, but it was unprecedented. No new clothes, no sweets, no prayers, none of the rituals that give Eid its sacred glow. Oh, the misery of life in Gaza! How much do we suffer in Gaza? And who else in this miserable world must endure what we do, witnessing the torn bodies of our brothers and friends everywhere we turn? Shame on this unfair world, where the blood of a fellow Muslim flows so easily and no one so much as flinches.

Still, on that Eid, we tried to go for a trip to Sawafi, the dunes. But the sky itself broke down in tears, weeping over the countless martyrs and the rivers of blood spilled in Gaza. The rain came pouring down. There was no way to play; the rain flooded our tent, soaking the worn-out fabric until it sagged and whispered to itself in surrender. If salt water can rust iron, imagine what it did to our skin beneath our tattered sheets.

Three days later, I went to the dunes, but I felt weak, exhausted, and dizzy. My mother decided to take me to the clinic for blood tests. Thankfully, my condition wasn't as severe as the other cases we saw there. Still, due to the lack of medical supplies and the overwhelming number of patients, we had no choice but to return to our tent. I was tired. My mother, alarmed by the yellowing whites of my eyes, decided to take me back to the doctor, hoping to find a reason for my severe fatigue. Maybe it was jaundice, hepatitis, or something even worse.

Her fears were confirmed. My readings were dangerously high. Questions flooded in; "What kind of diet should Yara follow? What can she eat?" Luckily dates were available then, along with some vegetables, though the prices had soared.

Still, how could I have gotten sick? We were so careful. We always washed our hands and kept things clean, despite the lack of access to food and water. We never ate uncovered meals. Eventually we discovered that it was because of contaminated water.

❀ ❀ ❀

The Rafah desert lies closest to the Sinai wilderness. The occupation had pushed us to the farthest edge of Gaza, as if we'd been exiled to Mercury, near the blistering sun. Living in the desert made safe shelter, proper homes, and clean food only a dream for children in that exile. Swarms of poisonous insects woke us at dawn like cruel alarm clocks, and the work shifts began at 4 AM. One day a snake slithered into our camp. We screamed. We had never seen creatures like that.

Still, this was not enough for the occupation. Soon they dropped evacuation leaflets again, announcing an urgent operation to begin in Rafah. This felt like the hardest displacement yet. The pieces of fabric and nylon we had used for making shelters were torn and couldn't be used a second time. Transport costs were unbelievably high, and we had so many belongings now that it was like moving an entire home. Starting over wasn't easy in that place, and it was all to no avail. They forced us to leave Rafah on May 15, 2024, when we were still counting the days, waiting for news of a ceasefire.

We returned to Al-Zawaida, owning only a ragged, battered tent. Five snakes were waiting at the door. On the fourth day, we found a hedgehog. Then a few days later came a turtle, a chameleon, an owl, and feral dogs.

Al-Sawarihah was the next spot we fled to, when the sudden operation in the Nuseirat camp began, to free hostages held by the occupation. Our bathroom there wasn't made of real walls, just some old curtains hanging all around and a worn-out cloth pretending to be a door. There was no privacy. Once a massive black snake, over two meters long, was sitting there when my father went to the toilet. Killing it wasn't easy. He asked my sister, Rwida, to call my brothers for help.

Two weeks later, something else unexpected happened: a large rat stormed the bathroom attached to our tent. It dug a tunnel, a deep one, as if it were laying siege, and then it invaded our space. My mother destroyed its nest over and over again, but the rat wasn't ready to surrender. One night, while she was asleep, it walked across her face, leaving a mark, as if delivering a warning that the land was his, not ours.

Like that rat, we won't give up our land. Despite the hardship of displacement, we memorize the Quran. We pray. We hold on to life, however fragile, whenever we find a way to do it. Yaffa Alezzah Camp gives us much help in investing our time in ideas we believe in—to remain a thorn in the throat of the enemy, armed with our knowledge, our faith, and our Quran. Whether we live in tents or in palaces, our goal is the same. Our Lord is the same. And we are still waiting for justice, for the triumph of the oppressed.

My thoughts are suddenly interrupted by the voices of my father and   grandmother: "Yara, where did you drift off to? The operation is done. Let's go back to the tent."

And still the massacres continue. The martyrs fall like a cluster of grapes, their lives scattering bead by bead. We offer the souls of our children, like the hidden pearls tucked inside a pomegranate's heart. We have reached nearly fifty thousand martyrs. Yet our cause remains: a headline of history, a story of defiance, and a symbol of unbroken will.

Written on May 8, 2024

Gazal Tareq Zad Alejel

Age: 10 years old

My name is Gazal. I am a ten-year-old Palestinian child. An intense attack on Gaza shriveled my childhood. The bombing was so frightening that it awoke us at night in panic. When I was woken up at night by the sounds of their terrifying rockets, everyone got confused, running to nowhere. I was crying out of fear for my parents and siblings.

"Get out with your family. Now! They sent a message that they would bomb your home," our neighbor shouted to my father. My father took us out in a blink of an eye. We fled our home, leaving all our fond and warm memories behind. The brutal enemy bombed it. Homeless is what my family and I have become.

Displaced from one shelter to another, we spend the days looking for safety. In Gaza, there is no safe place. We lost everything. We lost our dreams—past, present, and future. Woe is me! Our lovely people were killed. Whenever I remember my destroyed home, the home of my parents and grandparents, my heart bleeds. The beauty of the streets in Gaza is still stuck in my mind. I pray to return to my beloved city, Gaza.

Lastly, I can't help but say what my mother keeps saying, "Hasbuna Allah wa ni'ma al-wakeel." Allah is sufficient for us, and He is the best disposer of affairs.

Written on July 7, 2024

Dima Hasan Mohammed Alkumy
Age: 11 years old

"I don't want to leave our home. Where could we stay?" My mom tried to calm us down when I asked her to flee south of the strip. She failed to stop the tears that filled my eyes. Day after day, the Israeli tanks were approaching our area. The pain of it struck my head.

On October 7, 2023, our life was normal and I was getting ready to go school. But the sudden sounds of rockets stopped me. A few hours later, the Israeli occupation started its terrifying attack on Gaza. Evacuation leaflets spread more fear and panic among our family. We had no choice but to flee. On foot we headed south, despite risks and hardship. On the way, my eyes, the eyes of a naive young girl, caught sight of soldiers for the first time. They were so close. I was so scared that I fell to the ground. I couldn't move. My father picked me up and carried me as he continued walking.

Reaching the Nuseirat refugee camp, we collapsed on the ground. I was frightened. Thinking that I would spend the night on the pavement filled my spirit with fear. Then destiny came in the form of my father's aunt, who received us in her home for three months. It was so crowded. My father had lost his work since we were displaced to the south. Everything was costly, but it was my father's quiet sorrow that weighed heaviest on my heart. Each day the sadness in his eyes spoke louder than words, a silent ache I could never unsee. I longed to say something—anything—that might lift the heaviness from his face, but the words never came. They stayed tangled in my throat, small and helpless, just like me.

One day the planes came again not, with bombs but with papers fluttering down from the sky, ordering everyone to leave the Nuseirat camp. Then the bombing began. We could hear it getting closer, and soon the tanks weren't far away. Fear wrapped itself around us like a cold blanket. We had no choice but to flee again, to Deir al-Balah.

We walked there on foot and found shelter in a school, but it was just walls and floors, with no mattresses, no blankets, not even a scrap of cloth to shield us from the biting cold. At night the cold crept in like a ghost, and we had nothing to keep it out. My mother and father were responsible for finding a solution, for finding a roof over our heads. The pain of it struck us.

The next day, thank God, my father managed to gather some fabric, and we built a tent out of it. We spent ten long months filled with fear and sorrow inside it. At night, when I lay beneath that worn-out tent, I closed my eyes and thought of my school and the voices of my friends. I wished I could

143

wake up and find that it was all real again, and that the war had been nothing but a long, cruel nightmare.

But even in nightmares, the heart of my mom knows very well how to soothe us: "God willing, this won't last long... We'll go back to Gaza soon."

Written on July 27, 2024

Rawan, Fatemah, and Sahar Majdi Musleh Alamer
Ages: 19, 16, and 14 years old

The sounds of rockets broke that ordinary day, filling the air. They were unlike anything we had heard before. Soon all of our eastern neighbors near the border began evacuating their homes. In haste we gathered what mattered most, like our IDs, birth certificates, and a few pieces of clothing. There was a quiet belief that this war, like others, would soon pass.

Our first displacement spot was my aunt's house in the refugee camp. We stayed there for two weeks. But the situation got worse. Water, electricity, and internet were cut off. We couldn't even charge our phones. The bombings intensified. It wasn't the roar of bombs that robbed us of sleep; it was the dread of what might come next—the shelling of homes, the screams of people, the fire belts lighting up the sky. We couldn't afford to stay there anymore.

We moved to Al-Mufti School in Nuseirat Camp. It became our second shelter, for three months. At first things seemed manageable. The bombings were still going on, but they felt farther away. That didn't last. The school was targeted too. One day, without warning, the occupation forces bombed the school's solar panels. The explosion was sudden. Screams echoed. Body parts scattered on the ground. Mothers were frantically searching for their children. Ambulances rushed in to collect the martyrs.

On November 23, 2023, a blast tore through a nearby house, and I was caught in it. Shrapnel cut deep; the pain was unbearable. Still, through the blood and dust, I murmured, "*Alhamdulillah*"—praise be to God. There were no ambulances. We had to walk to the hospital.

As we made our way there, the third displacement happened. The occupation forces dropped leaflets ordering the evacuation of the school. We had no choice but to leave again. We fled to my aunt's home in Al-Maghazi Camp. They too were preparing to evacuate. There were no cars. We walked on foot from Maghazi to Deir al-Balah. That was our fourth displacement.

I was frightened. Thinking that I would have to spend the night on the pavement filled my spirit with dreadful nightmares. We spent that night on the street. Everyone was hoping that some solution would materialize from around the corner. The next day destiny came in the form of a kind man who offered us shelter. The following morning, we moved again. Opposite to Al-Aqsa Hospital, right there on the pavement, we built a tent out of old fabric, until we found some nylon to set the tent up properly. Still, it couldn't protect us from harsh winter. We got sick.

Whispers swept through the shelter like wildfire that Israeli forces were advancing toward Al-Aqsa Street. Panic spread before the tanks even arrived. We gathered our things and fled again. Just days later, the place we had called home was reduced to rubble. A direct hit. That marked our fifth displacement. This time we found fragile refuge in Ahmad Al-Kurd School in Deir al-Balah.

We've been here for nearly nine months. Life in the school is unbearably hard. Bread is scarce, and we can only get any after long struggles. Clean water is limited. Skin diseases spread among us, slowly eating away at our bodies, and there's no treatment. Next to us used to be Khadija School, a medical point and shelter. One day the occupation bombed it without any warning. We had to evacuate our school as well, but we came back later. We had no other place to go. That day we saw bodies scattered on the ground—children, women, and the elderly.

This is our story. We pray that this will be the last displacement. We pray for an end to this brutal war on Gaza, God willing.

Written on July 28, 2024

Elien Marwan El-Atawna
Age: 10 years old

One night, during the war, my mother was telling us a bedtime story. The room was dim, her voice soft, wrapping us in a fragile sense of calm. Then screams came loudly through the silence like blades. We jumped to our feet, hearts pounding, and rushed outside to see what was happening. People were running in all directions, shouting. Chaos filled the street. The news had come: the Israeli military had called, and everyone was ordered to evacuate the housing towers. Airstrikes were coming.

Panic set in. We grabbed what little we could carry and fled into the night, fear gripping our every step. We didn't think. We packed whatever we could carry and escaped into the night. Our destination was Al-Wafaa Hospital. As soon as we arrived, the bombing began. We watched in horror as the towers behind us were swallowed by fire and smoke.

At dawn, exhausted and cold, we sat on the curb of Palestine University Street. From 8 AM onward, fear and winter air clung to our skin. When the airstrikes finally stopped, we walked, step by step, to my uncle Basel's house in Al-Nuseirat.

Days passed. Then the building next to us was bombed. Fear returned like a flood. Hoping to feel safer, we moved again, to a relative's house nearby. A few days later, my father came to check on us. My little brother begged to go back with him to Uncle Basel's home. My mother refused at first—something in her heart made her anxious. But my father insisted and took him anyway.

Hours later there was a blast. My mother heard the explosion and began to pray, her voice trembling. "God, please, let them be safe." Her words were a plea, a shield against fate. Suddenly Uncle Omar arrived, carrying my little brother in his arms, blood covering his small body. He was screaming and crying: "Dad...Dad... Dad is dead!"

Uncle Omar told us the house had been hit. My grandfather and my aunt had been killed instantly. My grandmother was injured. We thought my father had been martyred too. We mourned him through the long night. It wasn't until the next afternoon that he appeared—wounded, broken, but alive. We cried. We thanked God. We wept for those we had lost and embraced the one we still had.

Later we moved to Ahmad Al-Kurd School, where we remain to this day. Still we await our destiny. Either the war may end, or martyrdom wants us. There is no third path. O God, have mercy on our martyrs. Heal our wounded. Free our prisoners. Protect our fighters. Lift this suffering from us. End this war without more loss, without more grief. Grant us patience and strength. And God, please protect my family.

To everyone reading this: please recite *Al-Fatiha* for the souls of my grandfather and my aunt. I love you all.

Written on July 7, 2024

Shame Alaa Jameel Aldeeb
Age: 7 years old

The TV was turned on. The screen flooded with breaking news. Bombing followed the roaring of rockets, sounds all Gazans are familiar with. Everyone was watching, hungry for the news. The air around us thickened with questions, fear, and anticipation. I scampered toward my mom. The Palestinian resistance had launched rockets, crossed the barriers into Israeli settlements, engaged in fierce battles, and inflicted significant losses on the Israeli army. In that moment something stirred within us, a strange mixture of terror and pride.

I remember the morning of October 7, 2023. The mosques erupted with chants of *Allahu Akbar*—Allah is great. Cries of victory rose from the streets, and pride swept through every honorable soul in Gaza. We were overwhelmed by a whirlpool of emotions—joy, fear, and anticipation. The uncertainty of what would unfold reigned over the body of the city, as if we were standing on the edge of something devastating.

The story didn't take long to shift. The Israeli military operation on Gaza began. The bombing became indiscriminate, brutal, and merciless. They targeted trees, buildings, and people. One by one, the names of martyrs poured in. The city began to drown in grief.

The decision came for us to evacuate, after one week of sheltering in our home, hoping the storm would pass. We moved to a nearby house, seeking temporary safety. We spent just one night there before the occupation forces dropped leaflets ordering the evacuation of the northern part of Gaza. The message was chilling: "Your area is now a dangerous combat zone. Evacuate south immediately, in preparation for a ground invasion." And so began our real journey of displacement.

We took whatever we could carry: a few belongings, some clothes, and our most important official documents. We left our home, forced to abandon the house we had built with love, our beautiful memories, and everything we owned. Our first destination was the Nuseirat refugee camp. We stayed there for about two weeks. During that time, we received the devastating news that my uncle had been killed. Grief consumed us; cries of pain filled the air. The sorrow of losing him shattered my family. I cried endlessly over the loss of my kind, gentle uncle. I knew he had gone to heaven and would never return.

The area we had moved to was under heavy shelling. We witnessed martyrs falling before our eyes. It was then that my grandmother decided we should flee once more, in search of safety and shelter in another part of Gaza. So we were displaced again to Rafah, a city the occupation had claimed a "safe zone." But "safe" means nothing here; not a day passed without airstrikes claiming lives and leaving others wounded.

The wireless network had been destroyed deliberately, and communication was nearly impossible, until a brief pause in the war. During the three long months we spent in Rafah, a one-week ceasefire was announced. For the first time, we were able to speak with my father. We checked on him and other relatives and friends who had remained in the north.

Six days later, the ceasefire shattered. Missiles rained again, and the Zionist war machine roared back to life. Then came the blow no soul can ever prepare for. The news struck like a blade: my father had been killed under the rubble in an airstrike, the second loss in the family.

Grief erupted. Arms clung to each other as sobs broke open like thunderclaps. A mother and her child were drowning in a sorrow too vast for words. What seared the heart deeper than the loss itself was the absence of a farewell. No final touch, no kiss on the brow. I had once lived a quiet happy life, despite the siege making Gaza like an open-air prison. We were an average lovely family, and now that family didn't exist. There was only silence. I burst into tears again and ran to embrace my mother. We wept together, grieving the unimaginable loss.

Six months after his death, his body was finally recovered from beneath the rubble, and buried without our getting a final glimpse or a chance to say good-bye.

I became a displaced girl who has lost my home, dreams, the warmth of my family. I miss my room, my paintings on the wall, my toys, my clothes. I was denied the right to continue my education, stripped of my right to learn and play like other children around the world. The war made me a girl much older than my seven years. Isn't being fatherless, deprived of his warm embrace forever, enough for the brutal occupation to stop?

Once again they announced a ground invasion, this time into the city of Rafah. All displaced families were ordered to evacuate to the central governorate. The agony of displacement has become recurrent. We gathered what little remained of our belongings and headed to Deir El-Balah in a large truck, surrounded by the relentless sound of shelling and the sight of endless bloodshed.

Here the true tragedy of displacement unfolds. It is a brutal normality, each day repeating the one before. On most days, our schedule begins after *Fajr* prayer, with the struggle to collect water. We line up in a long queue to fill gallon tanks, and sometimes return empty-handed after a fight breaks out over who gets to fill his first. When my mother bakes bread,

150

we queue again to use the communal oven. It takes hours to gather enough firewood and nylon to light the clay oven owned by our displacement camp.

Every family here lives in a tent made of nylon sheets, pitched on the streets. The heat inside is unbearable. All of us are living a life of misery that words fail to describe. The reality, the scene, speaks louder than any language. My mother handwashes our clothes until exhaustion gnaws at her worn-out body. We light the fire once again so that she can prepare our last remaining stocks of canned, unhealthy foods—just enough to sustain our bodies and carry us through the rest of the day.

Our exhausting day ends when the dark starts to fall, bit by bit. Night is different here. Its sky is lit not by stars or the moon but by enemy flares and missiles. Its silence is laced with dread, a stillness that stirs terror deep inside us. We wait for death with every passing moment. With each explosion or whistling rocket, we whisper to ourselves, "Maybe it's our turn now." We fall asleep reciting the *Shahada*, unsure whether we will wake or join the procession of martyrs.

The suffering doesn't end. Here lie many stories still untold—tales of agony, grief, and perseverance. Every soul in this sacred land bears a story, a tragedy, a wound. And the war still rages. The steadfast remain, bound to it until the Day of Judgment.

I can only hope this nightmare will end, and that I will wake to news that will fill our hearts with joy despite the pain: "A ceasefire has been announced. Return to your homes and your city, Gaza."

Written on July 28, 2024

Mohammad Nidal Al-Mabayed
Age: 10 years old

Our home was full of laughter. My mother used to prepare breakfast for us and call out, "Come on, hurry up! Get yourselves ready to go to school." She would hand us our sandwiches with quiet care, then stand at the doorway. Always her words were firm but gentle—reminders to pay attention in class, respect our teacher, and work hard for the monthly exam. Before we turned the corner, she would call out with a warming promise: "I'll cook your favorite dish when you return." And then, as if sealing us in prayer, she would whisper, "May Allah protect you and make you among the righteous."

This is what I remember, before my mother called out to me and my sisters from the middle of the road to come back home, after hearing the sounds of explosions and artillery shelling. We had no idea what was happening. Everyone shouted, "Has the Day of Judgment come?" No: the Israeli occupation airplanes filled the sky above, bombing every place in Gaza. In a hurry, we gathered some items into bags to carry on our backs. "I have an Islamic Study exam," I told my mother, "I'll take my book with me." And I placed it in my bag.

After leaving our small, warm, safe home for the unknown, I heard my mother telling us, "Keep running. Don't stop. Protect your heads. Stay close to me. Remember Allah. Recite the *Shahada*." If we didn't survive the random, insane shelling, we would meet later in Paradise. The sky was pouring missiles down and competing to kill and hurt more women and children. Martyrs and human remains were scattered on the ground. Mothers were screaming and wailing for their dead children. The smell of the earth was blood.

This was a war, but not just any war. We moved from one place to another, but all the places were unsafe. The sounds of shells and rockets didn't stop. Tanks were getting closer and closer. Where could we go? I looked at my school, our street, and the neighborhood I lived in; everything was destroyed. I couldn't even recognize my mother's face. Grief had redrawn it, etching sorrow into every line.

I was shocked when I found out about the deaths of some of my friends and my teacher. Teacher, what about the Islamic Study book I brought to prepare for the exam? You left me alone to test my patience, my faith, and my ability to endure all of this. I do not know if I will survive this war. Maybe I will join you soon in the Highest Companions' paradise as a little bird.

May Allah have mercy upon you, my lovely people.

Displacement and another displacement. My head can't bear any longer the sounds of explosions, the shelling, and the sight of bodies everywhere.

We fled south because of the orders and threats issued by the Israeli occupation army. My mother explained that we were looking for a safer place to protect ourselves. She was hiding her fear of losing us by showing only a belief that everything would be okay.

Oh, my mother, death has passed beside us many times! We have not died yet. We are alive, but we are not fine.

It was a terrifying experience. Everything was frightening. Tanks were everywhere. Shocking scenes I had never imagined, even in my worst nightmares, horrified me. We were not allowed to stop. We walked over bodies scattered on the ground, unable to help the wounded people lying in our way.

After our fifth displacement journey, we arrived at one of the open spaces in the Nuseirat refugee camp. The place was no better than the previous ones. A family was pitching a tent, another was searching for a place to rest. Many families had no shelter. We spread out on the bare ground, taking refuge under the open sky, like many other families. I closed my eyes as my mind started to remember.

The south used to be a place for our seaside trips, when we would enjoy the beautiful, charming areas and the vast farmlands in the summer. Today it was bleak and sorrowful. Worn-out tents covered the place, which lacked even the most basic necessities of life. In the summer, the heat turns those tents into boiling furnaces.

With thirst in our mouths and hunger in our stomachs, we lined up for a single meal each day, starving not only for food but for the announcement of a ceasefire. We stayed there for a month until we were forced to leave again, fearing the brutal attacks launched by the Israeli occupation forces on Al-Nuseirat camp. We had become displaced again within our own homeland, so we moved toward Deir al-Balah.

Our new suffering there was no less than in the previous displacement. The tents were overcrowded. We were experiencing death through displacement over and over again. There was no safe place, as the occupying forces falsely claimed. We set up our tent in the shelter area. We slept without mattresses on the floor. We waited for the charity kitchen to serve us our meals. Sometimes my mother would cook on firewood, but the smoke caused a range of problems to her eyes. She couldn't afford to buy cooking gas. There was nothing she could do but be patient and endure. May Allah reward you, my mother!

When a school was opened in the shelter, I joined it. I thank everyone who contributed to establishing this school. I am thankful to my teacher and the people responsible for it. You gave us hope again that our lives could go on despite the pain and destruction. We reconnected with beautiful memories of our schools back in Gaza. Thank you from the bottom of my heart. You gave us back a piece of our childhood.

Months passed, but we still woke up to the sounds of bombing and war-planes. We learned of the martyrdom of my uncle. I was deeply saddened; he had been like a father to me. Dear uncle, you are the winner. May your pure soul rest in peace.

Physical wounds may heal, but will memory ever heal? From Gaza to the world: do you hear us? I am a Palestinian child. The occupier has stolen all my rights and my homeland. I hope this war ends soon so that I can return home and find peace and safety. I wish to draw flowers, the sun, and my family, like I used to.

Our story embodies resilience, hope, and humanity in a war-torn city. One day, those war-planes will stop flying above our skies, and instead our dreams and future will soar. We will be victorious, God willing.

Written on July 24, 2024

Jana Ali Abu Qamar
Age: 9 years old

My name is Jana Ali Abu Qamar, a student from the Seeds of Goodness School, in the fourth grade. I want to tell you my heartbreaking story.

On October 7, 2023, when rockets rained down, the world turned upside down. We were forced to evacuate our home on the fourth day of the war. The occupation scattered us and forced us to leave the city. I lived in the north of Gaza. The bombardment was so intense that we left our home with only our empty hands—no shelter, nothing. We left for the south of Gaza without my father or older brother.

Terrible is my life; I'm living in a tent where nothing protects us. I can't manage without my father and brother. Tears never leave us. My heart is still in Gaza. Because of this occupation, we are living in a tragic and painful situation. Like all the other people in the camp, I live in a place with no water, no clean air, no food, and no electricity. Diseases and infections have spread in our bodies because of the heat and pollution.

I am counting the days, waiting for the war to end so that I can be reunited with my father and brother. Waiting is hard, and nothing is ahead of us but more waiting.

Still, our hope in Allah is great.

Written on July 21, 2024

PART TWO: THE LUMINOUS RESILIENCE OF GAZA'S DAUGHTERS

Jihan Al-Nimr
Age: 40 years old

It was Saturday, October 7, 2023. The day started with rockets and shells from the air, sea, and land. Tanks, warships, and war-planes moved to attack Gaza. No one knew that this day would mark the beginning of one of the deadliest wars in our lives.

I'm a mother of two orphaned children: Abdullah, eleven years old, and Nasser, seven years old. My family took me and my children into their home after the death of my husband.

In the first week of the war, we couldn't do anything but be afraid. We didn't eat or sleep because in Gaza we were under indiscriminate bombardment. The number of martyrs was rising. Entire residential buildings, with their residents inside, were being demolished.

I was living with my children near the Gaza port. When our home was no longer safe, we got out, searching for safety and security. The increased destruction, death, and bombing around us forced us to flee to the house of the children's grandfather. We stayed there, on Al-Jalaa Street in the Al-Taj building. My father-in-law's apartment was already housing forty family members. They had fled the constant bombing nearby.

On the next Wednesday, around two hundred displaced people came together in our five-story building. Each floor has four apartments. Surrounding us were buildings of the same type. Suddenly, at 5 PM, we heard a sound like a nuclear bomb, followed by a series of increasingly loud explosions. In the blink of an eye, everything around me collapsed. We fell to the ground.

At that moment, I could see nothing but dust everywhere. I kept reciting the *Shahada*, second by second, and tried to open my eyes. But I couldn't. I passed out. Those moments felt like the horrors of Judgment Day. I woke up after nearly five hours. I found myself at Al-Shifa Hospital, lying on the ground.

Inside the hospital, chaos reigned. Wounded people filled the halls. Mothers cried while children screamed. The stench of death was overwhelming. I wondered, "Where am I? What happened?" I was crying and screaming.

One of the nurses came to me, held me gently, and lifted me from the floor in order to set me down on a chair. She said softly, "Calm down. Thank God, you're safe. You survived miraculously. You're not hurt."

But I couldn't stop screaming, asking, "Where are my children? Where did they go?"

Oh, what a horrible moment! What a day! What unbearable seconds! I made tearful pleas to the nurse to call one of my brothers. I can't stand up. I was shocked, and the sounds were still pounding in my head.

Moments later, my brother arrived. He rushed to me and said, "Jehan! Thank you, Allah. You're okay. The kids are fine. They're okay. Don't worry. Calm down."

I dragged myself slowly through the hospital corridors. Each step was a struggle as I headed to my family's home. As I went, I caught the voice of a journalist on a live broadcast: "A massacre took place here in the Al-Taj building, and four nearby buildings were also bombed—sixteen airstrikes in total. Nothing remains of these buildings. None of the residents survived. The number of martyrs is more than three hundred."

I started screaming again, calling out for my children: "Somebody, please bring me my children!"

That's when I realized: they were still under the rubble.

At 3 AM, my brother brought me to my parents' house, since there were no free beds in the hospital. Then my brothers began searching the hospital. Hopefully, one of my children would be found and brought in. Maybe one of them was in one of the crowded hospital hallways. But they located no one except my children's grandfather. They found him in the hospital morgue, a martyr.

My children, my entire family, were still under the rubble.

The next morning, my brothers rushed to our destroyed building, desperately looking for my kids. They had no equipment and no excavators. Such tools weren't available in Gaza, and even if they had been, they wouldn't have been enough. The few operational tools in the city were already being used to clear rubble from other destroyed areas.

My brothers kept searching and removing the rubble, with their bare hands and simple tools. That day we found the bodies of my children's grandmother and their aunts. On October 27, 2023, we found the body of my eldest son, Abdullah. It was hard to recognize his face because of his blood and injuries and the rubble that had fallen on him.

Abdullah was buried alongside his cousins, who were also martyred, in a mass grave. We still hadn't found my younger son, Nasser. The bombing hadn't stopped. Anything moving was being targeted by the airstrikes. During the search, we came across the bodies of our neighbors. But Nasser's fate remained unknown.

We kept digging—digging with nothing but our hands and whatever tools we had. We searched under the rubble and the ruins for eight days…

Finally, on January 11, 2023, in the evening, we found him. Nasser was a martyr too.

The next day we went to say our final good-byes to him. The hospital, as always, was overflowing with bodies piled on top of each other. A question came to my mind: *In such dangerous conditions outside the hospital, how can all the martyrs be buried?*

A large truck normally used by merchants to transport goods arrived, bearing white flags as a sign that it was a civilian truck. They placed approximately a hundred and fifty martyrs inside, then quickly left to bury them in a mass grave, on land not far from the hospital. My heart went with them. My sons were buried.

A new chapter of pain, loss, distance, and death began. A new life without my children, without my family. We were forced to evacuate from Gaza because the area had become too dangerous. The occupation had taken over many places in Gaza and forced people to leave their homes and everything they owned behind them.

I fled with my brother and his family to Khan Younis. We set up makeshift tents, and we lived there in the rain. Life was impossible; there was no electricity and no food. It was only death, and the sound of bombs falling around us. Nothing on earth protected us from the missiles. Allah was our only protector. And we were still struggling to survive.

Then, once again, they forced us to evacuate, this time to Rafah. Every day brought more martyrs, more destruction, and more bombings.

In April, they ordered the evacuation of Rafah. By force, we were removed from our makeshift tents, displaced for a fourth time. We went back to Khan Younis, a city of destruction and endless ruins.

Now, we don't know what will happen. Maybe soon, Allah will reunite me with my children. I bear witness that there is no god but Allah, and Muhammad is His Messenger. Praise be to Allah for what He has given me, and praise be to Allah for what He has taken.

Written on July 18, 2024

Suheila Jamil Rajab Al-Toum
Age: 40 years old

Fear began to creep into me. Love, warmth, and tenderness for my home made it impossible to forget my memories of being there.

We lived all together, a lovely family. We used to wake up early to perform the *Fajr* prayer. Reading my daily *Athkar*, a set of prayers and remembrances to say daily, and reciting *Surah Al-Baqarah* were part of my routine to seek the care of Allah. Each morning I went to the kitchen to prepare breakfast with fresh milk for my kids, and sent them off to school. Then I'd continue my domestic chores. Usually, every morning would end with sharing coffee with my dear husband, in my home that brimmed with love.

Then, on October 7, 2023, history decided to change Palestinians' lives in Gaza. It was a day that will remain etched into our memories and the memories of our children.

That morning began as usual. I was getting my children dressed for school when suddenly the sounds of resistance rockets filled the air and rained down from every direction. We rushed to the windows to witness a breathtaking sight. We watched as rockets like flashing lights tore through the skies toward the cruel enemy. Our hearts trembled as we waited for the inevitable response. We gathered around the television to follow the news on the Al-Jazeera channel.

At first we assumed it was another assassination attempt of a senior figure, just as we had experienced in the previous wars. Then a powerful image of resistance fighters breaching the borders of our occupied land, despite the enemy's advanced technology, spread all over. We felt a surge of joy. Yet, deep inside me, a voice whispered, "What will happen to us? Will they kill us and melt our bodies away?"

What we feared came true. The enemy began bombing every-where—homes, gardens, and mosques. We stayed on our land. They threatened us by messaging and making phone-calls: "Evacuate the area. It will be bombed." But we stayed. We refused to leave. Displacement was not our choice.

One day the bombing in the Al-Tuwam area grew more intense. My children began to cry. "We want to get out of the house!" they screamed, as the airstrikes and bombing didn't stop.

The journey of our displacement began when we left our beloved home to go to Jabalia, where we sought refuge in our relatives' home. We thought we'd only stay there a day or two and return to our home, but the bombing kept growing more violent everywhere. Eventually we returned home, since all places in Gaza were being bombed; there was no safety.

The shelling was worsening. Soon it reached our home. We fled to one of the UNRWA schools in the Al-Nasr neighborhood, still holding out hope the we could eventually return to our home.

One day the Israeli occupation dropped warning leaflets on Gaza, telling people to evacuate to the south of Wadi Gaza, to Deir al-Balah. We refused. Instead, we went to the UNRWA schools in Al-Shati' camp.

Shelling, phosphorus bombs, and the killing of children, women, and men all intensified in the area. Out of fear, we fled again at dawn, back to Jabalia. The nightmare continued. There was relentless bombing, fire belts lighting the skies, massacre after massacre, and houses reduced to rubble with entire families buried under the debris.

Overwhelmed by the terror of destruction and death, we gave in at last, and fled to Deir al-Balah. The road was long, and the displaced ran frantically in every direction. The Zionist horror was waiting for us in Salah al-Din Street, where they had set up a checkpoint with tanks. Snipers and soldiers stood there, treating Palestinians as if they were animals. From afar, one Israeli soldier shouted, "No one looks left or right. Look straight ahead. No talking."

Suddenly a tank drove straight into the crowd of displaced people, crushing them. They arrested some men, killed other men and women. The street was littered with the bodies of martyrs and the scattered belongings of the displaced, as soldiers forced people to throw all of their possessions away. My children were crying out of fear. "Please, mama, don't look anywhere! The soldiers will kill us!" They treated us like slaves.

After all the suffering and torment, we finally reached an area where carts were taking the displaced people to Deir al-Balah. The Israeli soldiers took away my pregnant sister at that time. They tortured her and ordered her to keep sitting down and standing up until she lost the baby. Then they let her go.

After exhausting hours of walking, we reached the UNRWA schools in Deir al-Balah. But we could not find a drop of water in the school. We knocked on strangers' doors, pleading for a little to drink. A classroom became our shelter. The room was crammed full of a hundred and fifty people. Care was absent. My children and I slept on the cold floor.

Over time, famine broke out. We had no access to any food, not even bread. My youngest child, barely a year and a half old, cried often, asking for food. Cleaning supplies were rarely available. The disease in his body grew worse. Most of the time, he remained sick. His little body couldn't endure the pain.

Our displacements journeys were endless. We fled again, this time to Rafah. We pitched a tent at the Egyptian borders. We endured more pain, fear, and sleepless nights. We were determined to survive. Suddenly the Israeli occupation forces invaded Rafah, so we were forced to flee once more, back to Deir al-Balah. We took shelter in Ahmad Al-Kurd School. There we built a tent. Displacement was a life full of fear, bombing, and fear.

Despite the pain of the great war against Zionist occupation, unscrupulous drivers and merchants were waiting to trap us. Drivers demanded impossible fees from displaced families and took huge benefits. Greedy merchants battled each other with unaffordable prices. An internal war is harsher than that of the enemy.

Words can never tell you how painful it was when my daughter got married. She was a bride in a shelter school. We endured more and more. Patience protested.

One day four missiles struck the school. Shrapnel flew above us. Dust filled the air, and the children screamed, "Khadija! Khadija!" Then a man's voice shouted, "Get out! They're going to bomb the school again!" We ran.

Hours later, we learned that Khadija School had been bombed. Forty souls were killed, even though the Red Cross had declared that the school was safe to return to. When we went back, we found ruin: tents torn to shreds, buildings broken. There was no aid and no help, so we tried to repair the place ourselves. We tried to survive.

What could we do? What can anyone do when fate insists on destroying you? Even now, we still dream of going back to our beautiful house, even though it has been reduced to dust. We still pray that Allah will protect our children, guard our hearts, and keep us standing in the face of the merciless enemy.

In the end, it is hope that keeps us breathing in this place of exile. We pray for relief and pray for mercy. Hope is all we have left.

Written on July 27, 2024

Reem Hatem Abu Hussein

Age: 28 years old

I am a mother of three. The last moment of joy that we tasted was a Friday trip to the sea on October 6, 2023. We went as a happy family to enjoy the weekend. It was the last day we truly felt happiness. I write now with the feeling that ages have passed.

October 2023 marked the end of a vivid life and the beginning of an era of endless sorrow, marked by countless journeys of displacement. We moved from my home to my aunt's home, and later to a rented house, and then to many more, too many to talk about. Each journey of displacement carried with it a chance that we would die, which missed its target only by the mercy of Allah.

A short pause—a ceasefire lasting just six days—was a break from war. Though I wasn't in my home, the brief calm brought me a fragile sense of peace. The following day, I woke up to screaming and nearby shelling. We fled the house with shrapnel flying everywhere.

I was lying flat on the ground with my children when my husband was injured. At first I couldn't even assess the severity of his wound, but fortunately it was minor. As he stood by the kitchen window, speaking with a friend to convince him to leave, a bullet had come before his words, and he collapsed. Praise be to Allah, he survived.

Another friend approached to help him, and he was shot too. We had no choice. We had to leave. As we opened the door, we heard the buzzing of drones, quadcopters, circling above. We realized that we were trapped. Voices speaking Hebrew grew louder. The danger was increasing. We made a plan to climb over the walls and jump to reach my uncle's house.

We arrived after a struggle.

Twenty-seven people were squeezed into one small room. We survived on dates and the tiniest sips of water, for six days. No sound, no movement, just survival.

My mother-in-law decided to bake bread and give it to the children. Then we heard footsteps approaching. "They've found us," she whispered.

We were civilians, but the occupation targeted anyone with Palestinian blood. My mother-in-law tried to speak to them, explaining that we were just civilians. Still they forced us down the stairs. After five hours of interrogation, they arrested and tortured the men.

I looked around at the havoc they had wrought on the city. A flag with a blue Star of David on it flew over crimes and destruction. My husband had disappeared. He had become a prisoner under their cruel hands. Each day, I pleaded for international organizations to find him, but to no avail.

Again we left, but I felt that the occupation was chasing us. A house beside ours was bombed. My children were terrified. I looked around, panicked. Where was my son? Where was he? I ran outside screaming and searching. They pulled him alive from under the rubble, marked with minor injuries, the scars of which will last a lifetime.

Fifty-five days my husband spent in their prisons, knocked senseless each day. Finally they took him to the far south of the Gaza Strip, while I remained trapped in the north. With all the lines of communication cut, I couldn't even hear his voice, not the echo of his breath.

I stayed in the north, refusing to leave despite the destruction of my home and my parents' home. The months passed, and my children's stomachs twisted in hunger. I endured three more months before making the most difficult decision of my life. I was forced to move south.

We embarked on a painful journey, weighed down with our heavy burdens. On foot, my children crossed great distances of many kilometers. Along the way, I saw corpses strewn along the roadside, their flesh torn apart by stray dogs with no mercy.

I left the north for just one reason: to survive. We looked for food, for safety, and for peace. But nothing was different in the south. The same battles and the same killing were there, and adding to that were the misery of living in tents and the high prices of food and necessities. Everything available was expensive, and everything we wanted most was missing.

The only comfort in this life was reuniting with my husband and my family.

Mahmoud Darwish once said, "Nothing pleases me." And I feel the same. What joy can there be in a homeland held in the grip of brutal, inhuman hands?

Written on August 8, 2024

Zahiya Shamia
Age: 45 years old

Step by step, we were preparing for my son Ahmed's wedding, the biggest joy of my life. We were getting our home ready, rehearsing the moments of celebration, preparing every tiny detail. There wasn't much time left. The celebration was to be on October 30, 2023.

Everything faded away on October 7. My thoughts swirled in my head on that bleak morning, which began with joy and preparations for the wedding and ended with one haunting question: "Where are we going?"

We were forcibly displaced to the south of the Strip, carrying a heavy weight. Aimlessly, we moved from one place to another. My eldest son, Yasser, is a person with a disability and can't walk. I wandered in anguish, "How can Yasser endure all this pain and fear? O Lord, be with me; make me strong."

Heavy were the days that dragged on. Pain seemed to cling to us. Gradually the sound of rockets grew closer. Astonishment and shock were clear on Yasser's face. His small body and his tender heart were never meant to bear all these terrors and blows. We used to sleep to the sound of thunderous explosions.

When the morning of April 20 crept in, I reached out to feel his hands and wake him. They were cold. So very cold. "Why are your hands cold? Are you sick, my love?"

My beloved Yasser didn't answer.

People gathered around him, shaking their faces and sucking their lips. "He's not moving. He is dead."

"Please answer me!" I cried.

He was a martyr to fear and illness.

And my pain was not over yet. My heart was ripped apart in grief between the death of my firstborn and comforting my other son, Ahmad. For ten months he hadn't seen his bride, since she had remained in the north from the beginning of the war. I could do nothing for him but lay a gentle hand on his aching heart. I whispered to him words of hope all the time: "Days shall pass, and things will get better. No injustice lasts forever, and no trial remains without end."

My home with its warm and lovely nights had disappeared. My school, also, was the next to vanish.

No doubt dwells in my heart that Allah will compensate me for all of this with His mercy. No hardship will wilt me. No pain will defeat me. I am steadfast on my land. I am radiant and luminous despite the occupiers' cruelty.

This is my story to the world, and my aching heart is the witness.

Written on August 2, 2024

Alaa Al-Sayyed Al-Dahdouh
Age: 37 years old

October 7, 2023, was the beginning of the story. My children were on their way to school when the sounds of rockets erupted from every direction in Al-Shujaya neighborhood. We realized the truth: war was inevitable. In this area, people were usually among the first to be displaced, as it is located next to the occupied Palestinian lands. The most horrific massacres committed by the Israeli occupation forces took place here.

We fled from Al-Shujaya and sought refuge in the Al-Zaytoun neighborhood for a week, at my family's home. When the Israelis dropped leaflets ordering the evacuation of Gaza city toward the south, we moved and stayed for a month in a new sheltering school in Al-Nuseirat. Next, moving for the third time, we evacuated to Rafah.

On the following day, my husband received a devastating phone call, informing him that his sister and her children had been martyred. In their home in Al-Tuffah neighborhood, an airstrike had killed them all at once, in the blink of an eye. Unbearable sorrow struck us that day.

A classroom at a school was now the only destination for a displaced family looking for shelter. After surviving there for six long months, we awoke to an intense shelling and more leaflets dropped from the sky, ordering the evacuation of Rafah. They were aiming to control the Philadelphi Corridor.

We fled Rafah under the thunder of bombs. In fear, people poured out of the school; children were terrified. We climbed into a truck heading back to Al-Nuseirat. In the Al-Balata refugee camp, we pitched a tent made of a few fragile wooden poles and scraps of fabric, which give us no protection from the burning sun or the cold winter.

Still we wait for the moment when we can return to the Gaza of Hashim and to our old home in Al- Shujayia. We wait for the end of this war that has left no family untouched by loss. We wait for the world to finally hear our voice.

Today I work as a volunteer teacher at Budoor Al-Khayr School in the Al-Balata camp in Al-Nuseirat. The war shall come to an end; that hope has never left my heart. So we continue to teach children in a small class, in a makeshift, temporary learning space.

Written on August 5, 2024

Ikram Mohammed Jabr Abu Hussein

Age: 51 years old

My tale of displacement began when we were forced to leave our home. My family and I went to a nearby house within Jabalia camp. Six families were all crowded into the single house, lacking many essentials for survival. Rockets and shells were falling down from everywhere. We didn't taste a moment of rest or sleep, much less a quiet night.

I stayed for nearly forty days in Jabalia. The final five nights were among the most harrowing. Shells began landing directly on us, and we realized we had no choice but to head south. Here began our journey of torment—from a house in Al-Nuseirat to a tent in Rafah, and then to another tent in Al-Zawayda.

Those days were the hardest I have ever lived in my life, under bombardment, fear, and horror. Going to a bathroom was a luxury we no longer had. We spent four days in the street before we were allowed to shelter in a tent in a camp in Al-Zawayda. And our suffering was not over yet. The tent's roof did not protect us from the searing sun, dust, and wind. There were no blankets and no mattresses to sleep on. The lack of food and water took a toll on my health, since I suffer from spinal disc problems, diabetes, and high blood pressure.

Allah is all I need, and He is the Best one to rely on. I believe that Allah will hold accountable every person who has caused our suffering, displacement, and painful, bitter life.

We saw death with our own eyes. Corpses were strewn in the streets. The hardest day of all was when people in the thousands passed through the checkpoint to flee from the north. As we arrived, a bulldozer came, scooping up the earth and throwing it over our heads. We scrambled out of the area as if we were being pulled from beneath rubble. With tears streaming down our faces and hearts heavy with grief for what has become of us, we reached a safe place.

Alas, Allah is the only one to call on in this hardship.

Written on August 5, 2024

Fadwa Abdul Rahim Jouda

Age: 35 years old

We are war survivors.

We were living warmly in a small home. On October 10, 2023, our home was bombed to rubble above our heads, just at the beginning of the war. My husband, my four daughters, and I were pulled out by a miracle from beneath the debris, all with different injuries. Homeless, we started moving from one house to another, searching desperately for a shelter and safety. But finding these turned out to be impossible. Since we had lost our income, we could just barely provide our children with the basic necessities of life.

Journeying to Rafah was necessary, as the fighting was getting intense. Our area in Al-Nuseirat was no longer safe. Our miserable task was to search for shelter. We had to stand in neverending queues, waiting to get water and food. My heart ached when I saw my eldest daughter, Rahaf, who lives with cerebral palsy, struggling to adapt and meet her daily special needs.

We stayed in Rafah for four months. Eventually, since we were forced to share a single home with several other families, we decided to returned to Al-Nuseirat, and set up a tent near the ruins of our destroyed home.

But the cruelty of war didn't stop there. The pain grew heavier with time. My husband, Hazem Jouda, suffered a severe injury in the head, which has left him hospitalized up until now. Ever since, I have been the only one to take care of our four daughters, managing all their needs.

The war has not ended, nor has our suffering. Every day in the tent is a misery. The eyes of my daughters remind me every day of the bitter reality we're forced to endure. We pray to Allah for this cursed war to end.

Written on July 3, 2024

Asma Abu Matar
Age: 38 years old

A mother of six children, I gave birth to the youngest during this devastating war.

At first we were a typical family. I lived with my husband in our safe home in the Al-Saftawi neighborhood. Together with my kids, I had recently enrolled at the Islamic University of Gaza, to study English literature and translation. My eldest son had begun studying engineering, the next had joined the IT department, and the third was on the verge of completing high school. But he was robbed of that dream. My little girl, Hoor, stopped going to kindergarten. Najat, the last, has lived only in the deadly war that tore our dreams apart and bleached out the colors of life.

After our home was bombed, we moved to a relative's house in Jabalia. Our dreams were buried under the rubble of the universities when they were destroyed. My little Hoor was injured in her arm and had to undergo two surgeries.

We were forced to move constantly, under intense shelling and fear. Displacement, hunger, and deprivation became prominent in my story. The struggle to find water, firewood, and cooking gas was a daily challenge. When the war intensified, we were forced to flee to the south. I was burdened with my sixth baby in my womb. My husband remained in the north, and so all of the pain and weight of responsibility for my family were mine to take, much to my dismay.

We took refuge in a relative's home in Deir al-Balah. Hunger hurt us badly. We had to use water from the sea and wait in long lines for possibly carcinogenic food. My children fell ill with jaundice, and myresponsibilities increased: I had to provide them with healthy food and medication and do everything I could to prevent infection. Pregnant and exhausted, I spent nights darker than the darkest hours.

One day, a nearby house was bombed. I didn't realize what was happening at first. Flying shrapnel rained down from every direction, and screams filled the air. We found ourselves in the street. Everyone inside had been injured.

Winter came again. We tried to repair our damaged home with plastic sheeting and stones. In the bitter cold, we endured the harshest days of our lives; our space was flooded with heavy rains, and the chill gnawed at our bodies. With no firewood, no clean water, and no food, life became unbearable.

When we were evicted from the house, we had no choice but to enter the dreaded world of tents. It was cold, sandy, and full of insects. To make a living, I started making pastries. My children would sell them on the sidewalk so we could survive day by day.

The days passed. My pregnancy became heavier, and the time for delivery approached. Despite the cruel circumstances, I decided to search for a place to live near a hospital, and waited for the new baby without any help.

Once I had given birth safely, I returned to live with my children in Al-Nuseirat. Our home is an old storage room, which barely protects us.

Written on July 7, 2024

Suhaila Adel Muhammad Al-Sharif

Age: 32 years old

My name is Suhaila. I'm thirty-two years old. My home is in the Al-Shati' refugee camp, where the sea is my neighbor. I am a mother of four. My husband works on a fishing boat.

Vividness once ran through my life. Then everything was turned upside down. Day by day, we were dragged back into the Stone Age. A new chapter of Al Taghreba AL-Gazya, the Gaza Alienation, had started.

On October 7, 2023, at exactly six in the morning, I was preparing my children, Mennat Allah, Lama, and Shareef, for school. Out of nowhere, we heard the sounds of rockets, followed by chants of "Allahu Akbar" echoing through the streets. I clutched my children close, trying to calm their panic. That was the beginning. Three days later, the Israeli occupation army began their response, with intense missile strikes over the sea. My husband's fishing boat, our only source of livelihood, was destroyed.

We spent that day in the Al-Jalaa neighborhood, for fear of falling shrapnel. We returned the next day. As our area was still a brightly lit neighborhood in the early days of the war, the missiles kept falling. We fled again to Nuseirat, to my aunt's house.

We stayed there for four days and returned home later, though the threat still loomed over us. On October 31, at 3 PM, the area was bombed intensely. I held my youngest, Muhammad, in my arms while my husband rushed to safety with the other children. Amid the chaos, smoke, and blood-stained air filled with the scent of death, we left the place.

I watched my house crumble into rubble. My brother, Rami, was injured in that bombing. We spent the night at Al-Shifa Hospital, without sleeping a wink. I found all my family safe, and none of them lost. May Allah protect them all! I am stronger than the treachery of the enemy.

At that time I was two months pregnant. The next morning, we took the step to move to Nuseirat, where my cousin's home was located. We tried to evacuate to Rafah for two days, but the outrageous price of tents there forced us to return to my cousin's home.

Two months of suffering passed, with danger pressing in from all sides. One day I collapsed from exhaustion, and blood flowed everywhere around me. I had miscarried. I lost my baby. A cart became my ambulance to Al-Awda Hospital. There I was anesthetized so that they could remove the dead fetus.

During that period, we suffered a famine. Food was scarce and prices were high. Our bodies lost so much weight. My children would fall asleep with empty stomachs, their bellies aching from hunger. There was no clean drinking water, only salty water to quench our thirst.

Suffering was increasing. In December 2023, a neighboring house was bombed. The sounds of explosions scared us. After we fled to the UNRWA clinic in Nuseirat, we were ordered to evacuate again, to Rafah. But, since we were not able afford the trip, we decided to stay at the clinic for almost a month. At night we slept with almost no blankets or warm clothes. Only Allah knows what struggles we have been through. Our days went on. Life was lifeless. The danger was always present in that place. Drones buzzed overhead day and night.

In January 2024, we were asked to evacuate the clinic so that it could be prepared to treat patients. We moved to an unfinished building in Souq Al-Balata, in Nuseirat. Our fate was to live in suffering. On March 20, the area was bombed in a massive air raid, at a place where my children had been playing just moments before. Relatives of mine were martyred. My heart was crushed with sorrow. But Allah's protection was greater than the cruelty of the occupier.

Struggling to survive during the holy month of Ramadan in the midst of the genocide, our days slowly passed. On Eid there was no joy, only daily struggles to handwash our laundry, search for water, cook over a fire because all fuel had been deliberately cut off, and shower with a plastic jug.

In June 2024, the enemy invaded Souq Nuseirat. It was a deadly hour. At 11 AM, missiles and shells rained down on the area. My husband rushed to help the wounded and carry the martyrs. I fled with my children, terrified for their safety. In the middle of the crowd, I saw my brother's three children lost in the chaos. I took charge of them, and we continued walking until we reached Al-Zawayda, where I called my brother to let him know his children were safe.

When the bombing stopped, we returned with heavy pain. We kept moving, from one place to another, from one heartbreak to the next. Life continued. So did the shelling.

The war entered its tenth month in August. Another evacuation order has come. But where can we run to now? We're still suffering from the lack of medicine, clothing, and cleaning supplies. Diseases are spreading. We're torn between life and death. My children have contracted skin diseases, eye infections, jaundice, and severe anemia, without any treatment. I have begun volunteering at an educational center, Seeds of Goodness, to teach children in kindergarten. Under the direction of Dr. Maisa Helles, I spend my time with the kids, teaching them morals, numbers, and letters, trying to fight ignorance and keep the flame of education alive.

In Gaza, we stand firm. We ask Allah for urgent relief and victory. As long as life goes on, we hold onto hope. One day, we'll hear the mosques break into chants of "Allah Akbar," the sound of victory and celebration. I don't know what my fate will be, as the smell of death lingers in every corner. But I must survive.

Written on August 1, 2024

Fatima Darwish Al-Hawajri
Age: 30 years old

After the bombing of our home, I woke up to a new world. I ran my weary hands across the floor, trying to find my four-year-old daughter. I asked her to go to the bathroom, but she was afraid. The place was pitch dark; it was impossible to see well enough to catch any of my children. Dragging my aching feet, I saw a faint, terrifying light in the corridor, so I took them away. The horrors I have experienced stole sleep from my eyes. When I remembered what I had lived through, I found myself wondering, *Was it a punishment? Had I sinned?* But what were my kids guilty of, to deserve the silence of this failing world?

I will never forget that cursed day when I found myself homeless. Sitting on the pavement with my children, I wondered, *Where is my husband? Is he alive still?* A strange man looked at me and asked, "Why are you sitting like this? Why are you crying?" The words choked in my throat. I couldn't answer him. He gave me a sip of water and listened to my story as one of the many displaced people forced out of the area.

Yes, they had burned and bombed my home. I had no choice but to flee to the other side of the strip. I found it colder and more merciless than the bombs I had escaped. All of a sudden, I was without a shelter, food, money, or even a shoulder to lean on. My husband was the only person remaining to me, but he had gone into the unknown.

I pulled myself together. Still confused, I wavered between sleeping in a place under threat of bombing or on the cold street. I chose the place that might kill us. I didn't know then that the whole area was a target. I tried to find shelter in a school, but it was full. Despite the burning heat and freezing cold of the tents, I decided to search for one to stay in. It took me days and days to find one. Standing for hours in endless queues was a curse. My feet bled inside my worn-out shoes.

Was it the cruelty of life that created us only to drag us from one place to another, with my children carrying their hunger and me carrying my despair? Or was it "Fate"?

The next evacuation order may come at any time, telling us to run again. I no longer know if the next place might be safe or not. Being displaced more than five times has made us hate this tent. My children cry from hunger.

Once, with nearly empty pockets, I went searching for bread. The flour distribution centers overflowed with desperate crowds. There was no way in. Never in my life had I stood in such lines for food, for survival. Luckily, I found a shorter queue for bread. I bought five loaves to feed my children, and they went to sleep with full bellies. It was a small victory in a world of cruelty.

Half a loaf steeped with tears was left for me. My feet were cut and bleeding, but I wanted to sleep, to rest until tomorrow's suffering began. At that moment, unanswerable questions came to my mind again. *Until when? Where will we go? What's the next place? Will we live to see tomorrow?*

Written on July 31, 2024

Haneen Khaled Mohammed Abu Atiwei,
Teacher at the Arab Heritage Center
Age: 31 years old

October 7, 2023—a fatal day.

After carrying my dream for years, I was finally going to return to teaching. My family's happiness was even greater than mine. I got up early, did my chores, and set off for work, ready to pursue my dream. While filling the water tank on the fourth floor, I paused momentarily to take a few pictures of my beautiful village, Johr al-Deek, bathed in the soft light of the morning sun. That day I was going to sign the contract to become an official government teacher, in 2023.

I didn't care about the two rockets launched that morning: we were used to that noise in our area. Then, out of the window, I saw dozens of rockets and paragliders carrying fighters. I realized that this wasn't usual. It was war.

My dream faded away. After three days, the shelling around our neighborhood intensified. We made the decision to flee from our home and head north, to al-Zaytoun. Our four days there were unbearable, and I longed for death. The shelling was getting worse, so I decided to head south with some members of my family, while the rest went to the north.

On our way to the south, just before the Kuwaiti roundabout, a truck carrying displaced women and children was bombed. The road turned into a scene of scattered bodies and limbs. Never in all my life have I seen such a horrible thing. For three days, I remained shocked and drained after we reached our relatives' home in Nuseirat.

On October 16, I decided to return home to Johr al-Deek with my father and uncle. All along the way I saw horrors that will haunt me for my whole life. My father and uncles carried parts of farmers' bodies who had been working on their lands, doing what they could until sunset. The buzzing drones never left us.

Thanks to Allah, I spent nine days at home. A feeling of comfort and safety in my home was worth staying in such a dangerous area. I had been overwhelmed by a mixture of fear and discomfort since being alone. Nothing compared to the joy of living in *my* home.

Then a shell hit the back yard. The second hit our sheep barn. I didn't even hear the blast. The house was shaking; smoke filled the air. I ran a few meters, then came back. I didn't know the occupation was planning to invade Gaza that very night. We survived by a miracle.

After that, I stayed with relatives in Block C in Nuseirat camp. A ceasefire was announced. I walked through ruined streets and returned to

177

our half-destroyed house. We didn't sleep in our home but insisted on praying *Maghrib* with my father at home.

The most beautiful days I ever experienced had taken place in that village, even with a drone constantly hovering overhead. Our home was in an extremely dangerous place. It lay just two hundred meters away from the new road paved by the occupation, through the middle of Gaza. When the ceasefire ended, we lost access to our home again. For three months I stayed in my relatives' house, cut off from the world without internet and social media.

On January 2, 2024, the army tanks invaded the Bureij camp, reaching the Daawa Center in northern Nuseirat. Quadcopters began sniping into homes. We had no choice but to run away from the house in a rush. In a barren land, we put up a tent made of torn nylon and a few blankets we'd managed to bring with us during the temporary ceasefire.

Each time we were forced to leave our home, the ache in my heart grew deeper. I felt that there was an invisible canopy above me, enclosing me in a space of grief and heartbreak caused by being displaced from my home, trapping me in the tent, away from people and any kind of aid outside. My world shrank to my family.

On February 21, I received news of the death of my best friend. She had been killed two months before, on December 25. Since our relationship was sister-like, the shock shattered me. She was the friend who had never left me throughout the war, but we had lost connection in Nuseirat. Now we would have no more communication ever.

Every day I received a new pain. Someone was killed, another injured." Death had become daily news. In my extended family, over seventy-five people were martyred. On March 19, my brother was injured with a severe wound. Thanks to Allah, he started to recover from it.

I was exhausted, not just physically but deep within. Fear was with us all the time. A stray bullet could tear the fragile fabric of the tent and kill you in an instant. Every night we witnessed fights, gunfire, and chaos.

On June 26, I made the decision to go to Abu Orayban School in Nuseirat and start an educational initiative. It was a long walk, but it helped to silence my fear. I needed to survive what I'd been through. The streets were overflowing with people, and sewage was creeping in at the doorsteps of tents. It was hard to make my way through the filth.

Eventually I joined another initiative, run by the Arab Palestinian Heritage School in Canada. In Deir al-Balah, cruelty is part of our life. We struggle to educate our students and prevent literacy among them. Waiting on pins and needles for the moment when we can go home is not enough.

Though dangerous, I keep trying to reach Wadi Gaza Bridge, to catch a glimpse of my destroyed home, one among dozens flattened in our village.

Today, I stand here as an ambitious teacher and patient volunteer. A woman holding on tightly to her pain, as if it were a burning coal, awaiting her fate in Gaza.

Written on July 2, 2024

Hiba Zakaria Muhammad Samour

Teacher and Resident of Al-Shati Camp
Age: 33 years old

On October 7, 2023, we were forced to leave our home and go to Al-Shifa Hospital in Gaza. Later the hospital became too risky, so we moved to the UNDP center, which later also became too dangerous, so we sought refuge in Al-Nuseirat Camp.

I was pregnant at that time, yet I walked three kilometers to Al-Nuseirat camp. The occupation troops were standing ahead of us. They threw a sound-bomb. Fear gripped my heart, until I reached Al-Nuseirat Camp.

At 11 PM, I went to the Al-Awda Hospital in Al-Nuseirat on foot. I gave birth with no one by my side except my husband. At 3:30 AM, the new baby was born.

We were then forced to move to Rafah, where I stayed in Tiba Mosque. When Rafah was no longer safe, we returned to Al-Nuseirat and lived in a tent.

Praise be to Allah that Dr. Maysa Helles helped us and opened a teaching school, where I became a teacher.

On September 7, 2024, my husband got injured, but it was only a minor injury in his leg and abdomen, thanks to Allah.

Despite the pain, I am still teaching students, God willing. I pray to Allah Almighty to remove this sorrow as soon as possible.

Written on July 7, 2024

Rabina Basheer Albitar,
Volunteer Teacher
Age: 44 years old

While the sun sent its rays into the scattered holes of the tent's fabric, flies started buzzing endlessly. Our neighbor, Umm 'Abdo, had an uncontrollable voice. Like an alarm bell, it knocked into your brain every morning, and pain seeped gradually through your veins. Still, I refused to awaken from my restless sleep. I wanted to stay in the new bed that my husband had built from wood planks, once used to carry aid shipments to the Gaza Strip. I longed for the warmth of a proper family bed, where I could lie beside my husband or at least hold my children close. But, as the saying goes, "The soul is willing, but the flesh is weak."

My painful displacement memories failed to blot out my feelings of happiness in the moment when I first lay upon the makeshift bed. Now, as if it were the first time, I turned right and left. Restful though it was, it couldn't erase the memory of the tiles' cruel hardness, the ones that had hurt my body when I was first displaced.

We had sat on the streets like shoddy goods exposed to any passerby in a market. Our lives became not our choice, but the decisions of others. For fifty days I couldn't sleep because of living on the hard tiles. Sometimes, circumstances turn tough and the most painful things become companions who walk with you for a time. The floor was merciless toward me and my children. I tried to find solace in this life, but it insisted on giving me nothing but hardship.

My exhausted body finally found refuge from the biting cold we were trapped in, when I was taken in at a UNRWA school in al-Qarara, Khan Younis. I felt as if we had risen from our graves! We were disheveled, dust-covered, owning nothing but the few garments we wore like shrouds, clinging to us wherever we went.

Then, once again, this war carried us into another displacement, to the furthest point—Rafah. Against our will, we fled the arrogance of Zionism. History repeats itself, echoing Pharaoh's ancient proclamation to his people: "I am your lord, the High." Thus Zionism is tossing aside every international resolution that has called for an end to this genocide. Beware the wrath of a people; the universe might burst with anger in protest for them.

The sands of Rafah were cold and more brutal even than the tiles in Al-Qarara. The chill gnawed at our bones in the way a worm ate the staff of Solomon. All of us became mere shadows stripped of life, awaiting our turn to die. A neverending line exhaled smoke like a monstrous train, bound to reach us inevitably.

I stood at the entrance to my tent. By my side stood Umm 'Abdo, whispering sonorously in my ear, "Do you like the bed? You are one of the displaced, my dear neighbor, and possessing a bed, even if it is made of wood planks, is a luxury far beyond our reach these days."

I gave a weary sigh, then forced a smile and replied, "If only you could sleep on a bed like mine, you would know the depth of my happiness."

I paused to let memories into my mind. At that moment, I wished I could go back to being a little girl leaping upon her parents' bed and then leaving her laughter behind in sleep. Tenderly, hands of light carried her, and she found herself in her own bed the next morning.

Before we could continue our conversation, the sky was suddenly full of Israeli spy drones, fighter jets, and the deadliest drones, no bigger than toys and yet capable of slipping into the tightest spaces, as if our very brains were their targets. The Israelis tear our weak bodies apart with their missiles, as if we possessed the strongest defense systems. And indeed, it is through our faith in Allah that we hold great power.

Suddenly screams rose from all around. A powerful missile shook the ground near us. It terrified me. My children were crying. Everyone around us was terrified. Instinctively I took my five children into my arms, wishing I could return them to my womb and shield them from the death that was always coming.

I was alone with my kids. My husband had gone to fetch water for us. For the sake of my children, I tried to collect the scattered pieces of my soul and appear strong. I had to do something to distract my children from their fear. Maybe making hot tea together would release them from fear's hold. But I felt a surge of anger. Like a flood carrying embers that scorched deep down inside, I burst into speech, telling them that nothing mattered more to me than they did—that my whole life was less than a single tear they shed.

This pain shall pass. Undeniably, this shall pass.

"Come on, my little ones," I said. "Let's return to the teapot and make our tea together."

Then Karam, my eldest, shouted, "I don't want tea!"

It was the effect of the war. He hadn't been like this before. He had been quiet, barely a whisper coming from between his lips. That had been my main concern with his teacher, Miss Intisar. She had always complained about his lack of participation, about how little he spoke, even though his grades were always the highest.

Startled, I asked, "Why not?"

He replied with a tone full of discontent, "Because it has no sugar, Mama."

At the final words of his sentence, a fire shot from the soles of my feet to the crown of my head and seared every cell of my body. I struggled to put out the blaze burning inside me, sparked by those innocent words flung into my face. Trying to compose myself, I said inwardly, *Calm down. He's still just a child. I have to try harder. I must restore the balance that this cursed war has stolen from him. They are my children, who will always sleep in my arms no matter how much they grow.*

Then Masoud, my middle son, surprised me by saying, "Nor do I, Mama. How dare you call it 'tea'! It has no sugar, no mint, not even sage."

I drifted into silence, pain clenching my heart at what we'd become. I whispered to my weary self, broken by war and displacement, *Where am I supposed to find sugar? Sugar has become something out of reach, almost mythical.* Then I swallowed my anger. I turned toward my daughters and asked, "And you, my three little girls, what would you like?"

Sham, the youngest, answered in her soft, innocent voice, "Mama, I want to eat."

Her response was like a protective shield, saving me from being struck by the arrow that could have flown from "Where is the sugar, Mama?"

We waited for my husband, who used to leave early in the morning to wait in line for bread, salty water, and drinking water. One of our daily tasks was to collect a few scraps of wood for cooking.

I told my children, "Come on, let's make a family breakfast."

Then Masoud giggled and said, "I know milk that comes in family size, with banana, strawberry, or cocoa-milk taste."

I stroked his head. "I know you miss milk, my sweetheart." I explained to him, pulling him close, "A family breakfast means a meal that all the family helps to make. Come, help me light the fire so we can prepare it together."

Hours later, night fell. The sky was never free of spy drones. Sorrow and fear permeated us, as though our hearts were bracing for something unknown.

I looked at my children, falling asleep after a long exhausting day. The innocence on their faces—heavenly angels on earth—was stronger than the woes of war, and melted my heart.

The buzzing drones still howled above us, looking for prey to stalk on the ground. I froze with fear. My husband, the braver one as always, pulled me into his arms and whispered, "Don't be afraid. Calm down. The kids are asleep."

I tried to stay strong, but fear was stronger. I prayed to Allah to give me tranquility and return my torn heart to its place.

And then, without warning, intense missiles rained down on us from all directions. The whole area was like a hell that escaped the sky and collided with our world. I clutched my five children as I trembled, my teeth chattering and my limbs ice-cold, as though no blood had reached them.

I searched in my heart for a place to hide us. Both my husband and I, without thought, threw our bodies over the children, trying to shield them from the deadly missiles. I wished I were a mother cat, able to swallow her kittens when danger nears.

This filthy war devours our souls day after day. It's never full. We are its favorite dish. It doesn't know how to stop. It's always hungry for more. Will anything be left of our bodies when this war falls silent?

As the missiles rained down, a convoy of tanks stormed the crowded tents, unbothered by anything in their path or the consequences they left behind. Their iron treads would surely crush our innocent bodies.

Our sacred blood is a deep scar carved into the heart of the humanity they claim to uphold. The scattered limbs of our children strip the mask off of every face that ever fed on our blood.

My husband and I carried our children, and, like the others, we fled blindly into the unknown. All roads led to death. Through death we walked, and found it waiting for us in all places. Our children were howling in fear, and everyone screamed as if we were fleeing Judgment Day. We walked with eyes seeing only darkness. Our hands groped as if they might find some light to guide us, but to no avail. We walked for hours, carrying our children on one shoulder and, on the other, our souls.

Life here is a mixture of shrouds and death. Whoever finds their shroud in this burning patch of land has claimed the whole world.

My legs could no longer walk. I collapsed where I stood. The land embraced our bodies, longing for our return. Everyone around me had fallen too. All that was left of us was nothing. We wore our shrouds and waited for dawn.

When the white thread of dawn became distinct to us from the black thread of night, I lifted my head to see what happened to us. He was no longer beside me. He had promised to stay by my side, but he had left me to walk alone.

I still feel him stretching his hand to me. I'm holding his hand—but he is no longer there. Thirty days have passed, and I'm still waiting for his return. Carrying my wounds in both hands, I walk in the vain hope that I might find him—his smell, or his shirt—to bring back my life. But to no avail.

He shall return one day to carry me and our children, to take us back to our little home, to remove the rubble, and to cultivate life gently and slowly. Never does hope die. Muhammad shall return.

Name: Maisa Helles

Age: 45 years old

Our life was so vivid, full of work, learning, and dreams. What happened on October 7, 2023, that unlucky day, went against all expectations. Everything turned into a living hell. Life was suddenly all about bombings, killings, destruction. I lost the souls of many dear relatives.

The occupation destroyed my home, along with every beautiful memory of it. I was forced to flee to my parents' house, near Carrefour market. After fourteen days, the occupation threatened that area too, so we fled to Rafah, to the home of Abu Hussam Al-Shaer.

There a new tale began. They embraced me as if I were their daughter, with kindness and generosity. We shared food, drinks, and life together. Even amid the woe of loss and sorrow, we found a way to live—to coexist. Every day, I thanked Allah that I had fled to another home where I could feel safe away from exile.

Then came November 20, 2023. At four in the morning, I woke up to find myself injured in Al-Najjar Hospital. An Israeli airstrike had hit the house next door to Abu Hussam's home. My face and eyes were swollen, as my head had been hit badly. For a whole month, I lay in the same place, unable to see a thing. Fortunately, after a month of treatment, I recovered completely—I thank Allah. But those were very hard days. Were it not for Allah's mercy, I might have lost my sight, or even my children.

My suffering didn't end there. The displacement continued. The occupation dropped leaflets over Rafah, ordering the evacuation of every neighborhood, including Jenina. Where were we supposed to go? That day, I wished I could die.

I decided to seek refuge in the home of Dr. Ashraf Al-Qassas. He welcomed me, my husband, and my children with open arms. Once again, I felt a spark of happiness that I had found a real home to shelter in—not a tent.

But that happiness didn't last long. Soon, the occupation dropped evacuation leaflets over Tel Al-Zarab, where Dr. Ashraf Al-Qassas lived, and our suffering was renewed. The same question came again: where could we go now?

I made the difficult decision to move to Al-Nuseirat Camp and live in a tent. There was no escape.

Honestly, in the beginning, I was overwhelmed with despair. Memories of my old life flooded my mind—how I used to live in a luxury house with elegant furniture and a car. My family owned a chalet near the Sudanese beach. I remembered my dream from before October 7, to have a distinguished place in life. And now I found myself living in a small, fragile tent that lacked even the basic necessities of life, through no fault of my own. Dreams no longer had a place in our world. My only wish now was to return to my home, to my land, and to any of my family homes. It was heartbreaking!

But from amid the rubble, I knew I would rise. I had to help myself, and help others like me. I began offering whatever support I could, materially and emotionally, to the displaced around me. Eventually I launched my initiative, "Together to Ease the Pain of the Displaced." People here are suffering from the most basic shortages, with no shelter, no food, and no clean water. I started by distributing cash gifts to displaced families and the children of martyrs.

Then I began to think about bringing hope to the children in the camps. I decided to run classes inside makeshift tents instead of classrooms. I announced the establishment of a Seeds of Goodness school and started enrolling students. We interviewed and carefully selected qualified teachers. We welcomed the students warmly, encouraging them with activities like drawing and with toys, sweets, biscuits, clothes, and a communal breakfast almost daily. The number of students grew until we had over five hundred boys and girls. We expanded by opening additional educational tents.

I pray for Allah to bless our efforts and guide us in serving the children at Balata Camp, one of the largest displacement camps in the Middle area. And yet the question remains: will we ever return? My greatest fear is that history will repeat itself; that we will suffer another 1948 Nakba and never return; that the keys to the homes we once knew will remain all that are left to us from Gaza.

These difficult and bitter days will not stop me from publishing my new book, titled *Jerusalem and the Sociology of Refugees.* I wrote it before October 7, relying mostly on historical accounts to describe the refugees' suffering. Now I have lived through a catastrophe myself, one even worse than the Nakba. I have lived in the terror of displacement, the constant possibility of death, minute by minute, second by second. I have lived with the small details of suffering caused by living in tents. I have taught kids in tents and suffered from the overcrowding and the lack of simple school supplies and good ventilation.

Experiencing the war and life inside the tents has been far harsher and more painful than anything recorded in the history books.

Written on July 30, 2024

Mona Mohammad Kullab

Age: 47 years old

This is not the first war I have lived through. In Gaza, we measure our ages by the number of wars we have survived. But unlike any one I have ever witnessed before, this war is a genocide. Thousands are being killed. Thousands are being displaced and living under the shadow of exile.

We were forced to flee multiple times, as the occupation committed countless massacres in Sheikh Radwan. We escaped with no necessities to help us survive. We fled to Nuseirat and sought refuge in a UNRWA clinic. Some people sent clothing to us, the displaced. Heavy days rushed past, scarcely tolerable. On June 7, 2024, the occupation unleashed an unprecedented operation that destroyed and burned everything indiscriminately, killing over two hundred martyrs in a single day and place. By the grace of Allah we survived, miraculously.

Our life in the tents now is unbearably hard, since we're missing the most basic necessities. Diseases have spread within my family. Every single day brings a new and even harsher form of suffering.

Stop the war. Let peace prevail. I pray to Allah to put an end to this war soon, so that we can return to our homes in Gaza and the city that was stolen from us. Isn't eleven months of agony in all its forms enough to end the war, the pain, the agony? Enough is enough, world. We are exhausted. Our patience has worn thin.

But Allah is with us. And we await His near deliverance with hope in our hearts.

Written on July 15, 2024

Najah Hameed (Umm Mohammad), Martyr
Told by the Martyr Herself

"Nothing happens in Allah's kingdom except what He wills."

Success upon success, that is how my life was. I was life-loving. Pain could never break me down, regardless of the disappointments that came my way. I was always smiling, for I was a devoted teacher and a loving and tender mother. I offered many gentle words to comfort my friends, and much playful teasing to lighten my sisters' hearts, for they were the joy of my soul. I carried endless love within my heart, as big as the universe itself, for my sons, my daughters, and my family.

Out of loyalty and love, I refused to leave my beloved city, Gaza, not even under the rain of threats. Grueling days passed, troubling my heart with fear for those I loved. I wished I could gather you all into the shelter of my arms.

On a freezing December night, the warmth of my heart could not shield you with safety.

The sound of my beating heart competed with the roars of warplanes flying across the sky to release their fire. I prayed to Allah fiercely. I kissed my grandchildren and my daughter Aya, gathering them close to my heart. I calmed them down by reciting the Qur'an into their little ears, but the missiles did not wait.

The walls shuddered and fell, and in an instant our home was erased. My sons, Mohammad and Mu'ayyad, were thrown far by the force of the bombing. Mu'ayyad tried to come back to rescue us, but the planes struck again. He survived the first strike, but not the second.

Death is merciless, the result of a premeditated massacre to erase our names and our stories. Thirty-seven members of my family still lie buried beneath the rubble. We fought so hard to survive, but no one came to save us.

My dear Mohammad and Amna, stay brave and be full of hope. I could not bear to see sorrow in your faces. Hold tight to each other, and always remember that we are now in a place that is fairer and more peaceful.

To my colleagues: That joyful celebration marking the end of my years of service was one of the happiest days of my life. Everyone I loved was there. Your eyes sparkled with kindness and affection. I have tucked that memory safely into the folds of my heart. Thank you. I love you. You were my second family. Remember me in your prayers. I can still feel your love.

And remember that nothing happens in God's kingdom except what Allah wills.

Date of Martyrdom: December 17, 2023

Marwa Mhana, Um Ibraheem
Age: 35 years old

I was ruling over my beautiful kingdom. My husband was working hard, day and night, to provide us with a life of comfort and ease in our sweet home, a warm place that embraced me and my daughter, my three sons, and my husband. I cared for little details in my kingdom, and I nurtured my children with all my heart. Everyone spoke of their sterling characters, their kindness, their brilliance in school.

When the dreadful October attacks began, I vowed to protect my kingdom no matter what happened. Faster and faster, violence followed us. We fled to my sister's home, trying to shield our children from the bitterness of displacement, from the ache of being torn away from their own beds.

When the cursed occupation withdrew from our neighborhood on January 1, 2024, I raced back to my house, my heart pounding, eager to breathe again within the walls of my kingdom. But what awaited me was a home burned to ashes. My beautiful kingdom was gone, burned to the ground. Every memory and every corner had vanished.

I was determined to rebuild our home. I cleaned two rooms; we lived there for four months. Sometimes we were displaced; sometimes we returned—until a cursed day came when I lost my kingdom altogether. One roof atop the other, and I lost my princes underneath them. A brutal and merciless strike crushed our home. We were hurled into the air, landing on the roof of the neighboring house. Can you imagine the force of the bombs that could do that?

I froze, unable to comprehend what had happened. Somewhere amid the rubble, I heard a whisper near my ear: "Raise your right hand. Save yourself." I clawed at the stones above me, pushing them away, calling out into the chaos.

I heard my husband's voice, weak but alive. But I did not hear my children. I screamed their names into the rubble. "Where are my children?"

My legs were mangled beyond recognition. I was taken into the operation room. Again and again, I asked about my children.

My husband got out of the rubble only to bury my fifteen-year-old Janna, my nine-year-old Janna, and my eldest son, Ibrahim, who had bled through the night until death under the rubble. All at the same time were gone together. They were buried without even getting to say good-bye, without a final kiss, without a last breath shared.

A torrent of grief engulfed me, relentless and cruel. The doctors told me that Ayman, my other son, was in a coma—a state of clinical death.

Praise be to Allah that Salah, my youngest, survived with only minor injuries.

I was left with two broken legs, torn apart and stitched together with rods of cold, aching platinum. I sat now on the edge of a great abyss. My kingdom had fallen. Grief stalked me like an old enemy, hungry for revenge after too many stolen moments of joy. I wandered in the ruins of my own life.

And then a miracle happened. A call came from the hospital to inform us that Ayman had woken up. Oh my God, my son had returned to me! The doctors said it happened by a miracle. I laughed and cried all at once. Is it not a miracle that I, my husband, and two of our sons are still alive? Is it not a miracle that we found the bodies of Janna, Jouri, and Ibrahim, despite the unimaginable power of the missiles? I thanked Allah.

Salah and Ayman went to stay with their grandfather to escape death. Another strike came close, but Allah's mercy shielded them.

Still I am in Gaza. I will never leave Gaza, even though my family is separated. Each one needs special care to survive. I have knocked on the walls of the tank, pouring out my story. History must be written and told; our history must not be falsified.

Written on July 1, 2024

Ghada Al-Baz
Age: 30 years old

On the morning of October 7, 2023, I awoke with my four children to the deafening roar of explosions, unleashed by the brutal occupation upon the city of Gaza. The assaults were fierce, birthing massacres in their wake. And soon a new tale of death and destruction began. Shortly afterward, the occupation ordered the people of Gaza to evacuate the Strip, commanding us to head south into the illusion of so-called "safe zones."

My children and I fled without having any destination, our homeless souls adrift. From our neighborhood in Shujaya, we sought refuge in Deir al-Balah. There, no shelter embraced us against the cruel bite of winter. In the merciless cold, we put up a makeshift tent, stitched together from scraps of wood and blankets once meant to warm our sleep. Such was our life, as it was for every displaced soul. We wrestled daily with the scarcity of water, the high prices, the spread of disease and epidemics, and the rivers of rain that turned our shelters into swamps.

It wasn't one time but many and many. We were forced again to flee, this time toward the Nuseirat camp. Our misery deepened, as life was stripped of even its most basic necessities. The winter retreated, only for summer to arrive with its own arsenal of suffering: scorching heat, swarming insects, skin diseases, and the ominous spread of hepatitis (the yellow plague).

Each day was a battle—we lined up for hours just to get water and scavenged for food that barely silenced the hunger gnawing at my children's empty stomachs. Still we struggled to survive, within the ruins of a world that no longer knew the meaning of safety.

Written on August 16, 2024

Nasreen Qazaat
Teacher
Age: 35 years old

On November 19, 2023, a cowardly, treacherous missile refused to pass without sinking its shards deep into the pure body of my husband, Ata Muhammad Al-Daya. It inflicted a grave wound in his intestines. But Allah the Almighty and Merciful willed for the doctors in the Al-Ahly Hospital to heal him. Despite their meager resources, as if their hands were those of heavenly angels the doctors said, "By the grace of God, we will be able to save his life." For three and a half hours, he lay under the surgeon's knife.

O Allah, how unbearable that night was! My husband had been injured around nine o'clock at night. I had clutched his hand tightly as he slipped out of consciousness, whispering through my sobs, "You will be healed, God willing. Don't sleep, don't close your eyes, stay with me. You're going to be fine."

Around me, my children screamed, "Baba, are you okay? Baba, don't leave us!"

As his breathing grew faster and his pain intensified, I cried out for help, begging, "We need an ambulance, Red Cross, anyone!" But the medical teams in Gaza had been torn away from their duties in a city drowning in blood and rubble. I screamed, "Take him in any car, please!" But outside death rained from the sky, and fear pinned everyone to the ground. No one dared move through the hail of missiles and shells. What could I do? My husband was dying before my eyes.

At last his brothers and cousins said, "We'll carry him to the hospital ourselves, even if it costs us our lives." They set out with him into the night, and my soul went with them.

I whispered, wrapping my grief in prayer, "O Allah, surround them with Your mercy, guide them with Your care." I prayed. I wept. I fell to my knees in desperate supplication.

It was midnight, and I had received no calls, no messages, no news. Darkness tightened its grip around my heart. I wondered if they had even reached the hospital, or if the occupation's barbaric missiles had hunted them down on the way. As fear gnawed at my mind, deep within me a fragile flame whispered, "He will survive. Morning will come with relief and good news."

And the morning did come, after the longest night of my life. They returned, and with them the news I had begged the heavens for: "The surgery was successful." As soon as I heard this, I fell into a prostration of gratitude, thanking God over and over. Please, readers, keep my husband in your prayers, that he may recover fully.

After one hundred and thirty-eight days of steadfastness in Gaza, the land of pride and dignity, my family and I became displaced within our own homeland. On the night of February 21, 2023, the Israeli occupation forces invaded our beautiful neighborhood, Al-Zaytoun. We found ourselves surrounded from every direction by tanks and armored vehicles, hemming us in. The only sounds were the roaring of shells and missiles, the constant hum of drones, and the barrage of machine-gun fire. Everyone was crying. Children screamed in terror. The sound of tanks rumbled just beneath our house.

It might have been the last moment of our lives. We were breathless! What would happen to us? Would they demolish the house over our heads, leaving us to die beneath the rubble? Would they storm in, shooting and arresting us without mercy?

Until one o'clock the next afternoon, we stayed like that, all night, waiting. Then, a bomb! It exploded with brutal violence, and the door was opened. The occupiers stormed in, armed with the deadliest weapons, terrifying the women and children. They beat us. They hurled curses at us. They fired into the air.

The cowardly invaders forced us, the women and children, to leave and head south. We refused at first, saying, "We want to stay in Gaza, in our home." But they raised their weapons in our faces, fired shots above our heads, and forced us out at gunpoint.

As for my husband and the men of our family, they stripped them of their clothes, blindfolded them, tied their hands, and took them away as captives.

We walked five kilometers without a drop of water to drink and without our men. To God only could we complain of our misery. We'd left with nothing but the clothes on our bodies. The soldiers had refused to let us take anything with us. We walked for hours and hours, tears streaming down our faces all the way. We cried for our broken lives. We cried for our imprisoned husbands. We cried for the home we had lost.

Dear Gaza, you are the dearest of all lands to my heart. Had it not been that the enemies of Allah forced me out of you, I would never have left. But the will of Allah is supreme. For sure the dawn is near.

Written on July 7, 2024

Kholoud Younis Abu Hilal

Age: 45 years old

A tragedy lies somewhere between will-power and pride.

The sounds of rockets and artillery echoed around me, followed by cries and chants of "Allahu Akbar!" I didn't understand at first what was going on. But, within an hour, I realized that a brutal war was coming, inevitably. A suffocating ache lodged itself in my heart.

Fear gripped me, and as the hours passed, I realized the reason for this feeling. On the night of October 8, 2023, I woke up to the sound of my phone ringing, a sound that had become terrifying to me even at the earliest hours, since it had once awakened me with the heartbreaking news of my younger brother's death by drowning at sea.

More shocks came. I received the news of the martyrdom of three of my uncles, along with their families. The very first massacre in this war happened to my family. We lost thirteen martyrs in a single day— Alhamdulillah for everything. A single missile targeted his home and robbed me of my dearest uncle, the one who was more like a brother to me.

The massacre of my family members continued. One after another, the number of martyrs approached sixty souls. I received the news of each loss with a crushed heart, aching and helpless. We spent hard nights in the Al-Maghazi refugee camp. Missiles never stopped raining down on the fragile camp.

I pray to Allah to protect all my loved ones from harm. I prefer martyrdom, for I shall return to a just and merciful Lord.

The deepest wound of all was being away from my children. Since I had separated from their father and remarried, the war tore us apart. I was punished by being denied my heart's very flesh. Have you ever tasted the heartbreak and devastation of a mother who is stripped of her children, breathing the same air and living on the same soil, but unable even to hear a whisper of news about them?

The war grew fiercer, and the thought of displacement began to haunt me. Yet my husband refused. I couldn't sleep at night, as the house trembled with every missile that landed on nearby homes.

On December 28, 2023, my brother-in-law's house was targeted, and seven members of his family were martyred. It was devastating. Their house was very close to ours. I clung to the idea of leaving Al-Maghazi Camp and heading to Rafah City, where my family and children were. Maybe I could see them, even if by chance.

I stayed at my brother's house for about a month and a half. I sent a message to my daughter, telling her that I was displaced at her uncle's house. And she came to visit me, along with my youngest son. My happiness was priceless. I had been yearning to hold them in my arms, or at least to say good-bye before being martyred.

As for my stay at my family's home, it was not easy. I endured so much humiliation, but I was patient. I never made my husband feel the pain I carried inside. Still, my patience wore thin, and my decision to return to my home in Al-Maghazi came as a result.

After the occupation troops had withdrawn from the camp, I returned, and the scene broke my heart. My home was not as I had left it. It was full of widespread destruction and gaping holes in the walls. Nevertheless, we refused to give up. We worked hard to clean and organize what we could, sealing off the holes and repairing the walls so that it was possible to live there again.

An unexploded missile had landed in the apartment across from ours, but no one had known about it. A few days later, I learned what had happened, and terror filled my heart. The fear controlled me, knowing that the missile could explode at any moment. I couldn't sleep at night.

On the fourth day of Ramadan, just fifteen minutes before the call to *Maghrib* prayer, my husband went out to buy a Wi-Fi card. He came back in a hurry shouting, "Come down! Come down quickly!" The neighbors and I had no idea what was happening.

Missiles rained down like a storm upon our home, destroying it once again, exactly one month after we had worked so hard to repair it. There was no hope of repair this time. Our home was no longer a place where anyone could live.

I became homeless, without belongings, without clothes. We escaped wearing only our house clothes. Our home had been bombed, and our dreams were also shattered. But I thanked God that my husband and I had survived death.

We left for the third time, with no home to wait for us. After staying for a month at my brother-in-law's house, I left, for it lacked any kind of privacy. I tried to buy a tent, but tents were extremely expensive, around a thousand dollars and more.

I ended up renting an apartment in Al-Zawayda Camp, an area that was targeted by daily missile strikes, as if rain were falling from the sky. Many families were martyred there.

Despite the danger, I felt isolated. An idea of volunteering came to me, to serve the displaced people. I began visiting displacement camps to get to know the people, their struggles, and their suffering. I worked, and I still work, delivering their appeals and urgent needs to humanitarian and international organizations. I succeeded in getting some generous support from donors, so I was able to meet some of their immediate needs, like securing drinking water, distributing relief aid, providing food parcels, clothes, and medicines, and helping those who have no shelter or place to stay.

What pains me the most is looking at our children, who have been deprived of their simplest rights of education and play. They too need psychological and emotional support.

I started my initiative by setting up an educational tent in Yaffa Al-Ezza camp, near my home in Al-Zawayda, in partnership with some camp administrators. We organized a study schedule that included psychological support. We soon succeeded in attracting students; families rushed to register their children, searching for a better life for them. Our goal in this initiative was to mend what the war had broken: minds and souls. I reached out to Maraaseel Al-Khair, a charity organization, where I now work as a public relations officer. They provided our students with stationery, breakfast meals, and juices. The children committed to attending regularly.

Then an unfortunate military operation occurred in Al-Nuseirat, when the Israeli occupation reclaimed some of their captives. As on the first day, war flared up and families were displaced once more. Fear and terror filled our hearts. We were inside the school tent at that very moment. It was my responsibility to calm the children and get them safely to their shelters. The scene was horrific—shelling, missiles, artillery fire, bullets raining from the war-planes.

The students were forced to suspend their studies for several days. But I did not give up.

I visited their families and managed to gather the children once more. I continued my initiative by beginning with three consecutive days of recreational activities.

Then came the blow. On June 5, 2024, my dear father was martyred after being missing for thirteen days. It was the biggest shock in my life. Losing him, I felt like a bird who has lost a wing. The very next day, my uncle was martyred. Our eyes are still heavy with tears for my father and uncle. After that, my other wing broke when my husband and daughter were martyred. How can a bird with no wings fly?

I became a twenty-four-year-old widow, left alone with two little girls. Our grief was endless. The tragedies came one after another, as if determined to erase every trace of my former life. Days later, I lost seven of my cousins.

On July 10, our neighbors were ordered to evacuate their house before it was bombed. I fled, running for my life, carrying nothing with me, not even knowing where to go. We spent the night waiting for the missile of death to fall. Thanks to Allah, it didn't fall, and we returned to our rented home to continue our life under the shadow of this fear. At any second, death may strike us without warning.

This is my story in this damned war. I have written it with tears brimming in my eyes. It is a story too heavy for even the mightiest mountains to bear. I hate war, and everything about it. The occupation clipped my wings—my husband and my father. I am a wounded bird crying out for justice: "Stop the war."

Written on July 7, 2024

Iman Mohammed Youssef Al-Amrani

English Teacher

Age: 46 years old

What a shock! How dare the world begin and end with such a deep pain, all at once!

This tale of war started on October 7, 2023. Since then, we have lived in endless suffering and pain. At first, my husband and I fled our home in the great neighborhood of Al-Shuja'iya, along with our children, and sought shelter at my parents' house. My brother's house in Al-Rimal was the second place we moved to. When things worsened and the shelling grew heavier, we all moved to at Al-Nasr Children's Hospital. With no choice left, we spent two nights there.

Then my husband decided that we had to head south. We ended up in a UNRWA school in Al-Bureij refugee camp. Staying there from November to December, we passed days filled with a strange mixture of pain, fleeting joy, and crushing despair.

The bombardment intensified again, forcing us to flee with my family to Al-Shaboura in Rafah. Life, with its warts-and-all ordinariness, has vanished. The tender minds of children are too innocent to realize the reasons behind our displacement and the water lines we have to wait in. But they know they are living in a world stripped of joy, without toys or safety.

Life has turned sorrowful. We are heartbroken, torn away from our home. Our home is not just our house but our lands, schools, mosques, and trees—oranges, olives, and palms. Days pass, and we are all mortal. After Rafah was threatened with a ground invasion, people began to flee. I gathered my children, and we made our way to Nuseirat. Now we live in Souq Balat in Al-Nuseirat. All we can do is pray that we return safely to our homes. God willing…

Written on July 7, 2024

Safaa Abu Saqr,
Arabic Teacher

The word "displaced" consists of just four letters, but it carries so much suffering for the Palestinian people. Here I will tell you my story of displacement.

On the morning of October 7, 2023, we woke up to the deafening sounds of explosions. Our hearts were gripped by terror. The occupiers were brutal, launching their American-made missiles at everything, including homes, people, and trees.

At midnight, we received a warning about the nearby towers. In complete darkness, we left our home. The sound of gunfire from Apache helicopters terrified us more and more. The screams of children echoed from every corner. That night, we didn't know if we would survive.

We managed to reach a relative's house that night. By early morning, we tried to return to our home to see what had happened and to take some of the filtered water we had left behind, as it was increasingly hard to get clean drinking water.

But we couldn't reach our home. We headed instead to the pharmacy, to buy medicine for my mother, who suffers from chronic illnesses, and my father, who suffers from severe migraines. Their medicines were not available.

The occupation distributed leaflets telling people to leave the area and head south, claiming it would be a "safe" zone. Still looking for water and medicine, we decided to flee to the south, but to get there we had to cross Salah al-Din Street. There was a checkpoint there, and we had to wait for hours under the scorching sun.

Carrying only a few belongings that could not save us from hunger, we walked through the checkpoint, passing lifeless bodies scattered on the ground. We headed toward Khan Younis. That night we slept on the ground, as we had no tents or belongings with us.

The following morning, the building next to us was bombed. By a miracle we survived, though some of the shrapnel hit the building we were in. Then the occupation dropped more evacuation flyers, urging us to move to Rafah.

A lot of untold woes marked our journey, including a struggle with infection and the slow recovery from an epidemic of hepatitis. We also suffered from malnutrition and eating unhealthy canned food, and from the freezing cold in the tents, and the flooding from rainwater.

Then even the tents were bombed, and my brother carried my twenty-year-old sister, who has special needs, for a distance of several kilometers on his back.

We were displaced again, to a new camp in Al-Nuseirat. Out of a sense of duty to my people, I now volunteer at a "Seeds of Goodness" school, teaching Arabic to students in many grades, despite the harsh conditions and lack of resources.

We hope to return to our homes in peace and safety soon.

Written on July 7, 2024

Layan Khalil Al-Buhtini
Age: 21 years old

I am the daughter of the martyr Khalil, the daughter of the martyr Laila, the sister of the martyr Hajar, and the wife of the martyr Mahmoud Mushtaha.

One by one, my loved ones were taken away, like leaves torn from their branches, from October 7, 2023, until the day when we reached the so-called "safe zone." We prayed, with hearts heavy with grief, as we trudged through endless hours of fear to cross that narrow passage to safety. Allah granted us the power to pass through the checkpoint and to continue a journey that seemed endless. We moved like ghosts through the checkpoint, transported by the primitive means of carts and donkeys.

Finally we arrived Deir al-Balah. At a school that had been transformed into a shelter for displaced people, my brother hastily set up a tent. I am not exaggerating when I say that it was unlivable; it was only a hollow shell of the vibrant life we had known before.

Ramadan arrived, after days of waiting. We spent the sacred month away from our usual traditions, as everything we held dear had been torn away. Eid came as a sad day and went in a haze of sorrow, its joy swallowed by our tears as we missed our lost beloveds. We raised our voices in *Takbeer* as it was raining. Our hearts were heavy with the weight of memories that cut deeper than any wound.

Then came Eid al-Adha, and death was still there. We lost my grandmother, my grandfather, and my uncle, and each of those deaths is a wound that can never heal.

As the days passed, the occupation struck with relentless force, reducing the nearby school, Khadijah, to rubble. Amid the dead and injured bodies, we had been ordered to evacuate, leaving behind everything we had. A few hours latter, the school was a pile of debris, some of which scattered across our tent, leveling it to the ground and damaging our belongings.

We fled to a new shelter, the home of my husband's sister. There we set up another tent. Three days later, we returned to the school, our hearts heavy with fear. We began to gather what little we had left.

The shadows still loom over us, and the questions remain unanswered. How does a soul continue to breathe after losing a beloved? How do we survive in a landscape of heartbreak and grief? When will this damned war release its grip on our throats? When will we return to our homes? When will we reunite with those we have lost?

All remain unanswered thoughts, but we hold fast to the belief that Allah, in His infinite mercy, will one day grant us justice.

This is a fragment of my tale, woven with threads of pain and loss. May Allah grant us patience; only He can light our way.

Written on July 22, 2024

Eman Mohammed Rabah Bader

Age: 18 years old

A black day was followed by even darker days. There was no longer a safe place in this world. On October 7, 2023, a day that should have been like any other, I was preparing for school and putting on my uniform. I was studying in the secondary school, a critical stage for my future academic journey. Then, suddenly, the sky over Gaza was filled with the deafening sounds of rockets and explosions. We lived in a border area, where danger was always close.

We stayed in the house for two days, waiting for the worst to pass. But as danger crept closer, we fled to the Sabra neighborhood, seeking shelter in a UNRWA school that was supposed to be safe. Little did we know that nothing now is safe in Gaza.

We stayed there for several months, until a missile struck a home right in front of the school. The streets were littered with bodies and debris. Children stood frozen, their eyes wide in terror, witnessing these scenes of violence and horrors.

From that day forward, security and sleep no longer had places in our lives. Every night there was the constant threat of more bombings. Months later, the school was surrounded by occupation forces. We were paralyzed by fear, young and old alike. It felt as though we had already lost hope, life, and the will to continue. Everyone started to recite *Shahada*.

The soldiers stormed into the school and interrogated us. It was a moment that seemed to freeze time. We were ordered to leave and head south, to what they called "a safe zone."

On the road, we were a group of six families—including children, my elderly grandmother, and my grandfather. Exhaustion numbed my legs, and everyone was on the brink of collapse.

At last we arrived at the "Netzarim" checkpoint, which separated the north from the south. It felt like the Day of Judgment—a crushing, intense crowd that it seemed impossible to walk through. After eight hours of agony, we finally managed to get through, but that was only the beginning.

As we walked, in the dead of night, my mother and I lost our way and were separated from our family. We ended up in the Nuseirat refugee camp, where we spent the night in a shelter school, with no blankets and no means of contacting the rest of the family.

Our search went on, and eventually I found my brother, who had been looking for us. Our family was scattered. Some had gone to my grandfather's house in Al-Zawayda, others to my aunt's house in Nuseirat. I stayed with my grandmother, the one I loved more than anything, a woman who carried a love so deep that she was like a second mother to me. My mother and siblings stayed in my grandfather's house.

A few months later, we were forced to flee again. We were staying with a rural family, people we had known for a long time. But we couldn't stay there for long, as the tanks were now in front of the house. Without warning, we found ourselves forced to flee yet again, this time to Deir al-Balah. We found refuge in a tent in a shelter school, along with my grandmother.

She passed away five days afterward. It was such a harsh blow, it felt as though everything for me had shattered. The world turned black in my eyes. From that moment on, tears have never left me. My longing for her only grows with each passing day. I write my story with tears falling, soaking the paper. My grandmother died before she could rejoice with me over my success in Tawjihi, the general secondary exams. I couldn't bear to stay where she had passed away. We returned to our tent, and I have stayed there until this very day.

Soon after that, I received the news that my aunt and her children had also been martyred. I didn't shed a single tear, for the tears had dried in my eyes, my heart had already been torn apart by grief. My suffering was bigger than my years. I never imagined that I would carry this burden.

We stood in long lines for the bathroom, for water, for the charity kitchens. No one could ever fully describe our suffering. The year passed. And my future vanished.

We were displaced several more times, and I walked carrying my school-bag on my back. Hope was lost inside; finally I burned the books to stave off hunger. I should have been thinking about what university I want to attend. Instead, here I am, living in a white tent, which surrounds me like a white burial shroud.

To be in my home with my loved ones has become a distant dream. I pray that, one day, we can return to our homes after all this suffering. We are strong on the outside, but our hearts have shattered like glass. Yet, despite the destruction and bombing, we still thank Allah every moment, for we are still alive.

Written on August 20, 2024

Saidah Osama Al-Hasi

Age: 46 years

Since October 7, 2023, we have witnessed a genocide, the displacement of our people, and the agony of living amid severe famine and the deprivation of our basic rights. Countless are the stories of displacement, and countless are the times people have been forced to flee.

Here I write my own story of displacement.

Al-Nasser, the Gaza Strip. The first week of the war took place in our neighborhood. It was one of the most dangerous weeks of my life, with airstrikes and shelling relentlessly hitting our streets. As the destruction and bombardment intensified in our area, my family and I decided to flee. Fear gripped our hearts, as we were forced to abandon our home in search of a safer place.

When were about to leave, we were shocked to hear of the occupation's orders for the evacuation of the neighborhood, as it had become fighting zone. We were told to head south, to supposedly safer zones. We packed only what we needed, clothes and a few essentials.

But my husband and children hesitated. They asked me, "How can we go south, when we have no family there and no shelter awaiting us?"

We decided to go to my family's house—not far from our own home, but relatively safer. Upon our arrival, we found the house already packed with displaced people. We stayed there for almost two weeks, until we received another evacuation order. We were left speechless, unable to think clearly. Where would we go?

We stayed at a shelter school for a day and night. That night was one of the hardest I have ever lived through, as the school was dangerously close to the shelling and tanks. Then we found a place in another school, further away, and stayed for a week. It was still not safe, as it was close to the Al-Shifa medical complex, where the bombing and destruction intensified day and night.

I began to consider seeking refuge elsewhere, but all places in Gaza seemed to be just as dangerous. Fear had consumed every corner of this city.

On that Friday afternoon, around one o'clock, we decided to leave before the ground invasion of Al-Shifa hospital complex. The occupation refused to let us carry anything. We were allowed to enter only with empty hands. My heart was heavy with fear for my eighteen-year-old son, who has special needs. I was terrified that he might slow down or make a sound, and that the enemy would open fire on us—for the occupation shoots at anyone who makes the slightest unexpected movement.

We crossed on a path littered with decomposing bodies and the discarded possessions of people who had been ordered to threw everything away. As we neared the end of the path, a war-plane launched a missile at us. The scene was horrific, filled with screams and terror. Many people were killed, while others miraculously survived. That day, we became part of a displaced population beyond imagination. The fear of invasion in the Al-Shifa complex led many families to flee to the south.

We walked for hours, heading toward the Al-Nuseirat camp, searching for a shelter. But all were overcrowded with displaced people. So we continued on foot, searching for any available space. The time for *Maghrib* prayers arrived, and we were still with no food or shelter. We were exhausted. Finally we slept on a cold, hard spot on the ground, without blankets or food. We woke up the next day sickened by what we seen—dead bodies fallen on the ground.

We spent two weeks in that place. Then we received devastating news: my brother, his wife, and their children had been killed in Gaza city. My heart shattered as I heard this, far away from them. I had left behind in Gaza my mother, my father, and three of my siblings, steadfast in their land. A few days later, we received the news that my sister's daughter had been injured and her nine-year-old child had died. All I could do was mourn and accept Allah's will.

I spent nearly forty days in that shelter. Then the occupation issued another evacuation order and bombed the shelter with warning missiles. With empty bags, we moved to Deir al-Balah. There we found a makeshift shelter and spent two months there. One day we received more bad news: my sister and her family had been killed in Gaza. What grief we had to endure!

Two weeks ago, the occupation bombed a school near our shelter, so we had to evacuate immediately. We knew that our tent would have been damaged from the bombing, but it was our only shelter, so we returned, eager to begin patching it up as best as we could—only to find that it had been not only destroyed but burned completely.

Now I must look for a new place to seek refuge, away from the schools, as the danger there is unstoppable.

This is my story. A story of fear, disappointment, and agony. May Allah grant us patience and reward us for what has happened to us.

Written on August 25, 2024

Noor Al-Huda Hassan
Age: 21 years old

A great joy entered my heart: I was on my way to my dream. A knock came at the door. "Is this the home of Miss Noor Al-Huda?" My mother replied, "Yes, please come in." After offering hospitality to our guests, my parents asked officially to be related to the couple's son by marriage. Happiness filled our hearts. Our engagement was announced successfully. It was a beautiful day. Three months passed after that day, and our acquaintance was beautiful.

We were preparing for the wedding day. I had arranged my lovely new home, consisting of two rooms, a large living room, a bedroom, a bathroom, a kitchen, and a spacious balcony. Everything I needed was in my home. The wedding day was scheduled for October 2023. I packed my wedding trousseau, as the habit is in Palestine. On October 7, we decided to go to my home and arrange my belongings, two days prior to the wedding day.

And then, instead of hearing *Zaghreed*, a traditional joyful sound for celebrating weddings, we awoke to rockets, massacres, bloodshed, explosions, and genocide. We thought it would be like the previous wars and would end soon. But it became endless, and our forced displacement began.

I left everything behind. We packed up and left our home in a moment of hardship. Everything became ashes. The beautiful day turned into sorrow. We left our home with nothing, to face danger everywhere.

We were displaced from Al- Shujaya to Al-Daraj, and then to the Al-Tuffah neighborhood. We sought refuge at my aunt's house, but it was soon surrounded by heavy shelling. The house was about to collapse on us. The next morning, all outside communication was cut. We lost contact with the world. Gaza was divided into two regions.

We endured physical and psychological violence and forcible displacement from the north to the south, with nothing left for us. We fled on foot, not knowing where we were going. All along the way, we encountered soldiers. We crossed through checkpoints where they killed, arrested, and raped as they pleased. Fear engulfed us. "Raise your ID!" they shouted. "Look only forward. Hurry!"

Finally we made it to the "safe zone" announced by the occupation. We arrived in Al-Nuseirat, not knowing where to go next. After nearly a month of no communication, I received a call. My fiancé had been searching for me and brought me to his family's tent. They offered us everything we needed.

Winter crept in. The rain was relentless. We moved into a classroom-turned-shelter, crammed with five families. Life in the tent was desperate and unfair. We cooked over an open fire and washed in plastic basins. Food and water grew scarce. Diseases spread fast. The hospitals were reduced to rubble. There was nothing left to make life worth living.

Suddenly we were ordered to evacuate the school because the occupation planned to bomb it. I got married without a wedding or even a white dress. We fled to another area, not knowing where my family was. We reached Deir Al-Balah and set up our tent on a cold rainy night. Sixteen people were crammed into one small tent.

And the suffering grew worse—finding water, cooking inadequate food, paying sky-high prices without any income. I got married and started a family, but we had no job, no house, no decent clothes, and no appropriate supplies for a new wife.

As time passed, Ramadan came. I was sick, and later learned I was pregnant. Inside me was a small, innocent fetus who knew nothing about this cruel world. I was overjoyed, but that joy was overshadowed by the weight of our reality. Days went by, and I lacked medication and vitamins. The pregnancy weighed heavily on me. I couldn't wash or carry heavy objects. I faced great difficulties as I entered my fifth month.

I knew about a competition to write the story of displacement, so I began writing.

Boom! An exploding rocket hit nearby. The pen was in my hand. Fear spread in the air, and the pages shook in my grasp. That same night, pain woke me at midnight, as if I had reached the ninth month. My husband rushed me to the hospital in an ambulance. The doctor examined me and then, with great sadness, told my husband, "The baby is lost. Your wife must abort." In a breath, my child was gone, never to be born.

They made a new appointment for another procedure. I felt my baby's pulse inside me until he left. I felt his last movement at four in the morning. It was as though my soul had departed with him. I entered the labor room and endured a pain I cannot describe. At midnight I gave birth to my son, on August 12, 2024. He was beautiful, even in death. They took him away for burial, and I returned to the painful tent.

The birth was unspeakably difficult. My soul left my body, and I felt the pain deeply. Months have passed since then, but it has felt like years. I still feel him within me, my dear companion, my beloved.

My story has not ended yet, and the writing of pain continues. I don't know if I will follow my son, or if I will live to tell our story to my children. That night shattered me. It was more than grief—it was the ripping away of my soul. I still feel him near, my son, my little love. This story is not over.

Written on August 17, 2024

Faten Rafiq Mohammad Al-Siqali
Age: 39 years old

On the morning of October 7, 2023, like any mother, I was preparing breakfast for my kids as they got ready for school. As I finished helping them get dressed and packed, we were startled by sounds that warned of an impending disaster. But I didn't think that these were the bells of war ringing through my life.

Within moments, we realized this war would be unlike any other war. The Arab media claimed that the weaker side had initiated it. Never did I imagine that a war would be so monstrous. Never did I think I'd carry my children's bedding and clothes and a few of my most precious belongings away from my home—all I had left. I told myself as those before me had said, "Just two days, and we'll be back." We didn't know that those two days would turn into countless months.

I gathered my important documents and packed bags for my kids, grabbing some of their toys, their most precious things in life. Like all children in the world, they dream of play, learning, and feeling safe. In my home I left behind everything I owned—happy and sad memories, joys, sorrows, quarrels, reconciliations, laughter, and play. We all clung to the hope of returning home.

Day after day, the war intensified. Eventually I lost hope in going back. This would become the most cursed tragedy in the history of Palestine. I sought refuge in a UNRWA school in Gaza City. It was our first time being displaced. Our homes were no longer safe.

At that time, Gazans used to believe that schools were safer, but I couldn't endure the overcrowded rooms in the school. I moved to my sister's house in Al-Shujaya, near to the Souq area. I thought it would be far from danger. I stayed there for two days, but the overcrowding made it unbearable. Then the occupation threatened the neighborhood where my sister lived. With hearts hungry for safety, we packed up again, heading to another area to be safer. This time we lasted only three days before the occupation threatened that area, where my husband's relatives lived.

The Arab world has crushed the hopes of a woman wandering without her husband, dragging her children behind her, searching for scraps of bread in the war. Hasn't it been cruel enough for the world to stop the war now? All I have left is my faith in Allah that somehow, eventually, everything will be okay.

The shelling intensified. The occupation bombed every building near the house we were staying in, without warning. This went on for days.

Our lives were in constant danger. The occupation repeated its usual warnings about evacuating areas they designated as "red zones."

The city was heartbroken. Like all Gaza's people, we never believed such warnings. But massacres followed, one after the other. They bombed homes over the heads of their residents. They killed anyone who moved. They called every victim a terrorist. Danger bells rang loudly, and the situation kept getting worse. There was no shelter, no refuge but Allah.

I had no other choice. To the world, we became just numbers. I knew that if I stayed, I'd lose my children, to hunger or to bombs. I didn't want to die in a massacre that no one would even care to remember. So I headed south with my children. I thought that this would be my third and last displacement journey. I pinned my soul to hope and prayed to return soon to my city, my family, my siblings, and my loved ones. I left them behind in Allah's hands.

We stayed in a shelter school in the Nuseirat refugee camp for almost two months. The evacuation orders were a part of our life, following us like a monster wherever we went. Eventually I fled with my family to Rafah, to the so-called "safe zone." Life was unbearable; we lived in overcrowded tents, in extreme poverty. I couldn't endure life this way. The water was unclean, and diseases, insects, and rodents spread in the tents. But, as our grandparents used to say, "There's no choice in the matter." When all of my land was under threat, where could I go?

I stayed in Rafah for about four months. Then, once again, the occupation announced the area as a battlefield. What can a woman like me do, except obey the orders of an enemy who sees no difference between child and elder, between woman and man?

I was displaced for the fourth time, to Deir al-Balah. It wasn't our choice. It was their orders, after they claimed it was a "safe zone." The street was our shelter. Still I couldn't get used to life in a tent, lacking safety, privacy, and good infrastructure. I couldn't bear it. I gathered my things and moved into a school, where I pitched a tent.

For the fifth time, I was displaced. And maybe this will be the last. In the tent, we have to overcome the hardships of pain, cold, hunger, loss, and deep disappointment. Subjugation is being dominated by your occupier, losing your loved ones, your home, and your family, unable to do anything. Our health is collapsing. My children have lost their healthy bodies. Not a day passes without their suffering from skin diseases, psychological stress, hunger, and illness. They had no nutritious food, no safe place to sleep.

And the promise of the so-called "safe zone" was false. Death is everywhere in my land. When will this end? When will this nightmare stop? Will there be yet another displacement, or just a delayed death? Or maybe a return to the ruins once we called home?

The story isn't over yet. Tomorrow, the bird shall fly.

Written on August 8, 2024

Mona Safwat Aouath
Age: 19 years old

Sounds that had long instilled fear within me jolted me awake on the morning of October 7, 2023. I panicked and looked around... Had everyone else awakened, or was I alone? One of my brothers was as terrified as I was. I started shouting, and then I called out, "Father! Mother!" But no one heard me.

I rushed to the balcony and found everyone gazing at the sky with astonishment and bewilderment. Around us, the neighbors were looking at us, and we at them, in mutual surprise. My younger siblings were laughing, unaware. My parents stood there, utterly perplexed. We began to repeat, "Father, what's happening? What's happening?" Then we asked over and over, "Father, what is this?"

After a moment of heavy silence, he said, "Something momentous has occurred." He turned on the radio, but it offered no explanation. Shortly afterward, news began to trickle in from some people, and the truth became clear. Everyone started asking questions, young and old alike. "Will we go to school or not?" I peered out the window to see if any of the other girls had gone to school. The streets were teeming with passersby.

Just then some of my uncles arrived, and they sat watching the news. Minute by minute, what had happened became undeniable. We all sat before the TV, closely observing the unfolding events, bombarding my father with questions, until the first day ended...October 7.

My sleep schedule became erratic, and I couldn't stop thinking: "Will we return to school or not? Will there be a war? And how will the occupation respond?" Other thoughts swirled in my mind. Every time I drew close to sleep, my father awakened me, comforting me, "Don't be afraid... don't be afraid." We remained in this state for ten days.

Each time I looked at my father's face, I saw worry and confusion etched there. This became even clearer to me on the tenth day, when a mosque just one street away from my home was struck, on October 13. It was the Omari Mosque, one of the largest and most ancient mosques in our city, but they reduced it to rubble.

Many sides of our house were shattered, and it was no longer fit to live in. My father decided we should go to my sister's house, which was nearby. We all needed to feel safe. It was hard for us to leave our home, even though my sister's house was like a second home to us.

No sooner had we spent our first night there than we began to taste the bitterness of war. On the morning of October 14, my father, my sister's husband, and one of my uncles were sitting at the door of the house, drinking coffee. At exactly eleven o'clock in the morning, a missile struck about twenty meters away from my father. Three minutes after the first missile, another one hit the house adjacent to my sister's. The house filled with black smoke and stone dust. None of us could see each other, and we were deafened by the screaming and terror of the children and the weeping and wailing of the adults.

When the dust settled and we could see each other again, we found people in the house we didn't know. Shells rained down upon us, we didn't know from where. We were trapped inside the house and couldn't get out through the main door because it had been locked. Everyone started asking, "What do we do?"

My father asked, "Is there a hammer?" We were surprised. "Why a hammer?" Knowing the layout of the house, my father began to break through one wall of the house so we could escape another way. First the men got the children out, and then the women, until everyone had left the house.

We ran, shrapnel flying around us, not knowing where to go. Every time I looked right or left, I saw the same scene: women running, children screaming. Then I found myself inside my elementary school, this time not for studying, but for shelter—people had started gathering in the schools.

When night fell, the suffering intensified. Where would we sleep? And how could we sleep amid this intense fear? The night did not cast its usual darkness. Instead, the sky turned red with the light of rockets and missiles, and the buzzing of aircraft. Nights became a true nightmare; it was impossible to sleep, waiting for the break of dawn.

Every place we thought would be safe was not. The same nightmare haunted us every night. And what a night we had when we fled to the house of one of my father's friends! I realized then that death is inevitable. Eventually we returned with our belongings to the first place. The extreme destruction in the area was unbelievable.

"All residents of the northern Gaza Strip must head south of Wadi Gaza." The Israeli occupation spread the evacuation orders. Drones began dropping leaflets every day. We had known that this occupation was brutal, killing without warning, as had happened in previous wars. But the occupation was even more aggressive in this war. Leaving my home to go to my sister's home had been a difficult decision, so what about the decision to flee the city?

It was extremely difficult for my father to make such a choice. We had to convince him to make it. We left our home and our neighborhood, crying not out of fear but out of love. We heard in the news of the occupation destroying homes over the heads of their inhabitants. And every day the war grew more intense than the day before. We all got into a car, taking none of the belongings in our house.

As we were heading toward the city of our displacement, I thought back over my days of joy and the beautiful memories I had of this same road, which had once led me, as a little schoolgirl, on a wonderful trip with friends. Rubble now piled high over these memories. All the way I found only silence and dust. My thoughts blurred. I looked at my parents' faces and found worry settled deep into their skin; fear stared back at me through their tired eyes. I had never seen them like this before.

Our first shelter was in the city of Deir al-Balah, a place my feet had never trod until then. Now it was part of my life. We ended up in a shared school-turned-shelter. There my father began to recount the tale of displacement in 1948, the Nakba. The narrative echoed these days in a crueler, more profound way. Back then the displaced also said, "Just a few days. We'll go back home soon."

Yet here we are, in the ninth month of the war, July 2024. Each day has brought more death and more destruction. Since day one, a question has haunted every high-school student: "Will I finish my studies or not?" It's as if the year died before it ever began, like so many lost souls in this war.

I began to wrestle with even more pressing questions: How shall we eat? How shall we drink? Where will money come from, now that prices have soared and merchants have become merciless? My heart ached for my father, as I thought of how he would carry the responsibility of all of this— feeding us, clothing us, protecting us.

Three of my sisters had sought shelter with us. Their husbands were left behind, trapped by the Israeli occupation in the disconnected, northern part of Gaza. Each day, the suffering deepened. As my older sisters and I lay down to sleep, our voices hushed in conversation, the same question always arose, "How can we help our father?" He had no job, no income. Sometimes I thought we must be the wayfarers the Qur'an speaks of.

Time passed, and we came to know the refugee camp in Deir al-Balah that sheltered us. We walked its streets as strangers, waiting in the hope of returning home. We would barely emerge from one crisis before another came knocking. Sometimes it was food, or water, or clothes. I remember once being trapped inside for ten days because I had no shoes to wear. We would ration what little breakfast we could find—a dry biscuit, maybe a date if we were lucky. Hunger became a quiet companion. Lunch was to delayed until just before sunset. No one dared to mention dinner anymore.

Every day the news brought fresh talk of aid and hope. Promises flowed over us in words, but in nothing else. They told us to hope, but no one showed us anything. And all the while, our phones were silent. North was cut off from South. When communication returned, it carried sorrow with it—the deaths of people I knew and loved. Cousins, neighbors.

Never, not once, did I imagine that what I read in history books about our people's past—the displacement, the suffering, the Nakba—would one day become *my* life. But here I am, living inside the very pages I once read.

Each night, before sleep pulls me under, I ask myself, *What happened to me? Where did my dreams go? Where are the goals I once held so tightly?* My father set up a quiet corner with a desk for me to focus on my studies. I had high ambitions. Reaching them never felt impossible. My mother had always spoken about her preparation for the day when my test results would be announced. My father used to smile and call me "Doctor Mona." And I would answer him, proud and sure, "I want to be a university professor in the English Language Department, Baba." We dreamed so many dreams.

And now, here I am, telling my story. The war hasn't ended. Not yet. The whole world sympathizes with us, yet the war hasn't ended. We pray that it will end, for the sake of a generation nearly erased, for the sake of souls that can never come back, for the sake of an economy brought to its knees. The war has threaded itself through our veins; we breathe it, carry it, and bleed it.

Though the world has turned its back, our hope in Allah remains vast.

Written on July 7, 2024

Galia Nawas
Age: 53 years old

The Nuseirat Massacre—it happened to me. The scenes remain etched in my head, engraved deep within my mind, witnessed by every fiber of my being. They weren't mere moments passing by, not ordinary moments.

A few meters away, a frenzied air, land, and sea bombardment unfolded before my eyes. The bustling life of the marketplace was snuffed out in an instant. Everyone fled, abandoning their goods. Some left their money behind. A few merchants managed to close their shops; the majority could only escape. Without hesitation, they ran away under the rain of bullets, tanks, and war-planes bearing down...

Others were martyred in front of our very eyes, falling upon the market stalls that had once provided their daily bread. With every drop of their pure blood flowing into the dust, our hearts bled alongside them. Unearthly yells, pleas, and desperate cries for help came from every direction. No answer came. Oh, how dreadful! All hell had broken loose!

We froze there, perplexed and helpless. All I knew was that we had to do something in a hurry. But where could we go? North? South? East? West? Every way was swallowed by fire and bombardment. There was no place for safety, no escape. Was it a horror movie?

At last we chose to flee with the crowd. As the saying goes, "To die with the many is a mercy." We uttered the *Shahada* many times: In God we trust. Who knows? Death could claim us at any moment...

We escaped. Yet the bombardment did not stop. Bullets kept chasing us. At times we clung to the walls of houses, seeking protection, and at times we hid beneath roofs. So fierce was our terror that we crossed long distances without even realizing it. When no more strength remained for us to continue, we gathered what little will-power was left in us and turned toward an eastern road, thinking it might be safer. But Israeli tanks loomed up ahead, spewing fire and death in our direction. Once more we fled. Death was waiting everywhere.

Unforgettable, agonizing scenes are forever stuck in my mind. Martyrs and the shattered remains of their bodies were scattered in the streets. A frail, elderly, disabled woman was walking barefoot in the middle of the crowd, screaming and pleading for help as blood trickled from a wound on her head. Everyone was lost in their own desperate fight for survival. Some abandoned their families in the chaos.

Everyone was searching for someone. A mother was looking for her sons, screaming, calling, and scanning the faces of passing people in the hope that she might find them. An ambulance paused, unloading lifeless

219

bodies by the roadside to make room for the wounded, whose lives might still be saved. We saw trucks overflowing with martyrs and injured people whose limbs or arms had been torn away. Mothers clutched their children to their chests and ran Leaving their makeshift tents behind, families carried small bags, their faces wracked with sorrow and despair. Injured young men leaning on crutches stood there, unable to run.

Many are the scenes, few are the words. And no brush could ever paint what I have seen.

After hours of exhaustion and suffering, everyone was utterly drained. They collapsed along the roadside, trying to steal a few brief moments of rest before proceeding.

Written on August 25, 2024

Orchid's Mom
Age: 30 years old

It is nearly impossible to imagine, my sweetheart, that your soft body and beautiful hair are still stuck under the rubble of a three-story concrete house. I don't want to imagine that.

Vivid is your voice in my mind before the call was cut off: telling me that you were waiting for me to get you out of the rubble, taking care of your little sister, Carmel, and that you would never leave your shelter as the occupation snipers surrounded you. "I am so afraid that you didn't get out, Mama, that they bombed you while you were embracing each other…" I also don't want to imagine this scene.

You, Orchid, are not just my daughter. You are my friend and my darling. How happy I was when you would sometimes offer me your notes. Your intelligence and eloquence would amaze me. I loved your delicate sense of style, your excitement at being a little princess, twirling around in your fluffy dresses. You are a princess, Orchida. My princess, if only you knew!

I have been searching for you for a long time. I scan the faces of little girls in the hope that I might catch a glimpse of your eyes. I listen closely to every child's voice, hoping to hear your laughter among them. Then, suddenly, fear seizes me, and I stop searching.

I am terrified to find you in another's face. The faces of girls, their braids, their hair, their delicate waists all terrify me. And I am afraid of the word "Mama," when I hear another child calling her mother. I close my eyes and wish the sky would extend its arms and pull me away from this daily torment.

Do you know what has become of me, my darling? Can you imagine how I live now?

My child, Orchid—I lost contact with her and her siblings on December 13, 2023. She was living with her father. The criminal occupation besieged them, prevented them from leaving, and then bombed their house. Since that time, we have been unable to reach the house and remove the rubble.

Written on August 15, 2024

A Tribute to the Martyr Mohammed Jibreel
By His Mother

God, in His infinite grace, blessed me with my son Mohammed at the break of dawn, on a Friday morning, as the first call of "Allahu Akbar" echoed through the skies on May 14. From the very first moment he arrived, a strange fear gripped me, that a nurse might mistakenly swap him with another child. So I pleaded with the nurse to hand him directly to his uncle's wife. She laughed gently at my concern, but I could not help myself.

Mohammed grew into a child. I kept him inside out of fear, away from the chaos of the streets. Yet that very caution led to another fear, that overprotection might dim the spark of his spirit. So I let him go out to play with the children of the neighborhood. Nevertheless, fear consumed my soul, and I would find myself drawing him back in whenever he stepped out.

Mohammed began school, and with that change came another shade of worry. I feared that his marks might fall short, might be dimmer than those of his peers. At that time I delivered his sister, Lynn, through a cesarean. On the fourth day after my surgery, despite my pain and fatigue, I sat by him to help him study for his exams, ignoring my wounds.

By God's grace, Mohammed grew. He became a university student, a young man shaped by diligence and clarity of purpose. He excelled at every stage of his life, and the more he advanced, the harder he worked, the brighter he shone, the more he proved worthy of every hope I had placed in him.

So deep was my bond with my son that every morning, at half past seven, whenever he opened the door on his way to university, I would stand there watching and following him with my eyes, with love and longing, until he disappeared out of my sight. Only then would I close the door, to whisper a prayer and praise the Lord for His generous gift.

Mohammed completed his first university year with high honors, promising me excellence in the next.

But God's love for Mohammed was even greater than mine. In the days leading up to his departure, my beloved son would often repeat a saying: "Whoever longs to meet God, God too longs to meet him." He gave his heart to the Almighty, and the Almighty chose for him not just to live righteously, but to depart with glory. God took him from me, as a martyr. *To God belongs what He gives, and to God belongs what He takes.*

Mohammed did not receive the certificates of this world. Instead, he attained the martyr's crown in the hereafter. What triumph could be greater than that?

I pray that I was faithful to the trust God placed in me, that I upheld the treasure He had given, and that I returned it to Him as the Almighty pleases.

Praise be to God that my only son is a martyr.

Written on August 22, 2024

Name: Nidaa Adel Al-Sharif

Age: 41 years old

We were a dignified, modest family, grateful for the little we had, until October 7, 2023. That morning, I awoke with my children to the roar of merciless, thunderous strikes, launched by the occupying forces upon our city, bringing in terrible massacres. Death and destruction fluxed around us in waves of terror.

It was never enough for the occupiers. They commanded the people of Gaza to evacuate the north. We fled toward the coast, taking refuge in my parents' home. For a brief while, the coast too was evacuated, until only I, my family, and a few relatives remained. The sea became a place of relentless strikes. My mother got wounded, and my brother too. We fled again, this time to the Al-Shifa medical complex. But even there, among the wounded and the dying, we found no mercy. Tanks and shells surrounded us.

We decided to flee south, to a place we were told was "safe." We walked along the road known as Al-Hallabah, step after step, carrying nothing but our children and family. From Al-Shifa to Rafah we walked, not knowing where we were going. No home sheltered us from the biting cold.

When we arrived, we gathered scraps of wood and the blankets we clung to for warmth, and built a tent. The cold wrapped around me, my children, and my family.

This is not just my story. It has become the story of every displaced spirit. We suffered from the scarcity of clean water, the cruelty of rising prices, the spread of disease, and the merciless downpour of winter rain.

And still the war moved us like game pieces. We were told again: "Leave this place." So we moved to the Nuseirat refugee camp. For two months, my children and I lived in the home of my uncle, may God bless him. Then we were displaced once more, this time to my grandfather's home in Deir al-Balah. Again, only two months passed before war found us. My grandfather's house too was struck. By a miracle of God, we survived, but my grandfather was martyred. What an unbearable pain! So we fled again, back into a tent. Then the summer came, and with it the scorching heat, the flies, the illnesses.

O God, have mercy on us, forgive us, and write us among the martyrs. Please, I beg of you…stop the war. War brings nothing but sorrow, nothing but regret.

Written on July 7, 2024

Name: Nurhan Sharif Matar

Age: 35 years old

October 7, 2023, an ominous date etched into our memory, a dark birthmark of our destroyed life, the date when we were denied our homes and our beloveds.

That morning came not with light or promise but with the screams of rockets overhead. We did not understand what was happening. We felt panic and fear. It took only minutes to pierce through—war drums roared. A home beside ours was struck. We were forced to flee. From that moment on, we became wanderers.

Displacement upon displacement. The cruelty of being unrooted. Where to go? We never know. For a time, the pavements were our shelter. Sidewalks became beds. Then came the school, one of the many crowded shelters turned into refuges.

A new chapter of suffering began, one that cannot be captured on a page but only in the long, aching lines of a book. From a home to a tent. No food, no water, no place to rest without fear. I felt a horrendous pressure as I wept for my children's well-being. I rationed one single meal among my children and prayed that it would quiet their cries. Was it ever enough? I cooked what I could over an open fire, until the soot blackened our chests.

"Evacuate Nuseirat." We had barely found uneasy ground. The school that had sheltered us was struck—razed to the ground. Where to now? My soul collided with despair. With nowhere else to go, we turned to the UN clinic in Nuseirat. But its doors, though open, held nothing for us. A month passed. We left, and again we were back at the edge of the road. There we built a small tent. And still the suffering grows.

Isn't it time for this war to end? I raise my voice in a plea: To the world that calls itself free, will you not stop this war?

Written on August 20, 2024

Name: Nisreen Hamdi Al-Koumi
Age: 45 years old

On the morning of October 7, 2023, I sat with my family sipping tea, moments before my children left for school. Then the sound of rockets, a dreadful sound from past wars, shattered the calm. From that instant onward, our lives became hell, turned into a relentless nightmare.

Our electricity and water stopped. Life itself seemed to pause. Schools and institutions had turned into shelters for the displaced. Fathers and sons were consumed with the struggle to secure water, bread, and light from charged smartphones. Fear and anxiety swirled like a dark cloud, haunted by the ever-present thunder of bombardment.

Then came the ominous day, November 7, the day when we fled from Shati Refugee camp to Nuseirat. A terrifying day, a Doomsday. Along the road we saw spine-chilling scenes: corpses strewn everywhere, charred bodies, belongings scattered, tanks, snipers. On that fearful day the Zionist army fired upon us, the displaced, until we moved away from the "safe" passage. We walked on and on, exhausted.

By God's mercy, we eventually found people to help us, God bless them, people who were assisting the elderly, women, and children. We reached a relative in Nuseirat Camp, but alas, we soon wished we had never made it to the camp, for there was no welcome.

Later we sought refuge in Al-Orouba school, where, by God's grace, kind souls welcomed us and offered some solace. We tried to rest, yet soon the planes roared above us as if they had followed us from Shati to Nuseirat. That night was bitter and cold, especially for the children, who slept, hungry and shivering, until we were caught by the dawn light. What should we do? Why had our lives turned into such misery and suffering?

In the shelter-school, life became a series of endless queues—lines for water, for bread, for shelter, for a lavatory. We heard nothing but families arguing and the sounds of bombardment. We cursed the day when we were forced to flee the north.

Then, on December 25, the Zionist army dropped eviction leaflets on the school. The next day we fled again, to Ahmed Al-Kurd school. That day only God knows the suffering we endured, the desperate search for a place to rest.

Once again the lines grew longer, for water, shelter, and bread. The tents got hotter by day and colder by night. We tasted agony silently, weighed down by family stresses. Many of us needed healing that no therapist could provide. Praise be to God, the pain and suffering revealed the truth of many. Skin diseases spread like wildfire. Epidemics followed. Hunger gnawed at our bones. Grief settled on our faces.

All the while the world watched, witnessing our agony and our thousands of martyrs, wounded, and missing, yet it remained silent. We have been left with nothing but sadness, pain and misery in our spirits. What sears the soul most is the quiet erasure of entire families from the civil registry. Is a mother's mourning and grief not enough? Is the pain not yet enough?

Enough! Our hearts have melted; the weight of sorrow has turned our hair gray. Enough pain…enough, enough. My heart is broken with sighs. Enough. To whom shall I complain, when my blood has filled the fields?

Written on August 2, 2024

Name: Aisha Mahmoud Badr

Age: 17 years old

My name is Aisha. I am seventeen years old; I was born and raised in Gaza; and I live in Shuja'iyya. On the morning of October 7, 2023, like every other day, I woke early, preparing to go to school. Then war erupted, the violent clash between the Palestinian resistance and the Israeli occupation. It changed everything. Instead of going to school, we found ourselves grasping for safety, holding each other as the world around us collapsed, since I dwell in a district that lies along the border.

After due consideration, we decided to seek refuge in my aunt's home, just a stone's throw from our own but seemingly a world away from danger. We moved to my aunt's house that very day, our first displacement in this war and, as we then believed, the last.

That night, despite the chaos, we found fleeting moments of laughter and warmth, a brief sanctuary before the storm. We spent but a single night at my aunt's house, as my father and uncles set out to search for a place of greater safety.

We soon moved again, to a shelter in a school called Al-Sabra, west of Gaza. We carried only the essentials. There the reality of war and displacement revealed its harshest face to us. There was no electricity to pierce the darkness of night, for the Israeli occupation cut off electricity to the Gaza Strip. Getting clean drinking water became a torment. As the days passed, food became a rare treasure, and standing in long queues for bread was a daily test of endurance. I would go to one bakery and then another one, standing in long queues in pursuit of a mere loaf or two. At times I would spend the better part of my day doing this, and if I managed to obtain that precious loaf, a wave of indescribable joy would wash over me. Many days, all of my effort and waiting would be in vain, and I would return empty-handed. I lived on a single meal a day, and often hunger would visit me at night, robbing me of sleep. The simple act of brewing tea became a struggle, as we hunted for firewood in the streets across from the school where we had taken refuge. Yes, everything was unbearably difficult.

Time passed, and after Israeli occupation forces severed the north of the Gaza Strip from the south, the days blurred into the nights under the ceaseless bombardment. The sounds echoed from every direction, growing closer with each passing day. Fear crept into my heart. Yet I held onto the belief that we were in a place of safety. After all, we were sheltered within a UNRWA refugee center.

Forty days into our refuge, tanks and armored vehicles advanced into the Sabra neighborhood, leaving death and injury. Fear turned into panic, and we fled into the uncertain streets, leaving behind what little we owned for the second time.

That day, we were spared from death only by a miracle. Our footsteps led us down countless roads until we reached Salah al-Din Street. There we stopped and sat by the roadside, overwhelmed and directionless. East Gaza, where our home is, was no longer safe. West Gaza was occupied by tanks, and in the south of the Strip, which the occupiers claimed was secure, we had neither relatives nor friends.

Still, after agonizing deliberation, we resolved to flee to the southern part of the Strip, and thus a new journey of suffering began. We walked a great distance on foot, until we reached the Israeli checkpoint that divides the south from the north. There we stood for eight hours, waiting, before the Israeli occupation forces allowed us to pass into the south. We waited all that time without food or drink.

Exhausted by fatigue, hunger, and thirst, we had no choice but to keep walking after that, to reach the residential neighborhoods and find a place where we could obtain refuge and solace. Finally we arrived at the Nuseirat refugee camp, and there our family split for the first time. My aunt had taken refuge there, and my father, grandmother, and only sister stayed with her, while the rest of the family—my mother, my four siblings, and I—traveled further, to Zawaida, to my father's cousin's house. Now part of our family was living in Nuseirat, the other part in Zawaida.

We arrived there in the evening. I don't know how I managed to sleep in my exhaustion. When I awoke, I stepped outside into the street, eager to discover the place where I had been brought and to meet its kind-hearted people.

Forty-two days passed in a constant struggle against hunger and soaring prices, before the occupation forces advanced once more, forcing us to flee again and prompting my father to bring my grandmother to stay with us in Zawaida. I had missed her dearly. So the family was reunited once again. But our meeting did not last long. The Israeli occupation forces soon invaded the eastern areas of Zawaida, forcing us to flee yet again, this time to the city of Deir al-Balah.

Our new shelter was a nylon tent, barely five square meters in size, a fragile home in the schoolyard—our new home. It was far too small to lie down in comfortably, yet we lived there for seven months, enduring a bitter winter soaked with rain and a scorching summer. Rainwater leaked into the tent, and on many nights we remained awake, unable to sleep, as the ground beneath us was soaked through. Now, in the summer, the tent is unbearably hot, scorching, more like an oven than a shelter. Truly, as the saying goes, it shields us neither from the heat of summer nor from the cold of winter.

229

Life shrank to endless queues for bread, for water, for the dignity of basic human needs. Before the war, life was so simple. Now, every breath has become a battle, every step a hardship. Yet, through it all, the flame of hope burns quietly within me.

I long for the home I lost, my neighborhood, my friends, in northern Gaza. My journey of displacement is far from over, for the war has not come to an end. I sincerely hope that the day may come soon when we can return to our homes safely.

Written on August 24, 2024

Farah Daghmash
Age: 17 years old

My name is Farah. I am seventeen years old. In my own name, I freely express my thoughts and my being.

Since October 7, 2023, I have been living with my family of five in the heart of Gaza City, amid genocide, in a small shelter, far from the warmth of our home, which was demolished in November by the occupation forces.

I have two sisters: Marah, who is thirteen, and Mira, who is nine. As for the other side of the family, they are now scattered across different countries, due to many circumstances.

Fate decreed that my father be injured during the aggressive bombing. One day he went to perform the *Maghrib* prayer, and during the first *rak'a* the occupation forces bombed the mosque directly above the worshippers' heads. My father sustained a severe injury, and my grandfather and cousins were killed inside the mosque, on November 15, 2023.

That same night, my father was transferred to Al-Ma'madani Hospital. When he arrived, there were many wounded and injured people there already, and the doctors had no time to perform a surgery that would take hours. They decided that the only option was for him to lose one of his legs. My father refused; it was difficult for him to lose a part of himself, and hope continued to hover in him.

The next day, November 16, he was transferred to the Indonesian Hospital. On that very night, the occupation forces demolished our house and the agricultural lands in our region. After nearly a week of my father's stay at the Indonesian Hospital, due to the long list and the multitude of injured people, his turn to undergo surgery finally came, and the doctor fitted a device on his right leg. But when the time came for surgery on his left leg—the injured one that by now needed amputation—the occupation forces besieged the Indonesian Hospital. The doctors and the injured were forced to evacuate. My father's operation was left unfinished.

His condition was critical; he was unable to move or walk, and the location of his injury was sensitive, affecting both his legs and his pelvic area. He was transferred once again, to Al-Ma'madani Hospital, where several doctors agreed that he needed to travel abroad for treatment because of the deep wound on his left leg. Proper care and attention for his injury were not available locally. Unfortunately, this opportunity never came. By the grace of God Almighty, some doctors devoted themselves to his care, but by then my father had surpassed the critical stage by forty percent.

After nearly a month at Al-Ma'madani Hospital, the occupation forces threatened the medical staff and the wounded there, forcing them to evacuate so that they could inspect the hospital. The next day, my father returned home. My mother did everything she could, drawing on her prior experience to care for him, disinfecting and cleaning his wound daily, despite the wound still being sensitive and deep. There was no other choice.

To this day, my father still requires surgery, including another operation on his right leg, where the device was previously installed. That device alone has been insufficient for his recovery; he needs another device that is unavailable here in Gaza. Due to the severe shortage of medical staff, equipment, and supplies, my father remains unable to move or walk. His life is filled with patience and longing, an uncertain present, and a future entrusted solely to God.

Praise be to God. After being cut off from food for many months, after having been forced to taste things beyond what one could imagine, we know that God alone suffices us in everything. His generosity and kindness never cease. Praise be to God, who sheltered us, fed us, quenched our thirst, sufficed us, and made us Muslims.

As a description of the reality I live in: I feel as if I have forgotten how to sleep. Since October 7, 2023, we sleep with our eyes wide open. We are being wiped out every single moment. If it's not me, then it's someone else; if it's not my home, then it's someone else's; if it's not my neighborhood, then it's another area; if it's not my street, then it's the street next to mine. Houses are destroyed entirely, turning to ashes. Sometimes the owners survive only to mourn what they have lost—their years, their health, all that they had invested in their lives. They grieve a home wiped away in mere moments or shattered so severely that it can no longer shelter a living soul.

Children die from bombing, fear, hunger, or illness. The elderly perish. Women and men die. Youths at the peak of their lives die. Girls who were recently engaged or married, or perhaps just gave birth yesterday, die. Here, overnight, one can become the sole survivor of an entire family. Here is where orphanhood knows no age. Here a house becomes no longer a house; the place of the house no longer exists; the street of the house vanishes; the neighbors disappear; the family ceases to live; the owners have vanished. Everything has ended; nothing remains.

Here are the tents. Oh, what can I tell you about tents? I do not know how to describe them! They are tiny, yet they're supposed to be homes to us—I mean a home in every sense: people, kitchen, comforts, expenses, and so many other things. Yet, in fact, even tents are not available to many!

Here you must live in a tent where the rain of winter falls unhindered and where the summer sun beats down relentlessly. Here, you are a displaced person who must move from your home to a tent, or perhaps to a street corner, and this displacement will lead to yet another displacement after a short while. Maybe after only a day, you will have to move again, or maybe you won't even have the chance to move again. The tent itself has become one of the most vulnerable and threatened places, a place that might be bombed with all the things inside it, destroyed in a matter of seconds, without prior warning!

Here, suffering is endured for a single sip of potable water, or for a morsel of sustenance, for a shelter in which to spend the night, for a burden placed upon you, simply because there is no other choice. Here, even if you sleep with eyes wide open, you may never awaken except at the Hour of the Day of Judgment.

Here, the smoke rising from relentless bombing never ceases, engulfing the entire city. Here, every form of torture, killing, and starvation fall upon the living and the dead alike. Here, you fall asleep today and wake up tomorrow, if you wake at all, with military machinery at your doorstep. Here, a siege is declared in the very place where you are already besieged, leaving you a martyr, or perhaps a prisoner, or forced to witness the torture and killing of those around you, before your own turn comes, or doesn't, leaving you in endless sorrow.

Here, the mosques have been bombed. No call to prayer has been heard for ten months—glory be to God and to the Muslims. Here, churches, hospitals, kindergartens, schools, universities, and most institutions, whatever they may be, have been bombed.

Nearly a year has passed, and my final high-school year has been lost. I always wished that this year would end with joy, excellence, and hard work, that I could achieve the highest grades and fulfill my dream—which I still dream—of becoming a dentist. But now this is the reality for every student, whether a child in kindergarten, a grade-school student, or a university student, at whatever stage they have reached. This year has been lost, and the pursuit of education has been disrupted.

Here, there is no news coverage, no responding ambulances, no civil defense to protect families. Here, phone service and the internet are cut off for long periods of time.

Here, there is a great scarcity of many essentials, even those considered to be necessities of life—important things that once meant so much.

Here, the 365 square kilometers are divided into several sections: the north, which itself has subdivisions; the center, which is also subdivided; and the south, with its own divisions. Yet you cannot even travel within the section where you are staying. Here, you cannot visit the sea, the city's only breathing space, which lies only a few steps away from where you are. Here, there is a curfew from sunset to sunrise. Anyone found outside during these hours is risking their soul in the palm of their hand.

Here, the south contains what the north does not, and the north perhaps holds what the south lacks, and yet you cannot move between them. The distance between north and south is only an hour by vehicle, or perhaps more than an hour on foot. Yet both north and south endure suffering beyond what one person could witness.

Here, we face the whole world, with all its oppression, occupation, betrayal, silence, and shame. We cannot leave, nor can we stay. Here, we lack the feeling of security even in the smallest moments of this unjust life— security that this city has never known since its creation, stability that we have never known since our births.

Here, regardless of your age, your sole concern must be to survive the day with your people, to secure your daily sustenance, and then to wait for nightfall, hoping to survive until the next morning. Here, death speaks more to us than we speak of life. Here, hearts and souls are utterly exhausted. Here, clinging to a shred of hope is every drowning man's salvation.

And here we are, breathing the love of life despite everything. Our dreams do not cease, nor do we cease in their pursuit.

Here, we bear witness to God that we are content, and we ask Him to be pleased with us. Here, after all that we endure, we hope to be rewarded by the Lord of all servants. Here, only He can soothe our hearts, strengthen us, and help us. Here, only He will, by His own will, grant us victory over all oppressors. That is never beyond God's power.

Here is Gaza. Here is the city of love and war. Here, war has never ceased since the city's birth. Here is the ache of the heart, for this city was and will always be the dearest to my heart.

Here, we long for the land, for all that it holds, for all who dwell within it. We are those who remain in it!

Written on July 16, 2024

Sanaa Ahmed
\Age: 59 years

I am a lady with three married sons, and five married daughters as well. In the first month of the war, I lost my daughter, her husband, and their children. Only two daughters were left. Time passed restlessly, bringing me more and more loss.

Two months passed, and my eldest son was martyred while seeking an honest livelihood and sustenance for his children. His wife and their children remain, living without a father. They are still young; the eldest is only twelve years old.

After six months of war, my two remaining sons were taken captive, leaving me with no sons at all! The occupiers demolished my home, sparing nothing. They have ruined us, ruined our families, sparing no stone, no son, nothing at all.

O Lord, help us, O Lord, strengthen us!

We have not fled south. This is what we have become, my children and I. Now we suffer hunger, after witnessing countless forms of bitter loss. No flour, no rice is left—no food to silence our hunger, nor to quiet the cries of our little ones. I have embraced a heavy burden not easily borne. My grandchildren and my daughters-in-law are my responsibility, since they have no income to support them. My sons were employed at a meat and barbecue shop; their livelihood was daily. How am I to feed them now?

O Lord, return my sons to me safe…O Lord! My faith in you is great, O Allah; bring me my sons back and to their children, O Allah!

On the day after the withdrawal of the Israelis from Al-Shifa Hospital, on the twentieth day of Ramadan, I went searching for my sons, or at least their bodies. I learned that they were alive but held captive by the Zionists in Naqab Prison.

Has the hour not come for this nightmare to cease? Stop the war.

Written on March 30, 2024

Ghada Ibrahim Harb
Age: 48 years

On the morning of October 7, 2023, we awoke to the relentless sounds of missiles. A wave of terror swept over my children and over the people at large. In about six hours, a severe Israeli bombardment hit everywhere, and there was no safe place to hide. We stayed inside our home for seven days. Every member of our extended family sought shelter in our home. Then we received heartbreaking news: five family members had been martyred.

On October 19, at exactly 6:30 PM, after *Maghrib* prayer, loud voices arose. Trembling with fear and dread, we heard them saying: "Evacuation—the towers will be bombed." We rushed into the streets in fear. Everyone was disoriented. We endured the most difficult time—twelve continuous hours of shelling! Then we headed to Palestine University. That night was filled with panic and fear for children, adults, and the elderly alike.

After the bombardment ceased, we went to inspect our homes and the sources of our families' livelihoods, only to be shocked by the complete destruction. Not a single stone was left one upon another. There was no home left to shelter us. The house that had once sheltered more than thirty-five displaced family members and our children was utterly destroyed. Where could we seek refuge?

We were relocated to Deir al-Balah, to the home of relatives, where we lived for nearly five months. During this period, we faced death several times as houses near us were bombed. We endured great suffering from lack of water, psychological pressure, and hunger.

We decided to move again. Ramadan was nearing. Thus began our life in a tiny tent, no larger than four meters, on a street in Deir al-Balah city, where no safety existed. The biting cold gnawed at our bodies and those of our little ones, while the sounds of bombardment were everywhere. We had to leave the tent twice due to false alerts. We risked our lives in search of water and food, standing in bread lines. It was extremely difficult to obtain necessities, and diseases spread among us, such as polio, jaundice, and skin ailments. Medicines were nowhere to be found.

There is no life suitable for living here. Yet, despite all this, we ask God for help, believing relief is near, God willing. We call upon everyone to stop this crime.

As long as we can still take a breath, there is more to tell in the story. We shall remain persistent, resilient, with hearts united, full of hope in God as we await the imminent victory, by the grace of Allah Almighty.

Written on August 15, 2024

Nima Rabah Attallah Ghattas
Age: 42 years old

In speaking of Gaza's destiny, I always find myself repeating one sentence: "Grief and Gaza are inseparable." Now, amid this tragic circumstance called the "Al-Aqsa Flood," I have come to conclusion that death and Gaza are eternally entwined.

Less than a week into this savage war, my home was shattered, obliterated without warning, burying all the warm memories and fragile dreams we once held dear. Yet, praise be to God, we were unharmed: we had fled just two days before, seeking refuge in the home of a relative in Jabalia / An Nazla. My children cried hysterically and bitterly, grieving their possessions and their toys.

In less than a week, I was forced to flee, first to a school-shelter in Jabalia, which was believed to be safe but was soon revealed to be no sanctuary at all, and then to my daughter's home in Al-Wista-Nuseirat, where the raids were milder but the surge in prices was drastic.

I see with my own eyes what we lack, but I dare not speak of it, for fear my children's hopes will rise like flames I cannot quench. Our financial state has been dire, especially after all physical and emotional contact with my husband was severed. He has remained among the missing until now.

Our voices grew hoarse while flames of anguish ignited within our hearts over the loss of our loved ones, who were unable to reach the south due to a ruthless Zionist checkpoint whose sole purpose was to execute and imprison our rebellious youth.

For three months I have been tending my wounds, wiping away my sorrows, and striving to provide everything my children need, borrowing from my sisters to meet their essential needs. And meanwhile the enemy consciously strives to inflict pain and crush my spirit!

Leaflets of evacuation rained down, warning of an impending ground assault on Al-Nuseirat, followed by ceaseless shelling. We fled from my daughter's home to a school in Zawaida, only to be driven out by another onslaught. Then we went to Deir al-Balah, where tents covered the land, like rows of white shrouds laid out in mourning!

Life beneath these fragile covers feels like a slow death, bitten by the cold of winter, scorched by the cruel sun of summer, overwhelmed by fear and terror, which has established dominion over us. The thin plastic that shields us does not stop the shards of violence from piercing our bodies and souls.

By God, I have failed to provide safety and security for my children, bound though I am to do so, thanks to my helplessness. At last I have surrendered my affairs in the court of this earth, for the court of the heavens; the world has become too narrow before my eyes. I have done all that I can for my children, and I beg their forgiveness when my weary hands cannot cradle their needs; the conditions have been mightier than any of us.

This is a genocide, a violation of international laws, a contempt for the sacred blood of Gaza. Let all know that before October 7, 2023, I had a beautiful home. Now, as a mother of ten with no provider, I wander from one shelter to another, following the evacuation leaflets' orders.

Written on August 22, 2024

Afnan Ghattas
Age: 23 years old

No words or lines can suffice to recount what I have endured during this war. Yet I shall endeavor to gather the essence of my suffering and convey it.

My story of displacement began on October 7, 2023, the day I left my home. I departed with hope for a swift return. I went to Jabalia, believing it to be safer than my home, as it lay somewhat farther from the border. But no place is safe when the Israelis' shadow looms everywhere. The bombardment was fierce, and I could not grasp what was happening.

Our situation did not last long. Soon we had to move again, chasing the illusion of security. I went to Nuseirat, a decision made in the midst of pain, but nothing hurt more than seeing my family break apart before my eyes. Some stayed behind, guarding what was left, others went to Jabalia, and the rest with me went to Nuseirat. As the eldest, I carried a burden of responsibility I never expected, the weight of my siblings' lives resting on my shoulders.

Then the occupiers drew their cruel lines, separating north and south, and my mother came to us, trying to unite our torn family. Yet, bereft of backing without the cornerstone of our home, my father chose to stay alone in the north.

The situation worsened more and more. At that time, we knew nothing of my father. We waited, longing for even a single piece of news to soothe our hearts. Here came another difficult decision.

We made the hardest choice ever: to leave Nuseirat for Rafah, which we believed to be the safest place. I gathered our belongings, and we went there, to my grandfather's. I thought he would welcome us warmly; it had been a long time since he had last seen us, and surely, I thought, he must have missed us.

But his response was shocking: "I have no room for you."

We returned, broken, tears tracing silent paths down our cheeks, lost and wondering where to go, haunted by thoughts of my father. Yet we did not surrender. We moved on to Zawaida, determined to rise again, stitching together the scattered remnants of our spirits. We had no one to ease our burden or help us bear this heavy responsibility.

Then, on an ominous day, came the cruel blow—news of my father's injury and his transfer to a hospital. Not long after, the army stormed the hospital and took him away. Since that moment, we have known nothing of his fate.

Still the horrors did not cease. One dreadful night, driven by terror, we fled once more from Zawaida to Deir al-Balah, where we stitched a fragile tent.

Nothing can truly capture the depth of the suffering we endure here, from the bitter cold of winter and the scorching heat of summer. The insects never leave us, and infectious diseases spread all around. To make matters worse, we are in a place where we know no one.

Yet here we are, fighting every day, struggling each and every day to stay alive.

Written on July 28, 2024

Ahlam Adel Abu Dhaher
Age: 39 years old

People tend to exaggerate everything, even their sorrows—except what we have gone through during this time of distress. It's been like something out of a dream, almost unreal. I find myself compelled to speak, not exaggerating. I have seen my own end, my death, with my very eyes. Yet I continue to move forward, carrying the unbearable weight of survival.

There are six children who need someone to lean on, to feel a glimpse of the safety we lost on October 7, 2023, the day my journey of suffering truly began. Never mind the poverty and hunger that we endured before the war, or our barely standing house, because even in that fragile life we had our most beautiful days, our sweetest memories. Perhaps, just perhaps, they might return.

The war began, and so did the journey of our displacement—my husband, my children, and I—leaving behind our home in Al-'Amoudi, in the north of Gaza City. My children gathered what was left: our clothes, a gas cylinder, a sack of flour. We thought the war would pass quickly. We didn't know it would last this long. Yet it stretched ahead, each day heavier than the last.

We left our home and went to my parents' house in Al-Nasr neighborhood. I waited for a while until the bombardment stopped, so I could go out. But even that was nearly impossible. The car finally arrived. My husband, my children, and I left, gripped by fear. Along the road, I saw houses collapsed upon their inhabitants on both sides, the scent of death heavy in the air, and ambulances racing in every direction.

Our stay with my parents was not long. Homes were already destroyed; others were marked for evacuation. I spent ten days there, paralyzed by fear, caught between doubt and certainty, my emotions in turmoil. I could hear the voices of neighbors fleeing one after another, and I stood there, overwhelmed and torn: where should I go now? I held my phone tightly and began calling my friends, my neighbors, my sister, and the one brother I still have in Gaza. The rest of my family had emigrated a decade ago to a European country. Every voice I reached spoke the same truth: "There is no safe place."

I left my parents' house for the Al-Shati (Beach) UNRWA School, where my sister was sheltering. The place was flooded with people. We sat waiting for my husband, who had left us to search for a safer place, a place that could hold the weight of our heartbreak. He returned, and I saw him from a distance, waving his hands in helplessness. There was no space.

We left the school for Al-Mughraqa, in central Gaza, to stay with my sister-in-law. But we didn't stay long. Israeli threats loomed over every place, and the bombardment was relentless. I became convinced: God's mercy is wider than all this devastation, for no place has been safe since this war began. We moved again, to Al-Nuseirat, in a public school. Life regressed to its most primitive form: cooking over open fires, baking bread on stones. No doctor on earth could erase the marks left by the smoke and heat, the lines of hardship across our faces and bodies.

But our time there was also cut short. The occupation forces declared the area unsafe and dropped leaflets demanding evacuation. So we fled once more, to Deir al-Balah, and another public school. We no longer dreamed of the luxury of rented apartments. Again the suffering returned, as if it had never left.

Still we endure the silence of the world, the indifference to the cries and groans of our children. Harsh days, days so dry and barren… Perhaps they are the "lean years" preceding the blessed seven ears of grain. Surely, one of us will manage to survive this somehow. But for others, these days will cost them their very lives.

Written on August 25, 2024

Suheir Al-Lababidi
Age: 40 years old

How exquisite is the morning in my homeland! I never knew that this one would be my last beautiful morning. I awoke to a dawn unlike any other. It was the morning of October 7, 2023. Is there anyone among us untouched by the memory of that fateful day?

On mornings past, I would rise from my warm bed, wrapped in clean sheets. I would wake to the sweet songs of birds, the laughter of children flooding the streets, my favorite cup of coffee, and the call of the seller of sesame bread. Never did I imagine that this morning before would be the final one to hold such beautiful details.

On that morning of October 7, I awoke to the thunder of missiles launched from every direction, as if the Day of Judgment had come. Everyone jumped from their beds in terror. This was no dream. It was the beginning of a nightmare. I still remember how my children ran to me, one after another, trembling in fear. I had no answers; I was just as lost, just as terrified. I did not know what was happening.

Soon the news began to pour in. The picture began to sharpen. The alarm bell tolled. If only I had known then that it was the beginning of the end, the end of everything I called mine, the end of my dreams, the end of my ordinary, beautiful days!

The enemy started to send messages, one after another, laden with threats: "You must leave." Leave? To where? This was the most agonizing trial of my life. Should I stay? But what about my children? Should I leave? How? Where to? No, it was impossible.

Terror spread like wildfire. There was no time to think, and the warnings kept coming.

"Will you stay? Will you go?"

I had no answer. My mind ceased to think. Families began to flee, one by one. Homes emptied of their people. Everyone was escaping the grip of inevitable death. I stood there, frozen in place, wrung with pain as I saw every neighbor, every friend, and every loved one who departed.

Despite many desperate attempts to persuade me to leave, I stayed behind with those who had chosen to remain. But guilt gnawed at me every second. *You stubborn fool, how can you gamble with your children's lives? What good will it do you?*

The hour of truth struck. This was war, in its most merciless form! I felt as though I had descended into hell itself. The planes began to rain fire upon houses, upon streets, upon anything that stood. Nothing was spared. I could hear the groaning collapse of buildings nearby, and with each one I too collapsed a little further inside.

War had begun in earnest. Terror gripped every soul. Children screamed, seeking refuge with their parents, searching for peace. I still remember: I was preparing breakfast. The streets outside were empty, silence reigned. Then we heard approaching bulldozers. The ground began to tremble beneath our feet. Soon afterward, the roar of artillery echoed from every direction. Everyone scattered in panic. The enemy's tanks were here. We had never heard them before.

Everyone rushed to the basement beneath the house, seeking refuge from the storm of fire above. Time itself seemed to stand still in the face of such terror. Everyone blamed themselves: *If only I had left!* Looking at my children, I blamed myself more than anyone. What had I done? What sin had my children committed to deserve this? And what solace could such questions bring now?

Voices rose in desperate supplication, pleas, prayers, and cries to the heavens, begging for salvation. We did not know that we would spend nearly a month inside that basement without a whisper or a light. We would seize fleeting moments of silence to feed our children. We could not go back to our homes. Life as we knew it became the basement.

The first day passed, and the tanks returned, unleashing fire upon everything. We could hear the stones crashing down above our heads. Each person was silently wondering: *Was it my house that just collapsed?* I remember it well—how fear, like a dark tide, swept over us until all that remained was trembling flesh and weary souls. That night my children and I lay upon the bare ground. Weariness had drained us to the bone.

Night gave way to day, and with it came a desperate cry outside our home. Some of the men rushed out to see. It was our Christian neighbour, trying to reach the nearby church, but a quadcopter drone had opened fire on her. The men tried to help, breaking the chained gate, but each attempt was met with gunfire. The drone struck ruthlessly. Alas, the men could do nothing. Night fell again. We kept checking on her, moment after moment, with pity for her helplessness. She was only a meter away, O God, yet utterly beyond our reach! We couldn't save her.

We were whispering words of comfort to her from behind the door when suddenly the tanks returned with deafening fury. The thunder of artillery filled every corner; shouts of fear and desperate pleas rose from all around. The shelling raged on, mercilessly, for more than four hours, before a fragile hush fell over the ruins.

As ever, we were left shattered, our bodies weary, our spirits burdened, and our hearts aching. What, I wondered, had become of our

Christian neighbor? Everyone had drifted into restless sleep. But as the first light of dawn broke through, one of the men slipped quietly out the back to check on her. He returned, visibly shaken. We rushed to him, asking: "What did you see? Did she survive? Is she still alive?" He said, a rasp choking his voice, "The tank...crushed her. Flattened her into the ground."

O God! How could this happen? She was frail, elderly, helpless. How could they commit such cruelty against her?

Days began to pass in a haunting sameness. We were consumed by fear, exhaustion, and a surrender to God's will. At every passing hour, we anticipated our own deaths. We were living through hell itself. Our food supplies began to dwindle. Drinking water was no longer available. Would we perish from hunger and thirst, or by the enemy's shell? We did not know. Time had lost all meaning. Each day seemed to fold into the next, like a nightmare endlessly repeating itself. We felt dead, dead. We had nothing left but prayer, unceasing, desperate prayer.

The days crawled by; we found ourselves surviving on crusts of bread and sips of brackish water unfit for human intake.

Then...a ceasefire. Praise be to God! After a month of torment, fatigue, and gnawing hunger, we were allowed to go up again to our homes, to search for food and water, to search for life. "We shall live. We are still alive. We have survived."

We all poured into the streets. Some found their homes scarred yet standing. Others found only wreckage, splinters of lives once whole. Destruction blanketed every inch—the houses, the alleys, the roads. All the corpses had decomposed, and the reek of death filled the air.

The dead were buried right on our street, in front of the houses. It didn't matter anymore; the only thing that mattered was for the war to stop. We still held onto the hope that the war would come to an end. Some families came to our building, fleeing in fear of the war's return. I still remember a ten-year-old girl, pleading with her grandfather to take her to her uncle's house after their home was hit by shells and her baby sister died. She begged him desperately—before the truce expired and the tanks and planes started striking again, ferociously.

We had not yet regained our strength. What was happening? Once more, war had returned, more savage than ever, like a storm unleashed without warning. Dust choked the sky, stones rained down. I felt as though the entire building were crumbling beneath our feet.

We all rushed again to the basement. Moments later, a sound pierced the chaos—a cry, a wail, choked with anguish. It was the mother of the little girl who had begged her grandfather to bring her to this place, believing it would be safer. The child had died, struck by a shell in the head. Yes, she was dead. Her brother had been wounded in the eye.

The little girl lay lifeless until the Red Cross arrived, after many desperate pleas, and took her away. We begged them, "We want to leave. We need anyone who can to protect us and secure our path." Our pleas fell on deaf ears.

We stayed, and the situation worsened. We returned to the endless routine of living in the basement, in fear. Who among us would survive, and who would perish? It was as if we were trapped in a never-ending movie, *The Game of Death!* Days passed as though they were a repetition of October 7, looping endlessly, time frozen around us. But no. Life pressed on.

Our neighbor was eight months into her pregnancy. Yes, her time was drawing near. I would watch her and wonder, *Is she afraid?* She always pretended to be strong, speaking softly to her unborn child: "You will come safely. I will hold you, breathe with you. Rest easy, little one. You will see me."

The labor came on a night that, I remember, was unlike any other—quiet, still, with everyone asleep. I saw her, felt her pain. Her suffering grew more intense. We all knew what had to be done. She bore her pain silently, for this was not a hospital, this was the basement.

I still remember her silent suffering—how brave she was! While everyone else slept, I quietly went up to her home with a neighbor, just the two of us. Thank God, it took no more than half an hour. The baby was born safely, cradled in God's care. We had nothing but a laundry clip and some rudimentary items that might help, and yet she did it.

Another neighbor had kept asking, "When is the baby due?" We would laugh, wondering why he cared so much. He asked again and again, until the child was born. Only then did we understand his insistence: he had been hiding a small chicken, preparing it as a meal for the new mother, knowing that she would need nourishment. She was touched by his gentleness and deeply grateful.

The baby, this beautiful angel, joined our family in the basement, living out days with no change whatsoever. Nothing altered but the features of the little one, which changed with every passing day.

One day, the illusive calm of our devastated city fooled us. There was no sound of the enemy's machinery, no buzz of the cursed drones overhead. It seemed that they had withdrawn from our area. Anticipation began to rise. Truly, there was no sound at all. It seemed as if they had moved away.

One by one, everyone hustled back to their homes. How eager we were for everything—our plates, our dinner tables! We longed for the smallest comforts: sitting on our sofas, lying down on our abandoned beds without fear. Oh, how bitter it is to lose that feeling of safety! Just standing and looking out the window was a risk, but we yearned to see our streets, our houses, our cars...

If only we had not looked! It was as if an earthquake had struck the entire area. O God! What devastation was this? At last the locked door to our building was opened. We stepped cautiously onto the street, trembling with fear. Truly, the drone that had watched our every movement was gone. This was our chance.

The men began searching for places where lentils, rice, and legumes might be found. Flour was scarce, and food was nearly gone. Praise be to God, they managed to secure some provisions to keep us alive a little longer.

Days passed—one, two, three. Everyone moved carefully, cautiously. Two brothers in their late fifties ventured out to secure some necessities for their families, after much pleading, despite the danger that was looming heavily over the streets.

I remember my husband and son went that day to my family's house, since they had left everything behind, to secure some food for us. I was terribly afraid. I kept myself busy tidying the house; dust and stones lay in every corner. I watched the clock nervously. They were late!

Then I heard the cursed drone. Panic swept over me. I ran to the neighbors and asked for help. My husband and son were still out! How could I warn them not to approach the street? The drone had returned, and there was no way to contact them. *O God, keep them safe, keep them safe...* Then the enemy arrived. The sound of gunfire poured like rain. I screamed, "My son is gone!" I was screaming as bullets rained down. I heard my husband shouting, "Open the door!" The door was locked with bolts, and the gunfire never ceased.

Praise be to God, my husband and son returned safely. They had taken shelter at the corner by the door. Thanks and gratitude to You, O Lord! But I broke down. I could hardly believe, amid the hail of bullets, that they would come back alive. Thank you, Lord.

Once more the tanks returned, and we retreated again into the basement. Our neighbors, the two brothers, had not come back yet! How could we warn them that it was no longer safe? How could we tell them not to come near? The situation was perilous.

Their absence stretched on for two weeks. We remained as we were, with the same routine, the same fear. We comforted their wives, assuring them that, God willing, the two men would come back. Days passed—each one, for the two wives, like a year. The military vehicles eventually withdrew once more, yet still the brothers did not return.

We waited for days with no news. Their sons went out to search for their fathers, asking people around for news. A man claimed that he had seen them, had even helped one of them, and said he had been wounded in the leg. Another claimed that he had driven two men matching their descriptions to the hospital. Yet the sons looked in vain; there was no trace at all.

Where did they go? Were they taken by the army? Were they martyred and buried in the streets like so many others? Why didn't they come back? The two fathers' absence lasted nearly a month. No one knew their fate; everyone remained in bewilderment. What had happened to them? Where could they be?

Finally some people found them. They had been searching for firewood in a field near us, and came upon two decomposed bodies. O God... We had been searching everywhere, while they lay dead so close to us! A shell had struck them as they tried to reach home.

I remember how hard that day was. Words of consolation fell short, neither sufficing nor soothing. It was our fate, our destined share. God grant us patience, for we are believers.

The days passed as they always did, until at last one ominous day arrived. There was a firestorm in our street. One by one, all the buildings collapsed into ruin. It was then that I made the decision to flee. I grabbed my bag of papers, held my children's hands, and we rushed away.

O Lord, be with us... I bid farewell to my companions, my home, and my dreams. It was the beginning of the end. We walked a long distance, and we passed through the checkpoint. How did I do it? I do not know! I was walking among the enemy's tanks, wondering, *Will I survive? Will they take me? Or take my husband?* Those were moments that took one's breath away. My heart felt as if it would stop from fear, but, thank God, the soldiers were distracted by prisoners—handcuffed, barefooted, naked, being deported to the army.

We passed through. A car belonging to a friend awaited us. I could hardly believe myself. I had escaped from the hell of Gaza, and we still survived, O God! I watched the people, the gatherings, the noisy cars. There was a market, vegetables, food... None of this existed in Gaza!

At first glance, I felt as if I were in paradise. But alas, where was my family? All of them had traveled abroad. I was alone with my children in the middle of the unknown, inside a small tent. We burned under the scorching sun and froze in the winter days. We were in Rafah, the place the enemy bets on. And so began a new journey of agony.

Every night I weep with longing. How beautiful my home had been, with all its warmth, and I would wonder: *Where is my pillow? Where is my cup of coffee? Where is the chirping of the birds? Where are my family and friends, my school and the voices of children? How was I deprived of all this in a single day?* Everything was taken from me. I have lost everything.

I tried to console myself: *It does not matter. What really matters is that my children are safe.* But I still miss those little details. They are part of me, and I never truly valued them until they were gone. How wonderful my daily routine was, though I grew weary of it! If only it could return; how wonderful it was!

I could no longer see the beauty of my homeland. I knew that nothing of my old life would return. But still I was determined to overcome this ordeal, just as I had overcome my grief, the loss of my loved ones, and the panic attacks I endured. I still had the strength to do so.

Then the evacuation order came to Rafah. Where to, this time? Where was I to go? The world had grown unbearably narrow for me!

Thee was no time to waste. We dismantled our tent and moved to a piece of land in Deir al-Balah, where my close friend lives. For the first time, I had come upon a soul akin to mine! I wept with bitter sorrow for all that had befallen us. How had we ended up here?

The enemy still struck everywhere. It is a war of extermination, where no place is safe. Not everything said about the war is to be believed. Take the truth from the reality we are living through. Here I am, with my friend, all of us, in this small corner of the universe. You in the outside world see and hear nothing of us but fragments of scenes and captured images. The truth is what no eye has seen, no ear has heard, except our own.

We are still living through hell, with no shelter, no hygiene, no safety. We continue our journeys of homelessness here and there. Praise be to God for granting me the time and life to write my story. I do not know the end of it. The end will be my fate, either survival from death or survival into death. Both have become one, for we are buried alive, we die alive.

We die of fear, we die of hunger, we die of oppression, we die of humiliation. And so the death of the body has become salvation from all kinds of death! How cruel is this journey through hell!

Save us. Have mercy on us. Kill us silently. End our agony. We are the ones most worthy of a merciful death.

Written on July 20, 2024

PART THREE: THE YOUNG MEN'S STRUGGLES

Mohammed Al-Masri
Age: 19 years old

Until the day before the siege of Al-Shifa Medical Complex, I had been living there with my family. On the following day, just as the call to *Maghrib* prayer echoed through the air, the Israeli occupation troops ordered all the young men in the complex to descend to the ground floor. We were ordered to organize ourselves into groups, and the army officials called each group, one by one, into the courtyard of the complex. My father, my uncles, a few friends, and I formed a group of five.

The army call for our group filled me with dread. Suddenly, one of the officers told me to step forward. Tension and fear played havoc with my nerves. I obeyed. He ordered me to strip off all my clothes except my underwear and hand over all my personal belongings, keeping only my ID card.

The air was bitterly cold. Rain was falling heavily upon us. They forced me to sit on the wet ground, stripped of everything. I remained there for two hours. Then a soldier came and took me into one of their buildings. He recorded my details, then cuffed my hands tightly, with a plastic zip tie behind my back, and blindfolded me. I could not move. The cold bit into my skin, making my exhausted body shiver with cold.

The men beside me were called, and the officers conducted field interrogations with them. The sounds of beating and torture were terrifyingly loud. Once a man had been interrogated, he would be dressed in a white nylon robe and placed far from the rest. The officers did this with most of the young men around me. Whispers spread, saying that anyone dressed in white was marked for immediate execution.

I was waiting for my turn for interrogation, not knowing what would happen. A soldier came to the few who were still waiting and began to beat us savagely. Afterward, he loaded us into a truck—an open-roofed bus to expose us to the cold and the unrelenting rain. With no trace of mercy or compassion, they herded us into the truck.

We were so anxious. None of us knew what our fate would be. Why were they treating us this way? Where were they taking us?

The truck moved faster than light, it seemed. All the way, the soldiers continued to beat us half to death. The journey lasted nearly five hours. It ended up by throwing us into the hands of a new military group, and they too greeted us with beatings.

We were separated into groups again and moved to different vehicles that took us to a prison. Upon arrival, the soldiers forced us out of the vehicles with more blows and curses. We were ordered to sit on the ground for hours.

Then I was brought before a doctor who asked, "Do you suffer from any diseases?" The doctor wasn't there to serve our medical needs but to take note of our physical weaknesses, so that they would increase torture on these parts.

I told him that both my arms had been previously broken, a platinum implant in my left leg had recently been removed, and a disc had slipped in my back. He examined my body and found a gunshot wound. He asked about it, and I ended up in a special interrogation.

After a long time, a soldier untied my hands and ordered me to remove my underclothes. Then he handed me dismal gray garments, including pants five sizes too big and a shirt that hung loose over my body. I was forced to wear them. Then he put heavy metal cuffs on my hands and feet. At that moment, I realized that I had been imprisoned.

The soldier continued to beat me as we walked along the route to my prison cell. I was taken to Barracks Prison, a large metal barracks made of corrugated iron, encircled by barbed wire, and heavily guarded by soldiers outside.

They brought me inside, and I was approached by the assistant correctional officer, known as Shawish. He began explaining the prison rules to me. I was not allowed to speak to the person next to me, not allowed to remove the blindfold from my eyes under any circumstances, and not allowed to sleep unless I got approval from the army officer and had a medical reason. If he agreed, I'd be allowed to sleep for only ten minutes. I couldn't move from my place without the Shawish's permission. If I broke any of these rules, I would be subjected to punishment.

The Shawish led me inside the barracks, which were divided into two cellblocks: Section A and Section B. Each cellblock contained around a hundred and twenty people, so the total number of detainees was about two hundred and forty. Outside the cellblock, numerous soldiers stood guard and constantly watched the prisoners.

As I entered, the Shawish chose a spot for me to sit in. I was utterly exhausted. My body was numb from the beatings I had endured. Moreover, I was starving: I hadn't eaten in two days. It was the holy month of Ramadan.

I sat down and asked the Shawish if he could bring me some food, because I was hungry. He asked the soldiers to bring me something to eat, but they refused. They told him I had to wait until the designated meal-time.

My exhausted body lay down to rest. Suddenly the army officer called out for me and ordered the Shawish to take me to the gate. He punished me because I hadn't asked for permission to lie down. I was forced to stand for two hours with my hands raised above my head—the standard punishment inside the prison. They punished me with this method many times, at least once or twice a day. They punished me and others for the most trivial errors. Sometimes the officer would drag me out just to beat me severely—another form of punishment they often used.

After that first punishment I returned to my place, waiting for permission to sleep. Two hours later the officer arrived, and finally it was time to sleep. Our covers were thin blankets, useless in that cold. We were dressed in clothes that offered no warmth at all. My body was trembling from the cold. I asked the Shawish if I could have another blanket, but the soldiers refused to give me another. My body was about to freeze. In that prison, the cold itself was one of their torture methods.

It was not only the cold that stole sleep from my eyes; the iron handcuffs on my hands and the storm of thoughts in my mind also deprived me of sleep. I cudgeled my brain, trying to find an answer. What would happen to me now? What had happened to my family? What would be their fate? My body was worn out by pain, hunger, cold, and overthinking. Unconsciously, I would fall asleep.

All night the soldiers outside played football, shouting and yelling at the top of their lungs to disturb us and keep us from sleeping.

When the *Fajr* prayer approached, the soldiers brought us a suhoor meal: four slices of dry toast, a tiny dollop of cheese barely filling a spoon, and one small tomato. It was not enough to satisfy any hunger, and barely enough to keep us alive—nothing more. I ate with trembling hands, my body still shaking from the cold. After the prayer, they allowed us to sleep for half an hour only. Then they woke us all up and forced us to sit motionless for the rest of the day.

Going to the bathroom was a story in itself. You had to send a request to the Shawish and wait for your turn—half an hour, an hour, two hours. Each time, it felt harder to wait than the time before. We entered the bathroom handcuffed and blindfolded. For showers, each prisoner was allowed only four minutes. The water was unbearably cold, and the soldiers would shamelessly peek at us while we washed. We wore the same clothes every single day.

Unleashing the army's specially trained dogs on the prisoners was a common torture method. The soldiers would let the dogs scratch us with their claws. They were vicious animals, wild and terrifying. We were horrified by them. Sometimes the soldiers made the dogs urinate on our bodies or even defecate on us, while they stood by, watching and laughing loudly.

Dear human being who is reading this, imagine living only to be beaten, tortured, insulted, and deprived of sleep, food, and any form of comfort! They forbade us everything God has permitted.

Days passed...until, one day, an army officer called my name. I answered. He unshackled my hands only to secure them again behind my back, and shackled my feet together. Then he ordered me to walk forward. For about half an hour, soldiers beat me mercilessly, until at last they brought me to an unknown place equipped with a computer, which looked like an office.

A soldier uncuffed my hands and removed the blindfold from my eyes. I sat there waiting until an officer from the interrogation department walked in. He started questioning me, and I answered him. He interrogated me about every detail, big and small. He accused me of things I had never done.

The interrogation lasted about an hour and a half. When it ended, I asked him if I could make a phone-call to my father, to tell him I was still alive and being held by the Israeli Occupation Forces. He refused. He told me that they would notify the Red Cross to provide my father with the details of my circumstances.

After that I left the interrogation room, not knowing my fate. I had no idea what would happen to me next. I was taken away by the soldiers once again. They shackled me, blindfolded me, and transported me on a bus. Throughout the ride they kept beating me, until I was brought to a new prison, full of new faces.

The soldier brought me in to meet the new Shawish. Again he explained the rules, and he told me that this place would be even harder than the one I'd been in before.

He found me a spot, and I sat down. A storm of questions raged in my mind. My destiny remained a mystery, hidden in the shadows of the unknown. Here I was, imprisoned without any charges brought against me. I had been interrogated and moved again, and yet no conclusions had been made. I didn't know how many more days I'd be imprisoned.

The same suffering was repeated here—no food, no sleep, no words. My memories of the holidays, their joy, the gathering of my family, Gaza itself and its beauty—all of these memories made that prison different from the previous one. They cut me to the bone, but I couldn't stop the pain. All I knew was that I was in the custody of the Israeli Occupation Forces, locked in their prisons, being tortured, beaten, and humiliated. No one outside knew what had become of us. I had no idea what fate awaited me. I couldn't even speak with a lawyer and ask for help in getting out of this place. Everything felt impossibly difficult.

I began talking to some of the other men in secret, asking them to memorize my father's phone number. Maybe one of them would be released before me and could let my father know where I was. They kept transferring the prisoners, but we never knew what fate awaited those who were moved.

Eventually they transferred me to a second cell block, with the excuse that I had been a "troublemaker" in the previous one. In this new block, I didn't know a single soul. It was strange place with new faces but the same brutal rules.

The next day an officer called my name, so I stepped to the gate. He took me outside and forced me to undergo another interrogation, similar to the first one I had been through. They wrote the details of the interrogation on a paper titled "Statement." This type of questioning was called "Intelligence."

I asked the officer, "How long will I remain here in prison?"

He answered, "Until you die."

In that moment, I lost the last flicker of hope that I would one day reunite with my family.

Asking the officer that question exposed me to more torture. Then I was transferred to a new place, harsher and more unbearable.

The soldiers didn't allow us to use the bathroom except at specific times. Showers were permitted only once a week. The so-called meals were constantly delayed and consisted of scraps of food that couldn't nourish our hungry bodies.

After a while I grew used to it; I had been there for a long time. I lost all hope as I waited for my freedom. I was humiliated, beaten, and tortured. No one in the outside world knew what we were enduring. No one rose in protest against this occupation. No one cared. We remained there for so many days.

One evening an officer came and called my name along with those of a few other men. We stepped out. They shackled our feet and cuffed our hands behind our backs, then led us to a bus. We were moved to four consecutive locations, all similar to the previous place. The journey, as always, was filled with brutal beatings. In each of the four locations we sat for two hours, and then a soldier would call our names again, and again we'd be moved to another place.

The beatings and humiliation never stopped, until finally we arrived at a small new place. It seemed strangely luxurious. We sat there, and they brought more men, until a certain number had been reached. Then they told us to sleep.

Later, around midnight, an officer came and woke us up. He began taking us out of that prison one by one. He replaced the iron handcuffs on our wrists with plastic ties. At that moment, I thought perhaps we might be released back to our homeland, or else transferred to a new and strange location far away from where we had been. Or it could be an execution order. Death.

I was very worried. No one uttered a word about our fate; we had no idea where we were going. We sat in a large bus. After an hour it started moving.

Then something strange happened. The soldiers didn't beat us; they didn't humiliate us as they usually did. The silence was uncanny. Something strange was happening.

Four hours passed on the road. We arrived at a wide-open square. The army cut the plastic cuffs off my wrists and led us off the bus. Then they removed the blindfold from my eyes.

I saw a massive number of soldiers, tanks, and enormous military vehicles that I had never seen before. My eyes throbbed painfully because I had been blindfolded for so long. The soldiers arranged us in a line and handed me back my ID. In that moment, I realized that we were finally being released.

A military officer spoke to us, informing us that we had indeed been freed and that we were now standing at the Kerem Shalom crossing. He ordered us to walk forward without looking back. "Anyone who turns around will be shot," he warned.

I moved forward along with the other men, quickly, on foot. We walked a long distance. I managed to keep moving, but I was utterly exhausted. We hadn't been allowed to walk any distance for a long time. I hadn't seen sunlight in a long time. I hadn't even used my eyes in what felt like ages. I had to walk, but I wasn't capable of walking.

For part of the way, some soldiers strode alongside us. Then they stopped and ordered us to continue on our own. We kept walking until, at last, we reached the Palestinian side of the crossing. There we were met by staff from the Red Cross.

The terrifying ordeal was over. The humiliation and misery had ended. I was free! I could go back to my family, my relatives, and my friends. It was a moment of joy beyond description.

I asked a UNRWA staff member if I could make a phone call. He requested first that I wait a little while, so they could complete some administrative procedures. He took my details and then handed me his personal phone.

Though I was eager to call my father and my family, my heart was frightened. I knew nothing about what was happening with them. When the occupation soldiers had taken me, my family had remained at Al-Shifa Medical Complex, but were they still alive?

I took the phone, dialed my father's number, and called. It rang. He answered. I spoke to him. He was overjoyed to hear that I was free! I told him that in a few more hours I would be home with them. Thank God, they were all safe.

The Red Cross staff gave us some advice and offered each of us a small amount of money. Then they told us that we were free to go wherever we wanted. I went up to one of the Red Cross workers and asked him to help me return to my family.

It turned out that I was in the south of the Gaza Strip, while my family was in the north. Between the north and south of the strip stood an Israeli military checkpoint, a barrier that prevented me from going back. I pleaded with the Red Cross to help me return north, but they refused. They said, "It is impossible." The only option was for me to remain in the south, alone.

And so my family is in the north, and the Israeli checkpoint separates us. If I attempt to cross it, I will be killed without hesitation, whether from the land, the sea, or the sky. The idea of returning to my family has become an impossible dream. I am alone in the south of the Strip, far from them. I have no idea what to do, where to sleep, or what to wear. I am constantly hungry; I've been denied food. I have only a little money, not enough to buy anything. A friend welcomed me into his tent, but still I sit alone. I eat alone. I live alone.

Why are my family and I forced to be apart? Why must we remain miserable and isolated?

Stop this war.

Mohammad Mu'in Al-Khodary
Age: 42 years old

A Palestinian teacher from Gaza was pulled alive from beneath the rubble, after his death had already been declared in an Israeli airstrike in Al-Shujayia. Despite the trauma, he didn't hesitate to complete his lifelong mission, teaching.

Al-Khodary launched an initiative to teach the Arabic language to displaced school-aged children in shelter centers. In Gaza, these children awaken to their teacher's voice echoing between the tents, rekindling memories of a life they have lost. He specializes in Arabic-language development in the early years, handwriting, and overcoming learning difficulties. Al-Khodary's initiative seeks to rebuild the shattered academic memories of children in ways that resonate with the pain and disruption they've endured through war and displacement.

He defies the harsh and unsuitable conditions within overcrowded displacement spaces never meant for education. With remarkable perseverance, he does his best to teach children and offer them moments of joy and reprieve. Through creative and low-resource methods, Al-Khodary designs simple yet impactful learning activities. Given the scarcity of materials, he has turned to puppetry, storytelling, theatrical sketches, and face painting. These activities not only encourage participation but help the children to reclaim their sense of wonder, curiosity, and desire to learn.

He knows that the psychological state of the children is deeply troubling. They carry invisible wounds of fear, anxiety, and distress, caused by the war and their constant displacement. These wounds directly affect their ability to focus, engage, and absorb knowledge. Al-Khodary's initiative includes large numbers of displaced children who fled from the north of Gaza to its southern towns. His education system is the first kind in the Gaza Strip that covers not only education itself but emotional healing and recreational activities. It has quickly become a source of light in the darkness.

Parents have praised Al-Khodary's efforts, feeling deeply grateful for his role in teaching and easing their children's trauma amid relentless war. His efforts have allowed the children to escape, if only briefly, from the terrifying atmosphere that has gripped their world.

Al-Khodary appeals to the world for increased support to ensure the continuity of his initiatives—morally, financially, and through the media. A place where the educational system has been broken needs help to become a symbol of both resistance and rebirth. His initiative is a quiet revolution for the minds of next generations in Gaza.

Al-Khodary reminds us, "Palestinian children deserve to live. Like the phoenix, they rise from the ashes and will soar again into the skies of creativity and brilliance."

Written on July 7, 2024
Appendix: The Gaza Strip

APPENDIX

The Geography of Gaza, Prior to October 7, 2023

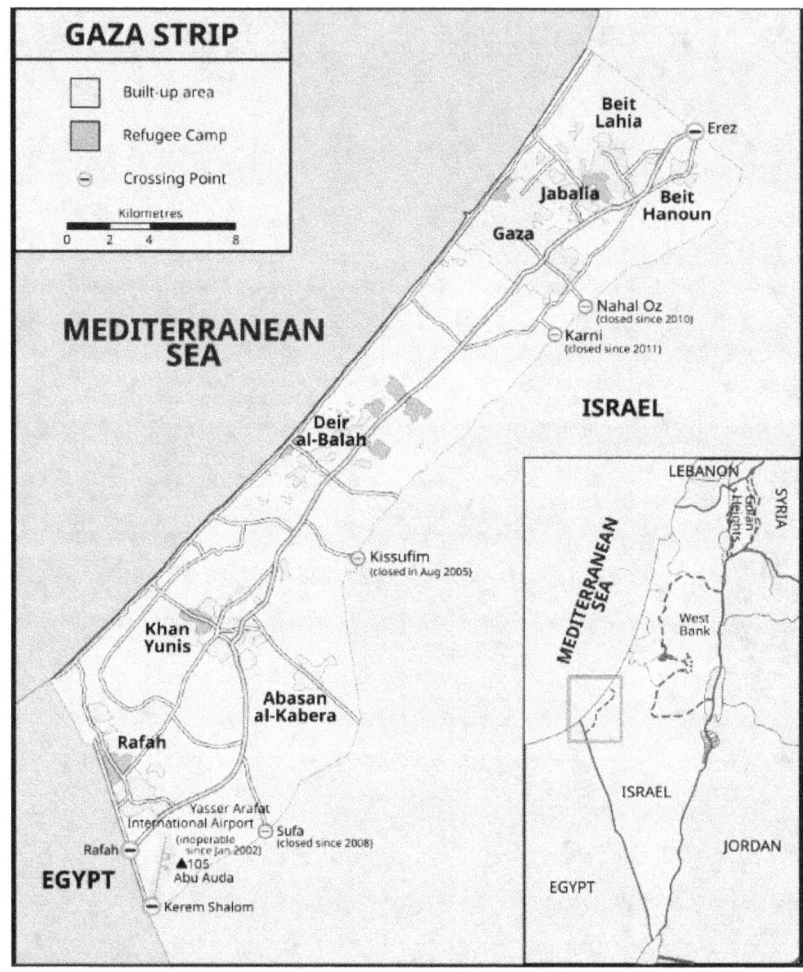

Map taken from: https://commons.wikimedia.org/wiki/File:Gaza_Strip_map2.svg

The Gaza Strip covers an area of 365 km² and is one of the most densely populated areas in the world. The Strip consists of five governorates:

North Gaza Governorate – Area: 61 km²
Gaza Governorate – Area: 74 km²
Al-Wusta (Central) Governorate – Area: 58 km²
Khan Yunis Governorate – Area: 108 km²
Rafah Governorate – Area: 64 km²

The governorates of the Gaza Strip have eight refugee camps in total: Jabalia Camp, Shati Camp, Rafah Camp, Khan Yunis Camp, Bureij Camp, Al-Maghazi Camp, Nuseirat Camp, and Deir Al-Balah Camp.

The Gaza Strip is named after its largest city, Gaza. It was an integral part of the British Mandate for Palestine until that was dissolved, in May 1948. Under the United Nations Partition Plan for Palestine, the Strip was designated as part of the territory promised to the proposed Arab Palestinian state. However, this plan was never implemented and became obsolete following the repercussions of the 1948 Arab-Israeli War.

Between 1948 and 1956, the Strip was under Egyptian military rule. The Israeli army then occupied it for five months during an attack on Egypt, which was part of the military operations related to the Suez Crisis. In March 1957, the Israeli army withdrew, and Egypt re-established military rule over the Strip.

During the 1967 war, the Israeli army occupied the Strip again, along with the Sinai Peninsula. In 1982, Israel completed its withdrawal from Sinai, under the terms of the Egyptian-Israeli peace treaty, but retained military control over the Gaza Strip, as Egypt chose not to reassert its authority over it.

Beit Hanoun

Beit Hanoun is a Palestinian city located in the northeastern part of the Gaza Strip. According to the Palestinian Central Bureau of Statistics (PCBS), in 2017 the city had a population of 52,227.

From mid 2007 until late 2023, Beit Hanoun was under Hamas rule. The city was completely depopulated, and all its buildings were either destroyed or severely damaged in the aftermath of Israel's war on Gaza in 2023. Beit Hanoun is approximately six kilometers away from the Israeli city of Sderot.

Jabalia

Jabalia is a Palestinian city located about four kilometers north of Gaza City, in the North Gaza Governorate. According to the PCBS, the population of Jabalia City in 2017 was 172,704. The Jabalia Refugee Camp lies adjacent to the city, to the north, near the village of Al-Nazla, which is part of the Jabalia Municipality.

The name "Jabalia" may be derived from the Roman name "Azalia," the Syriac "Jabalaia," meaning beauty, or the Arabic "Jila," meaning pottery and clay. Jabalia is known for its fertile soil and citrus orchards.

The Mamluk ruler Sanjar al-Jawli ruled the area in the early 14th century and dedicated part of Jabalia's land to the Mosque of Al-Sham'a, which he built in Gaza. The ancient Omar Mosque is also located in Jabalia. It is believed that the site has housed a mosque since the 7th century, with the arcade and minaret dating back to the 14th century. However, Israeli forces destroyed it during their war on Gaza in 2014. The arcade of the Omar Mosque consisted of three aisles supported by four stone columns. The aisles featured pointed arches and were covered with intersecting vaults.

Jabalia Refugee Camp

Located north of Gaza City, near a village of the same name, Jabalia Refugee Camp was established in the aftermath of the 1948 war. Most of the refugees who settled there had fled villages in southern Palestine. It is one of the largest of the eight refugee camps in the Gaza Strip, housing more than 116,000 registered refugees.

Beit Lahia

Beit Lahia is a city in the Gaza Strip, located north of Jabalia in the North Gaza Governorate. It is near Beit Hanoun and close to the border with Israel. According to the PCBS, in 2017 the city had a population of 89,838. As of January 2024, the city was under Israeli military control during Israel's war on Gaza.

The name "Beit Lahia" has two interpretations. Some historians believe the name is derived from the word "gods," and that it was once home to many temples and deities in ancient times. Others suggest it was a beautiful garden, with recreational areas near temples, thus becoming associated with leisure and amusement around the gods. In both cases, the connection between ancient deities and leisure is evident, leading to its name: Beit Lahia.

An ancient hill in Beit Lahia, near the ruins of an abandoned village, is believed to have been Bethelia, the birthplace of Sozomen, where a temple once stood. Byzantine-era pottery has been found in the area.

The mihrab (prayer niche indicating the direction of Mecca) is all that remains of an ancient mosque located west of Beit Lahia, dating back to the end of the Fatimid period and the beginning of the Ayyubid dynasty under Saladin. Two other mosques in the area date back to the Ottoman era.

Beit Lahia is located near Gaza City and is known for its many fruit trees, especially apple trees.

Gaza City

Gaza was an important city as early as the 15th century BCE, when the Egyptian Pharaoh Thutmose III made it a base for his army during a war with Syria. In later times, Gaza became one of the five royal cities of the ancient Byzantines. In the 8th century BCE, it was occupied by the Assyrians. From the 3rd to the 1st century BCE, Egyptians, Syrians, and Hebrew armies fought for control of the city.

In the 7th century, Gaza became a sacred Islamic city. It fell into the hands of the French under General Napoleon Bonaparte during his Egyptian campaign in the late 18th century. In 1917, during World War I, the city was occupied from Turkey by British forces under General Edmund Henry Hynman Allenby.

According to the United Nations partition decision in 1947, Gaza lay within the Arab area of Palestine. In 1948, during the war between Israelis and Arabs, Egyptian forces entered Gaza and its surrounding areas. The region came officially under Egyptian control according to the 1949 Armistice Agreement between the Arab countries and Israel.

During the 1948 war, about 200,000 Palestinian refugees migrated from the Arab territories occupied by Israel to the Gaza Strip, thereby doubling the population. Despite Gaza City having markets and some light industries, and despite the Gaza Strip being a productive area for citrus fruits, the economy cannot support such a large population. Therefore, assistance was provided by the United Nations Relief and Works Agency (UNRWA) for Palestine Refugees in the Near East.

Gaza is the largest city in the Gaza Strip, located in the southwestern part of Palestine on the shores of the Mediterranean Sea, with an estimated population of 1,300,000.

Al-Shati Camp

Located on the coast of the Mediterranean Sea, about four kilometers northwest of central Gaza City, Al-Shati is the third largest of the eight refugee camps in the Gaza Strip, and one of the most densely populated camps.

The camp was established in 1950 and gradually expanded east toward neighborhoods of Gaza City in the coastal area, north toward the nurseries area, and south toward the old building zone. It houses more than 90,700 refugees registered with UNRWA.

Deir Al-Balah

Deir Al-Balah is a city located in the middle of the Gaza Strip; it serves as the capital of the Deir Al-Balah Governorate. According to the PCBS, its population has reached 60,679.

Deir Al-Balah lies on a flat stretch of coastal land historically known as "Dārūm," a Semitic word meaning "south." The southern entrance to Gaza is still called "Bab al-Darum" (Gate of Darum). It is currently known as Deir Al-Balah because the first monastery in Palestine was built there by Saint Hilarion, who is buried in the eastern part of the town. It is also named after the palm trees that surround the area.

Deir Al-Balah is located on the Mediterranean coast, ten kilometers north of Khan Younis and sixteen kilometers south of Gaza City. The city covers an area of approximately fifty-six square kilometers. It is situated sixty-one kilometers southwest of Gaza City and ten kilometers northeast of Khan Younis. Administratively, it served as the center of the middle region of the Gaza Strip during Egyptian rule.

The economy of Deir Al-Balah relies almost entirely on agriculture, fishing, and livestock farming. The city is also known for its extensive cultivation of date palms.

Deir Al-Balah Camp

This is the smallest refugee camp in the Gaza Strip. Its area was about 156 dunams at its establishment, but later decreased to 132 dunams. It houses approximately 26,600 refugees.

The camp is located along the Mediterranean Sea, west of Deir Al-Balah City in the central Gaza Strip. Temporary housing was provided in the camp for the original refugees, who had fled their homes in central and southern Palestine due to the 1948 war.

Nuseirat Camp

Nuseirat Camp is located eight kilometers south of Gaza City and six kilometers north of Deir Al-Balah. The camp is situated in the middle of the Gaza Strip.

It is one of the largest camps in the Strip, in terms of both population and area, and includes a large gathering of Palestinian refugees from 1948. It is a crowded and densely populated camp, home to more than 80,400 refugees.

Bureij Camp

Bureij Camp is located in the center of the Gaza Strip, near the Al-Maghazi and Nuseirat camps, to the south of Gaza City. It was established in the 1950s to accommodate refugees who had been living in British army barracks and tents, many of whom came from cities in eastern Gaza, such as Faluja.

Bureij is a relatively small camp. It was originally established on an area of 528 dunams, which later decreased to 478 dunams. The camp houses approximately 46,600 registered refugees.

Al-Maghazi Camp

Al-Maghazi Camp is located in the middle of the Gaza Strip, south of Bureij Camp. It was founded in 1949 and is one of the smallest camps in Gaza, in terms of both size and population, with around 33,200 refugees residing there.

Most of the refugees who came to this camp fled due to the hostilities that accompanied the 1948 war. They originally hailed from villages in southern and central Palestine.

Khan Younis City

Khan Younis is the capital city of the Khan Younis Governorate. It is located in the southern part of the Gaza Strip, approximately a hundred kilometers southwest of Jerusalem. It is bordered by Rafah to the south and Deir Al-Balah to the north.

Khan Younis is a coastal governorate that overlooks the Mediterranean Sea to the west and borders the Negev Desert to the east.

Khan Younis City is the second largest city in the Gaza Strip, in terms of population and area, after Gaza City. Before the Palestinian-Israeli war, its population was approximately 242,714, representing about 16% of the Gaza Strip's total population.

The Mamluks founded the city in the 14th century. It remained largely unchanged throughout the Ottoman period but flourished toward the end of that era, particularly before the British Mandate over Palestine in 1917. In 1948, it was administratively annexed to Egypt, along with the other cities in the Gaza Strip. Israel occupied it in 1967, and it remained under occupation until 1995, when it became the center of the Khan Younis Governorate under the Palestinian National Authority.

The city serves as an administrative and educational hub for southern Gaza, hosting numerous government offices and dozens of schools for boys and girls at various educational levels. The Khan Younis

Governorate is considered the agricultural backbone of the Gaza Strip, known for its fertile lands, abundant water resources, and diverse farms. It plays a vital economic role in the region.

The city's name consists of two parts: "Khan," meaning "inn" or "hotel," and "Younis," named after Prince Younis Al-Tawrizi Al-Dawadar. Caliph Umar bin Abdul Aziz was the first Islamic ruler to establish khans (inns) for travelers. These khans played an important role, especially during the Mamluk era, when global trade flourished across the Arab Mashreq. During the Ottoman period, hotels gradually replaced khans, and so their importance diminished, with only a few continuing to function traditionally during the British Mandate over Palestine.

Khans, including Khan Younis, served as stations for commercial caravans along trade routes. Merchants would stay in these khans with their goods and livestock, to rest, replenish their supplies, and access water. The khans also provided security and protection from thieves and fraudsters. Ibn Battuta described khans in his travels, noting that they consisted of rooms for travelers and separate areas for their animals. Outside each khan, there was a water fountain and a shop where travelers could purchase necessities for themselves and their animals.

Some historians suggest that the ancient name of the city might have been "Ganis," as mentioned by Herodotus. Regardless, modern-day Khan Younis is relatively young, dating back no more than six hundred years. Sultan Barquq, a Mamluk ruler, sent Prince Younis Al-Tawrizi Al-Dawadar to build a fortress, which was completed in 1387 CE (789 AH) and bears Barquq's name inscribed on its gate.

Khan Younis Camp

Khan Younis Camp is located about two kilometers from the Mediterranean Sea, north of Rafah and west of Khan Younis City, which is a major commercial center. Refugees fled to the camp during the 1948 war, most of the coming from the Beersheba area.

At its establishment, the camp covered an area of approximately 549 dunams, and later expanded to 564 dunams. It houses around 88,800 registered refugees.

Abbassan al-Kabira

Abbassan al-Kabira is a city located in the Khan Younis Governorate in southern Gaza. It is connected to Khan Younis City by a local road that passes through other villages, such as Bani Suheila and Khazaa'a. In recent years, Abbassan al-Kabira and the neighboring village of Abbassan al-Sughra have been developed into a larger urban area surrounding Khan Younis.

According to a census conducted by the PCBS, the city has a population of 26,767. It relies primarily on agriculture for income. Additionally, small industries produce construction materials like bricks and farming tools, while some residents work in trade.

The community is heavily influenced by tribal structures, with large extended families such as Al-Qadhi, Al-Shawaf, Al-Daghmeh, Masbah, Abu Youssef, Abu Mustafa, Abu Tayr, Abu Daqa, Abu Tabbash, Abu Daraz, Abu Matalqa, Abu Hamed, Abu Sabha, Abu Amer, and Abu Taimeh. Families generally rely on customary law to resolve disputes among themselves.

Abbassan al-Kabira is located southeast of Khan Younis City, about four kilometers away and seventy-five meters above sea level. A paved local road connects it to the villages of Bani Suheila and Khazaa'a, while a main road links it to Beersheba via Amariya. Abbassan was established over a thousand years ago on flat land in southwestern Gaza, where the Negev hills meet the southern coastal plain.

Its name probably originates from the Banu Abbas tribe, a branch of the Lakhm tribe that settled east of Khan Younis before Islam. The name "Abbassan" is also attributed to the presence of two villages: Abbassan al-Sughra and Abbassan al-Kabira (home to the shrine of Prophet Ibrahim Al-Khalil).

South of the shrine, there is a beautiful mosaic floor featuring colorful designs of birds, plant motifs, decorative scrolls, and inscriptions, including a Maltese cross. This mosaic dates back to 606 CE and can still be seen today. Abbassan al-Kabira also contains several shrines, such as the tomb of Sheikh Salem and Sheikh Umm Ahmed, among other sites.

Abbassan al-Sughra

Abbassan al-Sughra is an agricultural town located two kilometers southeast of Khan Younis City, in the Khan Younis Governorate in southern Gaza. According to the 2017 PCBS census, its population is 9,290.

In 1886, toward the end of the Ottoman era, Abbassan al-Sughra consisted of about ten huts made of ancient stone.

Al-Mawasi

Al-Mawasi is a village on the southern coast of the Gaza Strip. It is approximately one kilometer wide and fourteen kilometers long. Before Israel's unilateral disengagement from Gaza in 2005, it was a Palestinian enclave within the Gush Katif Israeli settlement bloc. According to the PCBS, in mid 2005 its population was 1,409.

In December 2023, during Israel's war on Gaza, the Israeli military classified Al-Mawasi as one of the few "safe zones" in the Gaza Strip. Hundreds of thousands of Palestinians fled there, only to find a barren strip of land lacking basic resources like food, water, and sanitation.

In February 2024, when Israel announced plans to expand its operations to Rafah, hundreds of thousands of civilians again sought refuge in Al-Mawasi, as a last resort, with the Israeli occupation describing it as a relatively safer area.

Rafah City

Rafah is the capital city of the Rafah Governorate. It is located at the southernmost tip of the Gaza Strip, under the Palestinian Authority, approximately 107 kilometers southwest of Jerusalem. As the largest city in the Gaza Strip on the Egyptian border, it covers an area of 55 km² and has a population of approximately 190,000.

Rafah is one of the oldest historical cities, established over five thousand years ago. It was conquered consecutively by the Pharaohs, Assyrians, Greeks, and Romans. After the Camp David Agreement, when Israel withdrew completely from Sinai in 1982, Rafah was divided into two parts: Rafah on the Palestinian side and Rafah on the Egyptian side. This division caused harm and displacement to many families, who were separated by barbed-wire barriers. The center of Rafah was destroyed by both Israel and Egypt in order to create the border between Egypt and the Gaza Strip. Approximately 4,000 dunams were annexed to the Egyptian side, leaving 15,500 dunams of land, of which about 3,500 dunams were allocated for settlements.

The city has been known by several names throughout history. The Pharaohs called it "Rubi-Hui," the Assyrians called it "Rafihu," the Romans and Greeks called it "Raphia," and the Arabs called it "Rafah." Its historical importance grew due to the railway line connecting Cairo and Haifa, which ran through Rafah's lands until it was rerouted in 1967.

Rafah is an ancient city with deep roots, carrying many names over the centuries and witnessing numerous famous battles. The Arabic encyclopedia describes Rafah as an ancient city on the Egyptian border in the Sinai Peninsula on the Mediterranean Sea. During the Ottoman period, a road connecting Egypt to Bilad al-Sham passed through Rafah, making it one of the ancient Canaanite cities.

Rafah experienced significant historical events due to its strategic location as the gateway between Egypt and the Levant. In the 8th century BCE, a major battle occurred there between the Assyrians and the Pharaohs, allied with the King of Gaza, resulting in an Assyrian victory. In 217 BCE, another battle took place in Rafah between the Ptolemies of Egypt and the

Seleucids of Syria, leading to Ptolemaic control over Rafah and Syria for seventy-one years, until the Seleucids regained control.

During the Christian era, Rafah became the seat of a bishopric until it was conquered by the Muslim Arabs under Amr ibn al-As, during the reign of Caliph Omar bin Al-Khattab. However, in the 7th century AH (13th century CE), Rafah was abandoned and reduced to ruins, before experiencing a revival later on.

Napoleon passed through Rafah in 1799 during his campaign in Bilad al-Sham. Later, Khedive Ismail and Khedive Abbas Helmi II visited the city. Abbas Helmi II marked the border between Syria and Egypt using two granite columns placed under an ancient Christ's Thorn tree.

Rafah Camp

Rafah Camp is located in the southern part of the Gaza Strip near the Egyptian border. It was established in 1949 and soon became one of the most densely populated refugee camps in the Strip. Over time, thousands of refugees moved from the camp to a nearby housing project in Tel al-Sultan, making the camp blend almost indistinguishably with the adjacent city. It houses approximately 133,300 registered refugees.

ACKNOWLEDGMENTS AND GRATITUDE

Words race against each other and phrases crowd together, striving to weave a necklace of gratitude that is worthy of you. To you, a pioneer in the journey of education and knowledge; to you, who gave without expecting anything in return; to you, I dedicate these words of thanks and appreciation.

To the brilliant novelist and researcher, Nawal Halawa, Founder and President of the Arab Heritage House in Canada, who carried out the project of educational initiatives in resilient Gaza amidst the demonic war on our people and homeland—thank you. I tasted the sweetness of gratitude in your kindness, and the tears of the eyes are a measure of emotion. For the first time, now, my eyelids have savored the taste of tears that flow from joy.

Gratitude also extends to the esteemed teachers whose significant contributions brought this work to light, as well as the experts and educational supervisors:

Ms. Walaa Zaqout
Ms. Ghaliya Nawas
Mr. Mohammad Al-Banna
Ms. Raghda Badran
Dr. Shaimaa Al-Azzayza
Ms. Haneen Abu Atwi
Ms. Zubeida Shawwa
Mr. Mahmoud Shaqli

Translators:
Shaima Abu Jubbah
Doaa Isleem

And to the bearer of excellence and enlightened ideas, I extend my most sincere, beautiful, and heartfelt greetings, with all due love, respect, and loyalty. Words fail to capture the depth of admiration and esteem my heart holds for you, nor can they fully describe the admiration and praise filling my soul. How beautiful it is when a person becomes a candle that lights a way for the lost: Dr. Zaher Mohammad Al-Banna.

Arab Heritage House – Canada

ABOUT THE EDITOR

Nawal Halawa is a writer and a novelist. She is the founder and president of The Arab Heritage House in Canada. A Canadian citizen of Palestinian Jordanian Arab origin, she is a researcher who specializes in Arab heritage. She is a Member of the International Federation of Journalists, and earned a degree in Journalism and Radio from the International Institute of Journalism Werner Lamberz, based in Berlin, in 1981. As an editorial secretary, she was honored with a certificate from the Kuwaiti Journalists Association, and she contributed to both the first Arab television station in Chicago and the first Arab newspaper, *Al-Mir'at*, from 1987 to 1993, in Montreal, Canada.

Her books and novels include *Prisoners of the Bekaa* (1983), interviews with six Israeli prisoners in the Bekaa Valley in Lebanon; *Sitt Zubaydah* (2014), about the first Palestinian exodus before and after the Nakba, later translated into English to be adapted into a film; *Al-Ankriziyyah* (2017-18), about the second Palestinian exodus; *The Shunt* (2021), published by Dar Al Maaref in Egypt, about human suffering overcome by defiance and faith; *Scheherazade* (forthcoming from the Sharjah Authority for Culture and Heritage), an illustrated cultural and artistic heritage volume inspired by the One Thousand and One Nights Festival at the Place-Des-Arts Theatre in Montreal; and the novel *A Girl's Paradise Lost* (2023).

Nawal.halawa@gmail.com
514-362-9067